THE WORLD'S CLASSICS

THE LIGHTS O' LONDON
AND OTHER VICTORIAN PLAYS

THE PLAYS in this volume were all successful in their time. Edward Fitzball (1792–1873) was a prolific writer of melodramas, and *The Inchcape Bell* (1828) contains the Gothic and nautical elements then popular on the stage. Joseph Stirling Coyne (1803–68), who wrote *Did You Ever Send Your Wife to Camberwell?* (1846), was principally an author of farces, and the play is typical of the kind of farce with a humble domestic setting and characters to match, popular in the 1840s. George Henry Lewes (1817–78) wrote relatively few plays, but *The Game of Speculation* (1851) is a cutting comic satire upon greed and duplicity, softened by the usual Victorian sentimental ending. George Sims (1847–1922), the author of seventy plays, specialized, like Fitzball, in melodrama, but melodrama on a much larger social and urban scale. *The Lights o' London* (1881), which has never been printed, is the most famous of Sims's plays, with a stage history that stretched into the 1930s. *The Middleman* (1889), a play about capitalist exploitation and how the tables are turned, is a good example of the way in which the older melodrama became that staple of the late Victorian theatre, the 'drama'. Its author, Henry Arthur Jones (1851–1929), soon came to be ranked with Pinero and other important dramatists of the 1890s.

MICHAEL R. BOOTH is Professor and Chair of the Department of Theatre, University of Victoria, British Columbia. Among his many publications on the Victorian theatre is *Theatre in the Victorian Age* (1991).

MICHAEL CORDNER is a Senior Lecturer in the Department of English and Related Literature at the University of York. He has edited George Farquhar's *The Beaux' Stratagem*, the *Complete Plays* of Sir George Etherege, *Four Comedies* of Sir John Vanbrugh, and, for the World's Classics series, *Four Restoration Marriage Comedies*. He has also co-edited *English Comedy* (Cambridge, 1994) and is completing a book on *The Comedy of Marriage, 1660–1737*.

PETER HOLLAND is Judith E. Wilson University Lecturer in Drama in the Faculty of English, at the University of Cambridge.

MARTIN WIGGINS is a Fellow of the Shakespeare Institute and Lecturer in English at the University of Birmingham.

DRAMA IN WORLD'S CLASSICS

THE WORLD'S CLASSICS

EDWARD FITZBALL
The Inchcape Bell

JOSEPH STIRLING COYNE
Did You Ever Send Your Wife to Camberwell?

GEORGE HENRY LEWES
The Game of Speculation

GEORGE ROBERT SIMS
The Lights o' London

HENRY ARTHUR JONES
The Middleman

Edited by
MICHAEL R. BOOTH

General Editor
MICHAEL CORDNER
Associate General Editors
PETER HOLLAND   MARTIN WIGGINS

Oxford   New York
OXFORD UNIVERSITY PRESS
1995

Oxford University Press, Walton Street, Oxford OX2 6DP

Oxford New York
Athens Auckland Bangkok Bombay
Calcutta Cape Town Dar es Salaam Delhi
Florence Hong Kong Istanbul Karachi
Kuala Lumpur Madras Madrid Melbourne
Mexico City Nairobi Paris Singapore
Taipei Tokyo Toronto

and associated companies in
Berlin Ibadan

Oxford is a trade mark of Oxford University Press

British Library Cataloguing in Publication Data
Data available

Library of Congress Cataloging in Publication Data
Data available

ISBN 0–19–282736–7

1 3 5 7 9 10 8 6 4 2

Typeset by Pure Tech India Ltd., Pondicherry, India
Printed in Great Britain by
Biddles Ltd.
Guildford and King's Lynn

CONTENTS

ACKNOWLEDGEMENTS

THE text of *The Lights o' London* is reproduced by permission of the Department of Drama at the University of Manchester, which possesses the performance copyright; the manuscript is retained in the Departmental library. Anyone wishing to perform the piece (the orchestral score by Michael Connelly is also available by permission) must apply to the Administrator of the Department. I am personally most grateful to David Mayer of the Department for his kindness in making the text available to me, and also for his clarification of points of difficulty in the stage directions. I would also like to thank Pieter van der Merwe of the Maritime Museum at Greenwich, who has helped me to an explanation of ship's carpenter's terms for the Explanatory Notes. My wife, Judy, whose computer skills produced a copy fairer than ever I could have managed, deserves, as always, my utmost gratitude for her invaluable assistance.

INTRODUCTION

THE five plays chosen for this volume span the years from 1828 to 1889, a period in which the English theatre changed substantially in response to population expansion, urbanization, industrialization, and new patterns of transportation, with all their social and demographic implications. A close examination of nineteenth-century theatre would have to take these areas into account, since, like any other art, theatre is a product of its age, and without an understanding of that age there can be no full understanding of the theatre.

In 1828 England possessed an extensive system of provincial theatres, based upon the Theatres Royal of important towns and upon the circuit system in which a group of theatres was controlled by one management, which moved its actors from theatre to theatre at socially appropriate times of the year like fairs, assizes, and race meetings. This system was then decaying, having reached its apogee in the late eighteenth century; it was now suffering the consequences of economic decline and social change occurring since 1815. The London theatre still gloried in its two headquarters theatres, Drury Lane and Covent Garden, to which ambitious provincial actors aspired and from which leading actors sallied out into the provinces during the summer to star with the local stock companies. These two great theatres, however, were also in decline, suffering badly from mismanagement and a lack of revenue, victims, like their lesser provincial counterparts, of theatrical hard times. The rumbles of discontent over their legal monopoly position in the performance of the 'legitimate' drama—generally the standard repertory of tragedy, comedy, and farce—had been audible for years; they were to result in a parliamentary committee in 1832 and the passage of the Theatres Regulation Bill in 1843, which removed their prerogatives and allowed any theatre in the country to play what it liked, subject only to the censorship powers of the Lord Chamberlain as exercised through his officer, the Examiner of Plays—a restriction that effectively kept religion and politics off the stage. Although the many London competitors of Drury Lane and Covent Garden, before 1843 known as 'minor' theatres and confined to performing 'illegitimate' theatre—mostly melodramas and light comedies with songs—found themselves on the whole no stronger, no more prosperous, and no more adventurous in repertory because of the new Act, the legislation at least removed their fear of prosecution for infringing upon the dramatic domain of the two 'majors'.

The audience for London theatres varied widely according to theatre, class status, and neighbourhood; theatres were careful to tailor their repertory and performance style to the taste and social composition of their audiences. One significant new factor in the early Victorian period was the growth of a huge working-class audience, centred in the East End of London, on the Surrey side of the Thames, on the fringes of the West End, and in provincial towns and cities, especially in the industrial Midlands and North. In 1828 this growth was just beginning.

By 1889 the provincial stock company and circuit had disappeared; in its place came the touring company dispatched from London to perform in the surviving Theatres Royal and in lesser venues. Such touring, in which a major company could take its scenery, costumes, and properties as well as its actors, was only made possible by the railway, which was as powerful an agent for change in the theatre as it was elsewhere in society. The West End of London was now given over to the long run, which had slowly replaced the old system of a constantly changing repertory. The West End was also dominated by the actor-manager in control of his own theatre: Henry Irving at the Lyceum, Beerbohm Tree at the Haymarket, John Hare at the Garrick, and so forth. These managers were their own stars, and combined what we would describe as the functions of an artistic director with those of a general manager or administrative director. They actively promoted the gentrification of the West End and established the middle-class audience as the heart of their operation. The working- and lower-middle-class audience now stayed in its own neighbourhood theatres (in 1889 fewer in number) or patronized the flourishing music hall, which had experienced a lively and vigorous expansion from modest beginnings among the taverns and clubs of the early Victorians. In order to understand how the plays in this volume worked in the theatre, it is necessary to have some practical understanding of how they were produced and what the production resources of the nineteenth-century theatre were.

The actual structure and operation of the nineteenth-century stage was inherited from the eighteenth century. What the audience saw was a rectangular proscenium opening, behind it a working space larger than the auditorium itself. On both sides the stage extended into the wings to a distance more than equal to the width of the proscenium opening. At the very top of the backstage space, high above the stage, was the gridiron. When the Victorian theatre began to use the space above the stage more extensively than did the Georgian, employing flying mechanisms for scenery as well as for special machines like chariots and clouds descending from the heavens, the stage roof had to be raised. Thus the modern fly-tower was born. From the gridiron, by a system of drums, ropes, and pulleys depended everything that had to be flown and hung out of sight of the audience. Below the gridiron was at least one fly-gallery on each side of the stage, running from the proscenium to the back wall. From these galleries the stage crew—carpenters, they were called—pulled on the ropes to which the scenes were attached, and the limelight men operated their lanterns. Attached by grooves to the underside of the lowest fly-gallery on each side and fitted into corresponding sets of grooves in the floor of the stage—most theatres had four such sets—were wings and shutters that were slid on or off by stage carpenters to form complete scenes: a forest, a street, a country view, a prison.

This was the traditional system, which served a theatre whose public knew perfectly well that they were watching a play and did not insist on the illusion of reality. Scenery was a selective and aesthetic representation of the interior and exterior world, not a replication of it. By the second half of the nineteenth century, however, to many Victorians these methods seemed inadequate and unrealistic; the idea of realism in art was growing more powerful. Gradually the groove system began to disappear. It was replaced for interior scenes by the box set with walls and a ceiling, for exteriors by solid three-dimensional scenic structures. Scene changes now took longer and had to be concealed from the audience by the increasingly frequent use of the curtain.

The machinery beneath the stage, as vital to production as the grooves, wings, and shutters above it, was responsible for anything appearing from below or sinking out of sight, including actors. The stage floor itself was largely made up of removable planking so constructed as to drop and slide off, when necessary, to right and left beneath the wings. Scenery and actors were raised to stage level by a system of bridges, traps, and narrow cuts in the stage floor called sloats, all attached to winches, pulleys, and ropes operated from the mezzanine floor below the stage. To the uninitiated the mezzanine must have seemed a veritable forest of traps, posts supporting the stage floor, sliders, tackle, sloats, and bridges. The comparison with the 'tween decks area of a ship was often made, and many stage carpenters had previous shipboard experience. They were perfectly at home in the theatre.

This mechanical system, operated in the large and better-equipped houses by huge numbers of stage carpenters, made it possible for theatres to meet the heavy scenic demands placed upon them by the more and more elaborate and spectacular kinds of Shakespeare, melodrama, and pantomime favoured by audiences. Advances in the technology of lighting were also crucial for the success of pictorial and spectacular display. The nineteenth-century theatre went from candles and oil lamps to electricity in two generations, an even faster progression than the society outside its doors, where electric light was pretty much confined to factories, public buildings, and wealthy homes until well after the First World War.

Gas lighting, first introduced into London theatres in 1817, was by the Victorian period arranged in three main sections: the footlights, shielded from the audience by tall metal reflectors but glaring hotly and fiercely upon the actors, the wing lights, arranged in ladders behind each wing that lit the scenery behind rather than the actors, and the long, heavy, overhead battens stretching the full width of the stage ranged from front to back. There were four or five battens in medium-sized theatres, and they were concealed from the audience by sets of cloth drops called borders. Each batten contained scores of burning jets; it was their light that made the flies and the gridiron so hot and caused most of the very real risk of fire during performances. The battens added immeasurably to the brightness and glare of the stage, of which many complained, but they did make it finally possible for the actor to stay behind the proscenium arch and still be seen clearly.

However, gas could not project a beam of light and could not be focused. Limelight could do both, and by the 1850s it was in regular use and an indispensable part of stage lighting. It was produced by the burning of lime, or calcium oxide, in an oxy-hydrogen flame, and cast a light much brighter than gaslight. When coloured it was also a beautiful light in the effects it could achieve, being much employed in the depiction of sunrises, sunsets, and any sort of romantic spectacle. Indeed, spectacle effects of any kind would have been almost impossible without limelight, and the fairy scenes of pantomime were especially in its debt. A few colours—red, blue, and amber usually—were possible in the Victorian theatre. Painted glass slides could be inserted into a limelight box; coloured silks could be drawn over the battens and coloured glasses could rotate in front of footlights.

The final step in the progress of Victorian theatre lighting was, of course, electrification. In 1881, the Savoy Theatre in London was the first in the world to be lit entirely by electric light, although like other theatres it kept a complete back-up gas system for years. It took a long time for electric light to achieve the degree of aesthetic sophistication finally achieved by gas and limelight, but it did almost completely eliminate the omnipresent threat of fire. In the next century the demands and challenges of stage electric light led to the new position of lighting designer.

Victorian stage production was as much painterly as mechanical, and in fact machinery was a means to a pictorial end. The art of the scene-painter was essential in providing not only a pictorial representation of the world of a play, but also—depending on the talent of the scenic artist and the quality of lighting—a beautiful impression of the natural world, if the scene were exterior. Early Victorian theatres had their resident scene painters; later it became common practice to contract painting out to specialist studios that might be working on scenes for several theatres simultaneously. Because Victorian theatre production was dominated by a pictorial aesthetic, the scenic artist was an important figure; the closer production came to painting the more important he was. With the development of three-dimensional scenery this importance declined, but for a long time such scenery coexisted with painted cloths and canvas. There is also a practical reason for the primacy of the scene-painter in the Victorian theatre. For the first time his work was adequately lit and perceived in richer colour and detail by the audience. The retreat of the actor behind the picture frame also drew much greater attention to the picture itself, now a bright and living scenic environment rather than a dim background.

Thus a combination of new and traditional technology, the skills of the painter, a large labour force, relatively low wages—except for star actors—dominant trends in theatrical taste, and a West End long-run system that ensured, for the successful manager like Wilson Barrett of the Princess's Theatre and Augustus Harris of Drury Lane, that handsome profits could be made even from the most expensive productions. The most vivid and striking illustration of these developments on the late Victorian stage was the performance of large-scale Shakespeare, melodrama, and pantomime.

Even before the Victorian period audiences had demonstrated a taste for the pictorial and spectacular, notably in these three areas. The conveying of a pictorial image was a vital function of production technique, and audiences were used to looking at performance as at an illustration in a book or painting in a gallery. The stage direction 'picture' or 'tableau', found in many early nineteenth-century playtexts, indicated the freezing of actors in a striking act-ending pictorial arrangement that would heighten the emotions and character relationships just then exhibited on the stage. From the late 1820s the technique of 'realizing' famous paintings known to the audience, a technique borrowed from the French stage, replicated the actual painting by a combination of actors, scenery, and properties, frozen at a particularly climactic moment in the play.

Indeed, the stage was moving with architectural inevitability toward its final Victorian form: the picture-frame stage. The idea of the stage as a picture and the proscenium as its frame had been in the air for many years. This development was concluded architecturally in 1880, when the manager Squire Bancroft put a moulded and gilded picture frame, two feet wide, around the proscenium of the Haymarket, flush with the front of the stage. No longer could the actor come downstage into the auditorium in a close relationship with the pit in front of him and the stage boxes on either side of him. Fixed behind the proscenium, he was now part of a stage picture, integrated with scenic effect and lighting in a manner previously impossible.

An important feature of all nineteenth-century stage performance, which we are entirely unused to in today's acted drama, was the presence of an active theatre orchestra. Even in the humblest theatre a few musicians would have accompanied the play, and in large urban theatres an orchestra of some twenty performers was common. (In 1885 the orchestra for Henry Irving's production of *Faust* at the Lyceum numbered thirty-five or thirty-seven musicians.) These orchestras did not simply play overture and entr'acte music. They heightened the emotions of the scene and special moments of stage business by playing under the voices of the actors, and they cued the entrance and exit of characters with music appropriate to each character, especially in melodrama, where hero, heroine, villain, and comic man at least had distinctive motifs to bring them on stage and take them off. The numerous music cues in, for example, *The Lights o' London*, suggest that at times musical accompaniment was almost continuous, one cue segueing easily into the next, depending upon the development of the plot, the mood of the scene, and the particular characters on stage. Actors must have used the music to enhance their own vocal delivery, and music played loudly had the more mundane purpose of concealing the inevitable noise of a heavy backstage scene change from the audience. Music was woven into the very fabric of stage performance, and to imagine the nineteenth-century theatre without it would be about the same as watching innumerable modern films without the powerful emotional effect of their musical scores.

When we return to 1828 and the drama itself, we find that *The Inchcape Bell* was one of the earlier effusions of the prolific Edward Fitzball (1792–1873), who wrote over 150 plays and opera libretti; and whose play-writing career extended from the Regency to the middle years of Victoria's reign. Fitzball's real name was Ball; he added as a prefix his mother's maiden name in order, he claimed, to avoid confusion with a song-writer also called Ball. After managing his deceased father's farm near Newmarket, Fitzball became a printer in Norwich. Following a modest success as a budding author in the Norwich theatre, he sent plays to the London minor theatres, soon following them himself to take up residence in Lambeth as a professional playwright. He wrote mostly melodramas, of which *The Inchcape Bell* is a sterling example, not only of his work but also of a whole school of early nineteenth-century play-writing. At the Surrey, a Lambeth theatre near the Thames, with an audience containing a heavy representation of sailors, carpenters, shipwrights, and tradesmen who lived close by, *The Inchcape Bell* received eighty performances, then a substantial number. In the late 1820s the Surrey was the principal London theatre for the performance of nautical melodrama; this is not surprising, given its audience catchment area.

The play combines notable aspects of two kinds of melodrama, the supreme dramatic form of the nineteenth-century stage that was equally popular in all theatres and with all classes, although in the 1820s one critic commented acerbically, 'A minor theatre is the proper region of *melodrame*—an entertainment to which we have no objection, provided it be found in its right place.'[1] The most prominent kind of melodrama had, for over twenty years, been the Gothic, the kind that offered apparitions, grim-visaged tyrants, mutes with mysterious pasts, wild and forbidding landscapes, dark forests solely illuminated by flashes of lightning, and the by now familiar character stereotypes of hero, heroine, villain, comic man and woman, good old man and woman—a basic list, capable of variation and also

[1] George Daniel, 'Remarks' on *The Inchcape Bell* (London: Cumberland, n.d.).

capable of performance by the nineteenth-century stock company, whose members specialized in the 'lines of business' that gave life to the essential characters of melodrama as well as the *dramatis personae* of Shakespeare. The Gothic melodrama, which held the stage of East End theatres until the 1870s, was rivalled in the 1820s by a new subgenre, the nautical. Fitzball or his publisher entitled *The Inchcape Bell* 'A Nautical Burletta', the word 'burletta' meaning, in general, a short form of illegitimate drama played at the minor theatres, with songs. Nautical melodrama derived ultimately from the existence of a large British navy and its exploits against the French (or any other nation), as well as from a new theatrical fascination with pirates, smugglers, storms at sea, and shipwrecks—the last two made possible on stage by developments in machinery, scene-painting, and lighting. Nautical melodrama used the same stereotypes as other kinds of melodrama, and particularly developed the character of the heroic sailor, usually a member of His Britannic Majesty's fleet. Like the Gothic, the nautical did not forgo domestic interest for the sake of sensation and spectacle. By the end of the 1820s it had surpassed the Gothic in popularity, especially with two plays, Fitzball's *The Pilot* (Adelphi, 1825) and Douglas Jerrold's *Black Eyed Susan* (Surrey, 1829). In the nautical form, Fitzball also wrote *The Floating Beacon* (Surrey, 1824), *The Flying Dutchman* (Adelphi, 1827), and *The Red Rover* (Adelphi, 1829).

Many of the general characteristics of Gothic and nautical melodrama are adroitly combined in *The Inchcape Bell*. Melodramatists were not purists, and in choosing to blend two of the most popular entertainments on the stage Fitzball showed how skilfully he could write a stirring melodrama suited to contemporary taste. The Gothic elements of *The Inchcape Bell* are evident in the Dumb Boy who turns out to be Sir John Trevanly's son, the 'ancient castle' inhabited by the mournful Sir John, and the mysterious legend of the Bell itself, which takes on superstitious, if not supernatural force, at the end of the play. The nautical elements are present in the brave Captain Taffrail, the smuggler's ship, the concluding storm and shipwreck—which provide a satisfying colouring of excitement and the natural catastrophe so common to melodrama—the smugglers and marines and, especially, the character of Hans Hattock the Rover, or pirate. Such a character was the villain of many a nautical melodrama, and was full-bloodedly played by the Heavy Man of the stock company. The dramatist Tom Robertson described the dressing-room transformation of the actor into the character:

The baggy trousers of private life are discarded for tight-fitting pantaloons of the brightest red. The well-trodden boots, familiar with the pavement, give place to a pair of pointed-toed patent-leather curiosities, which run up the leg considerably higher than the knee, and which are lined with morocco as scarlet as the tights. The Heavy Man is dressing for Ruthven Rudderblood, captain of the Ocean Helldog, pirate schooner. A short white skirt, bordered with a broad stripe, still redder than the tights or the morocco of the boots, descends from his waist to his knees. . . . A striped Guernsey shirt covers his herculean chest, over it he wears a scarlet waistcoat, infinitely more scarlet than the hem of the petticoat-trousers, the morocco of the boots, or the colour of the tights; and a queer garment that in shape and trimmings combines the brigand's jacket, the ancient drawers, jerkin, and the pilot's pea-coat. A blue silk handkerchief is loosely knotted round his throat, he has pistols in his belt, and a cutlass by his side. His face is a concentration of compressed marine villainy and highly-salted atrocity. With a black wig, black whiskers, black moustaches, black eyebrows, and a broad black line under each eye, intended to represent black eyelashes, every trace of the good-humour of his face has vanished, and his mouth looks fit only for treasons, stratagems, and spoils.[2]

Special acting techniques as well as a special costume were necessary for the pirate villain, or any villain. Melodramatic acting was entirely appropriate to the content of melodrama: larger than life; highly externalized; extravagant in gesture, movement, and facial expression; rhetorical in speech; and intensely emotional. This kind of acting, necessary for the serious characters, was not required for the comic characters that liberally populate the genre, exemplified in *The Inchcape Bell* by Sampson Sawdust, Jupiter Seabreeze, and their sweetheart Beckey Butterfly. Such characters were played with farcical emphasis by low comedians who drew their material from their compatriots in the working and lower-middle classes outside the doors of the theatre.

The emphasis on low comedy and the skill of its practitioners is an important element of nineteenth-century farce, which abandoned the upper-class love intrigues and the clever servants of an older farce tradition. Early Victorian farce, indeed, went to the opposite extreme: its class status is much lower, its characters and settings socially humble; its comedy deals in misadventures with food, drink, and domestic paraphernalia of all kinds. Domesticity is the key word; no more utterly domestic drama has ever been written. In no other drama have furnished lodgings, articles of clothing, and the contents of

---

[2] Tom Robertson, 'Theatrical Types. No. X: Heavy Men and Character Parts', *Illustrated Times*, 26 June 1864.

kitchen cupboards and larders afforded so much opportunity for confusion, misunderstanding, and comic business of all kinds. The central character of such farce is usually a perfectly ordinary man, often married, who either through his own mistake, or through a combination of unfortunate circumstances of which he is in no respect the author, finds himself helplessly and inextricably involved in a sequence of disastrous events over which he has neither control nor influence. They drive him, willy-nilly; his world disintegrates around him. Most good Victorian farces, like W. S. Gilbert's *Tom Cobb* (St James's, 1875) and Pinero's *Dandy Dick* (Court, 1887), are structured in this way, as are the farces of Feydeau, but the concept originated in the English farce of the 1820s, 1830s, and 1840s.

The author of *Did You Ever Send Your Wife to Camberwell?*, Joseph Stirling Coyne (1803–68), an Irishman, became in 1856 Secretary of the Dramatic Authors' Society, founded in 1833 to protect the legal interests of dramatists under the new Dramatic Copyright Act, which for the first time gave a playwright sole property in a performed but unpublished play. As a professional journalist, Coyne was a contributor to *Punch* in its early years and later became drama critic of the *Sunday Times*. Like Fitzball, he was a productive dramatist, his career spanning the years from 1835–6, when three of his farces were produced in Dublin, to the year of his death. During these years he is credited with sixty-four plays, the vast majority of them farces and comedies, not an exceptional number for a busy Victorian dramatist.

In another Adelphi farce by Coyne, *How to Settle Accounts with Your Laundress* (1847), the tailor Whittington Widgetts is convinced that his laundress sweetheart has drowned herself in his water butt because he has rejected her. His dreadful fear of discovery, which sends him into paroxysms of duplicity and comic business, is matched by the behaviour and predicament of Chesterfield Honeybun, the lowly attorney's clerk of *Did You Ever Send Your Wife to Camberwell?*, who believes that he has squashed a baby under a chest of drawers, not to mention discovering a strange woman in his bed just before his wife returns, and being physically assaulted by an apparent madman. Both Widgetts and Honeybun suffer for engaging in illicit flirtation, but their suffering is out of all proportion to its cause, which is how farce of this kind works.

The part of Honeybun was created by Edward Wright, the admirable low comedian of the Adelphi, whose presence on stage sent his audiences into fits of hysteria. The journalist Edmund Yates saw Wright in many parts, including one of a travelling showman in

J. B. Buckstone's melodrama, *The Green Bushes* (Adelphi, 1845). Yates remembered that Wright would,

without uttering a word across the footlights, give the audience a confidential wink and send them into convulsions. . . . Never have I heard such laughter as that which he evoked, never have I seen people so completely collapsed and exhausted by the mere effect of their mirth. In some of Wright's scenes in *The Green Bushes* I have fallen helpless, spineless, across the front of the box, almost sick with laughter.[3]

The low comedian was equally at home in farce and the provision of comic relief in melodrama. His style was broad and his effects carefully contrived; he was often, as in the character of Honeybun, ludicrous in his role of the powerless victim of coincidence and misunderstanding. The low comedian was an essential member of every stock company; his presence in thousands of farces, comedies, and melodramas attests not only to his indispensability but also to the fundamental desire of English audiences to have a good laugh in the theatre. As West End theatre grew more refined and serious toward the end of the century he died out, at least in that area of the theatrical world, but his lineal descendants continued to supply more or less the same ingredient of comic drama.

If low comedy and broad fun are major characteristics of farces like *Did You Ever Send Your Wife to Camberwell?*, the comedy of *The Game of Speculation* is different altogether. Writing under the pseudonym of Slingsby Lawrence, George Henry Lewes (1817–78) adapted the play from Balzac's and Dennery's *Mercadet*, first produced in Paris in 1851, writing it, as he stated in a note to the published play, in less than thirteen hours. Adaptation from French drama without any payment was common and legal until the Berne Convention in 1886 prevented this sort of international pilfering. *The Game of Speculation* opened at the Lyceum after only two full rehearsals and achieved a notable success, with ninety-two performances in its first season. Although he wrote some dozen other plays, half of them farces, Lewes was a literary critic, a biographer, a philosopher, a physiologist, and a psychologist rather than a dramatist, publishing many books in these areas. Perhaps he is now best known for his long association with George Eliot. He was, however, a keen student of the theatre: in addition to writing plays he served as drama critic for the *Leader* in the 1850s, wrote essays on the drama for the *Pall Mall Gazette*, and published one of the best

---

[3] *Edmund Yates: His Recollections and Experiences* (London: Bentley, 1884), i. 197–8.

nineteenth-century works on acting, *On Actors and the Art of Acting* (1875), a collection of essays upon leading French and English performers of the day, as well as upon the state of the theatre in France, Germany, and Spain. A Londoner, Lewes was the grandson of a leading eighteenth-century comedian, Charles Lee Lewes, acting with the Dickens amateurs and in his own tragedy, *The Noble Heart* (Olympic, 1850).

The Game of Speculation, with its themes of feverish, obsessive stock-market gambling, selfishness, duplicity, and gullibility—a sort of *Volpone* of the financial markets—has a distinctly modern feeling about it. Affable Hawk, one feels, would have made his fortune in insider trading or junk bonds in New York in the 1980s. Similar in some respects to Caryl Churchill's *Serious Money*, the play is both contemptuously satiric of human greed and benevolently redemptive about human nature; thus it is fundamentally a sentimental play rather than a nightmare about human rapacity. Hawk displays a whole armoury of manipulative weaponry, including fraud, to achieve his financial objectives, but ultimately these are useless and he is only rescued by the *deus ex machina* intervention of his now repentant and wealthy partner, Sparrow. In any case, Hawk is at bottom a good person with the best interests of his family at heart; it only needs the restoration of financial equilibrium to give him peace and remove the incentive to double-deal and manipulate. So is Sparrow a good person, and young Noble, too, who refuses to give up Hawk's daughter when told the family is ruined. Even the creditors may be good people, though they deserve to be cajoled and cheated into giving more money to Hawk, and they are not objects of pity. The happy ending is typical of innumerable Victorian dramas and comedies that raise dark themes and mighty subjects, but end up subordinating them to the necessary success of a romantic love interest, or simply walking away from them and taking refuge in trivial sentiment or a most improbable plot outcome, as long as all concludes pleasantly. *The Game of Speculation* has faults of this kind, but it is more hard-headed, at least until the end of the third act.

The subject-matter of the play is also representative of a school of Victorian comedy and melodrama that dealt in themes of business and the world of finance. Here the theatre was reflecting its times: the development of commerce and the financial life of the City of London necessitated a considerable expansion and sophistication of market mechanisms and the concomitant growth of financial institutions. Villain and hero alike become involved in this world, and their struggle is carried on in an environment of banks and broking offices, spilling over, of course, into the home and threatening the family with destruction. Notable in this category of business drama are Dion Boucicault's *The School for Scheming* (Haymarket, 1847) and his *The Streets of London* (Princess's, 1864),[4] as well as three plays by Tom Taylor: *Payable on Demand* (Olympic, 1859), *The Ticket-of-Leave Man* (Olympic, 1863), and *Settling Day* (Olympic, 1865).

The star of *The Game of Speculation*, Charles Mathews, was among the leading comic actors of the century. His brand of comedy, as Affable Hawk, was quite different from that of Wright as Chesterfield Honeybun. Although he always rejected classification as one kind of comedian or another, Mathews's comedy was essentially light comedy, as opposed to Wright's low comedy. Light comedy was another of the essential stock company lines of business. Hawk is a character whose performance clearly requires great energy, charm, quickness, vivacity, control, and the power of overwhelming other characters with sheer style. On stage, Mathews possessed all these qualities in abundance. Many parts were written for him in which to display his unique talents, and when he died at 75 in 1878, bright and buoyant on stage to the last, a whole comic repertory died with him. Nobody else could succeed in his parts. The decline and ultimate disintegration of the stock company, and the practice in the West End of casting for a long run, meant the end of lines of business like low and light comedy—affectionately memorialized in Pinero's *Trelawny of the 'Wells'* (Court, 1898)—and the entire range of the old character stereotypes so well suited to the structure and histrionic abilities of the stock company.

These stereotypes are still in evidence, though used with great skill and variety, in *The Lights o' London*. As well as being a successful playwright, its author George Robert Sims (1847–1922) was also a journalist, writer of fiction, social critic, and balladeer. For many years his poems were the very stuff of dramatic recitations. Such poems as 'In the Workhouse: Christmas Eve', 'Billy's Rose', and 'Ostler Joe' can still be given from the public platform with great effect. That mixture of narrative strength, unabashed simple sentiment, and intense emotion that also characterizes his best plays made Sims as popular a versifier as he was a playwright. His plays were performed in a variety of London theatres, especially the Adelphi, with the Princess's the headquarters of West End melodrama in the 1880s and

---

[4] This play opened in New York in 1857 as *The Poor of New York*. 1857 was a year of financial panic, as was 1837. Both panics figure in the plot.

1890s, and he went on after *The Lights o' London* to write *Romany Rye* (Princess's, 1882), a melodrama about gypsies, and a military melodrama, *In The Ranks* (Adelphi, 1883), in collaboration with Henry Pettitt. His output of seventy plays, mostly melodramas, stretches well into the twentieth century. Sims's other career as a journalist—he wrote under the pen-name of Dagonet for the *Referee* from the 1870s—was a long and full one. He was an acute commentator on London life and to some extent a social critic sympathetic to the urban poor, with such a work as *How the Poor Live* (1883). This vein is apparent in *The Lights o' London*.

It was the manager Wilson Barrett who took a chance on *The Lights o' London*, which had been rejected by half a dozen London managements, and who enabled Sims to graduate from struggling journalist and playwright heavily in debt to affluent and popular man of letters. The play ran consecutively for 228 performances at Barrett's theatre, the Princess's, and the royalty agreement Sims was offered brought him £150 in the first week; within a fortnight Barrett and Sims had been paid £1,000 down for the American rights, and Sims's income, £1,400 for the year before the first production, was £14,000 the year after. Two companies were soon touring the provinces, and according to Sims the number one company would stay four to six weeks in each large city playing to record business. By 1916, *The Lights o' London* had been playing steadily all over the world for thirty-five years, not only in English. It was translated into several languages, and in that year Sims records performances in Danish in Copenhagen and forthcoming productions in Swedish in Stockholm and in Norwegian in Christiania.[5]

The Lights o' London is one of innumerable melodrama titles incorporating the name of London, and an example of the continuing fascination of Victorian melodramatists with the metropolis as a setting as well as a symbol of moral and material darkness and suffering. They also found the contrast between countryside and metropolis both dramatically powerful and morally instructive; it was a common device to counterpoint an initially idyllic village setting with the later squalor and vice of London streets and low life. In *The Lights o' London*, although the rural setting of Armytage Hall is none too happy an environment for the hero, it is nevertheless the old home of an innocent and virtuous heroine who reaches her nadir at the forbidding doors of a London workhouse. Under extreme pressure

---

[5] George R. Sims, *My Life* (London: Eveleigh Nash, 1916), 126–31.

her mind wanders: 'My dear old home! I seem to know every hedgerow, every wild flower—how sweet the honeysuckle smells—and listen to the birds. Look, Harold—yonder's the Lodge, and there's father standing at the gate waiting for me.' Such a speech is typical of the fixation of countless village heroines on their country home, and Bess's subsequent collapse into Harold's arms in front of the workhouse is also characteristic of their suffering in the contrasting dark world of London. Such a heroine at the end of her physical and emotional tether is a traditional figure in melodrama; the interesting thing here is that the collapse occurs outside that grim symbol of the darker side of Victorian class and social relationships, the casual ward. The brief scene that immediately follows, where Bess and Harold are refused charity by two gentlemen in evening dress, is Sims's own special social contribution to an endlessly repeated melodramatic leitmotif.

Thus *The Lights o' London* partakes of that significant melodramatic world of country innocence and city experience, of riches and poverty (the scene of the lavishly appointed villa in Regent's Park is succeeded by the scene outside the workhouse), as well as belonging to the familiar urbanized melodrama of betrayals, suppressed wills, repentant assistant villains, crimes, detectives, and the police. Bursting with plot and strongly coloured, it is packed with exciting incident and unexpected reversals of fortune, and in the usual way of melodrama the disasters and pathos are varied by comic relief. In 1881 the staging of the play was considered the last word in realism. Particularly acclaimed was the first scene of Act 5, the Borough Market in Southwark on a Saturday night. Great care was taken to ensure the duplication on stage of a street market and the shops behind. Eight costermongers' barrows were set out and stocked with goods such as vegetables, fruit, haddock, bloaters, whelks, and oysters. There were also 'scales and weights to those barrows requiring them. Lighted candles in the glass shades to each barrow. An ice-cream and baked potato barrow combined with hot potatoes in can and cornflour boiled to represent ice, 2 colours. Glasses, wooden spoons. Piano organ. Walnut basket and walnuts.' In the greengrocer's shop, 'plenty of greengrocery in bushel baskets. Heap of coals in one corner of shop. Coal scales, shovel, etc.' A cobbler's shop and a public house were also appropriately furnished.[6] Not only was the detail of

---

[6] This information is not in the initial stage direction to 5.1 but is given in the unpublished biography of Wilson Barrett by his son Alfred Wilson Barrett, 'And Give Me Yesterday', i. 88–9.

verisimilitude considered praiseworthy; critics were also much impressed with the management of the crowd in the street, which was compared favourably to the crowd scenes in the recent visit of the Meininger Company to Drury Lane. The drama critic, Clement Scott, made just such a comparison:

I really do not think there is any necessity for us to 'sing small' to German stage managers. . . . This scene of the Saturday night marketing in the Borough, with its hundreds of varied supernumeraries, men, women, and children; its grim squalor and hideous depravity, its drunkenness and its dirt, its fierce unbridled animal passion and wild-beast fighting, its street row and police-court mêlée is realism out-realised.[7]

Thus, although its fundamental character and machinery had not changed—the struggle of good against evil was as clear-cut and sensational as ever—the technique and content of melodrama had been considerably adjusted since *The Inchcape Bell*. Realism in staging meant the replication, as far as technology allowed, of actual urban scenes like the Borough Market and the Slips in Regent's Park in *The Lights o' London*. Melodrama also reflected urbanization and the growth of huge cities, and showed the vicissitudes and material sufferings of domestic life, whether that life was comfortably middle class or socially more humble in character and setting. Although earlier melodrama could be noticeably tinged with domesticity, despite its romantic cast, Victorian urban melodrama had moved some distance from the Gothic and nautical drama of the 1820s; the same thing happened to the novel in its progress from Scott to Dickens and Mrs Gaskell in more or less the same period. Out of the later Victorian melodrama grew a serious theatre whose heritage is apparent, yet is recognizably a different kind of drama.

The Middleman is just that sort of play. Its author, Henry Arthur Jones (1851–1929), who for some years worked as a draper's assistant and a commercial traveller, achieved his first great theatrical success in Wilson Barrett's Princess's Theatre a few months after the run of *The Lights o' London* with a strong melodrama of the old school, *The Silver King* (1882), following that with *Saints and Sinners* (Vaudeville, 1884), conventionally melodramatic in many respects but daring (and thus giving offence) in its attack upon religious hypocrisy. *The Middleman* in 1889 was really a turning-point; it ran for 182 performances. After that, together with Pinero, Jones dominated the serious theatre of the 1890s with dramas and comedies like *The*

[7] *Illustrated London News*, 17 Sept. 1881.

Dancing Girl (Haymarket, 1891), *The Case of Rebellious Susan* (Criterion, 1894), and *The Liars* (Criterion, 1897). Jones was a great proselytizer for a theatre of ideas (yet reacted violently to Ibsen) and published two important collections of essays and lectures vigorously advancing his beliefs, *The Renascence of the English Drama* (1895) and *The Foundations of a National Drama* (1913). In the twentieth century he grew out of touch with public taste: having been ahead of it he was now behind it, and with a few exceptions like *Mrs Dane's Defence* (Wyndham's, 1900) and *The Lie* (New York, 1914; New Theatre, 1923) his plays were far less popular.

Unlike the treatment of subject-matter in *The Inchcape Bell* and *The Lights o' London*, the main problems of the Blenkarn family in *The Middleman*—Cyrus Blenkarn being the brilliant potter exploited by his profiteering master—are rooted in the social and economic situation, although Jones makes little attempt to analyse this situation from the social and economic point of view and even less to offer solutions. At the end of the play the tables are turned; the former employee is now the rich capitalist and his bankrupt employer is at his mercy. Blenkarn offers him a managerial position in the works of which he is now the master. Jones seems to suggest that kindness, fairness, and good treatment are the best means of developing harmonious and fruitful relations between capital and labour; he who does not practise these industrial decencies is, literally, the loser. This may be superficial, but Jones and the melodramatists before him were writing plays, not economic tracts. *The Middleman*, indeed, comes from a long line of nineteenth-century plays, stretching back to John Walker's powerful *The Factory Lad* (Surrey, 1832), that are concerned with problems of labour and capital, of work and wages, of strikes and unemployment, of machine-smashing and victimization. John Galsworthy's *Strife* (Duke of York's, 1909) is the culminating masterpiece of this line. There is also, in *The Middleman*, a subordinate but significant theme of the clash between the *nouveau riche* industrialist and the old landed interest, represented by Joseph Chandler of the Tatlow Porcelain Works on the one hand and Sir Seton Umfraville, displaced by Chandler from Tatlow Hall, on the other. Since Victorian drama is riddled with class conflict, melodrama especially, it is not surprising that the theme of class also finds expression here, as it is not only capable of forceful dramatic expression but also a significant aspect of Victorian society. Plays like Robertson's *Society* (Prince of Wales's, 1865) and Taylor's and Augustus Dubourg's *New Men and Old Acres* (Haymarket, 1869) deal in the same material. Although Blenkarn's feeling for his daughter Mary is strongly emotional, Jones does not go in for melodramatic effect; his characters are not stereotypes; and situation, character, and dialogue are socially credible and convincing.

Like the nineteenth-century novel, nineteenth-century drama responded to and expressed its age. The texts in this volume demonstrate that conclusively. Not only are the financial and industrial concerns of *The Game of Speculation* and *The Middleman* a clear reflection of the Victorian obsession with making money and the relationships between management and labour, but also the Gothic and nautical content of *The Inchcape Bell* gave voice on the popular stage to the Romantic movement and to the almost mystical glories of English maritime prowess. *Did You Ever Send Your Wife to Camberwell?* illustrates in comic microcosm the modest material preoccupations of Victorian domesticity. There is a subtext here of respectable poverty, and poverty—one of the Four Horsemen of the Victorian age—is a prominent theme in *The Lights o' London*, which conveys striking images of the difficulty of living in great cities and the sheer hardship of life for the underclass.

These plays are representative, not only of their age, but also of the theatre of their age. None of them has been reprinted in modern selections of nineteenth-century plays, and *The Lights o' London* has never been printed at all. One of the principal reasons for the selection of these particular texts in this volume has thus been to present the interested student of nineteenth-century theatre with a fresh new selection of texts that otherwise might be difficult of access, a selection of plays previously neglected by editors in their understandable tendency to recycle the obvious and well-known choices from Boucicault, Gilbert, and Pinero. The plays chosen here are leading representatives of their genres, melodrama, comedy, and farce, all three important and dominant dramatic forms in the nineteenth century;[8] all five were extremely popular with audiences. Much of the vigour of performance and the variety of dramatic expression in the nineteenth-century theatre can be found in these texts alone, and since possibly 30,000 plays were performed in England during these hundred years there is no shortage of material for further exploration.

---

[8] If it had been possible to add a pantomime to this volume, then one could have spoken of '*the* dominant dramatic forms'.

NOTE ON THE TEXTS

THE text of *The Inchcape Bell* is that printed in the first volume of *Cumberland's Minor Theatre*, a series which started publication in 1828. It was also published in vol. 79 of *Lacy's Acting Edition of Plays*, but this series did not begin until 1851. The *Cumberland* edition of the play advertises on its title-page that the play is 'printed from the acting copy' with 'entrances and exits, relative positions of the performers on stage, and the whole of the stage business, as performed in the Theatres Royal, London,' indicating the immediate popularity of the play across the river in the 'majors' after the run at the Surrey.

The text of *Did You Ever Send Your Wife to Camberwell?* first appeared in vol. xii of the *Acting National Drama* series, which began publication in 1837. It is described on the title-page 'as performed at the Theatre Royal, Adelphi . . . correctly printed from the prompter's copy'. A much later acting edition of the play is no. 955 of *Dicks' Standard Plays*, a series which began publication in 1883.

The only printing of *The Game of Speculation* is that in vol. 5 of the *Lacy* series, which was eventually taken over by *Samuel French*; that publisher reissued the same *Lacy* texts under its own imprint. The text here is that of the *Lacy* edition.

The Lights o' London has never been printed. The text in this volume is that of Sims's master copy, a bound typescript which he leased to managements wanting to stage the play. Its date is uncertain, but it appears to be an early version, probably the one performed at the Princess's Theatre in 1881. In later versions Sims updated his topical references and made cuts to accommodate twice-nightly performances; there is evidence of neither practice in this text.

The text of *The Middleman* is that of the first printing of the play, in *French's Acting Edition* no. 6, published in 1907. As is common with modern *Samuel French* acting editions, appended to the play are full property and lighting plots, together with a floor plan of the stage setting for the first three acts. These floor plans have not been reproduced here, but in the interests of obtaining a complete picture of the stage action the detailed marginalia indicating virtually every move, every stage position, and every piece of business not recorded in the stage directions within the body of the text have been included.

Since the edition also contains the cast lists of both the London and New York (1890) productions, it is not clear which prompt copy was used—unless the London and New York productions were identical in plan, which is quite possible. A foreword by Jones, dedicating the published play to E. S. Willard, who played Blenkarn, indicates authorial approval of the text; there is no evidence for any of the other plays that the printed text was validated by the author.

Throughout this volume, punctuation, which can be fairly haphazard in nineteenth-century acting editions, has been regularized, and spelling has been modernized. Very occasionally a clarification has been added to the stage directions, such as '*to him*' or '*aside*', to make the relationship between speakers on stage clearer to the reader. Characters' names have been expanded from the abbreviations commonly used in speech prefixes and sometimes in stage directions.

The positions of exits and entrances as marked in the stage directions of nineteenth-century playtexts display a bewildering variety of alphabetical and numerical abbreviations; they are not, however, as confusing as they first appear.

Before the box set became common on the English stage in the mid-Victorian period, entrances and exits were made—unless specifically indicated as through a door in a flat—at the fixed positions for the wings or grooves (in which the wings slid on and off) on either side of the stage. These positions were numbered from the front of the stage to the back. Thus R2E (or 2ER) was at the second wing or groove from the proscenium arch, on the right hand of the stage facing the audience. L1E (or 1EL) was at the first wing or groove position on stage left. These directions, unfortunately, were not printed consistently. We also have such directions as RH1E (right-hand first entrance), RDUE (right door, upper entrance—indicating the stage position of a door in a flat), RSE (right second entrance), and RUE, or UER (right upper entrance). LC and RC need no comment. The simplest stage directions here are those for *Did You Ever Send Your Wife to Camberwell?*, which has only one set, and *The Middleman*, which used a box set for each act.

SELECT BIBLIOGRAPHY

OF the authors represented in this volume, only one, Henry Arthur Jones, is available in a recent collection. *Plays by Henry Arthur Jones*, ed. Russell Jackson (Cambridge: Cambridge University Press, 1982) contains *The Silver King*, *The Case of Rebellious Susan*, and *The Liars*; the introduction is substantial and informative. An older but much fuller collection of Jones's work is *Representative Plays*, ed. Clayton Hamilton (London: Macmillan, 1926), 4 vols. Two melodramas by Fitzball, *The Devil's Elixir* and *The Flying Dutchman*, have been printed in *The Hour of One: Six Gothic Melodramas*, ed. Stephen Wischhusen (London: Gordon Fraser, 1975). Coyne's farce, *How to Settle Accounts with Your Laundress* can be found in vol. iii (1973) of *English Plays of the Nineteenth Century* (Oxford: Clarendon Press, 1969–76), 5 vols., and *The Magistrate and Other Nineteenth Century Plays* (Oxford: Oxford University Press, 1974), both edited by Michael R. Booth. No plays by Sims and George Henry Lewes have been reprinted; in fact almost nothing of Sims's large dramatic output found its way into print, while Lewes's plays, like those of Coyne and Fitzball, are easily available in nineteenth-century acting editions. Jones's plays were first published in *Samuel French* acting editions and Macmillan reading editions.

The most useful bibliography for the student of nineteenth-century drama is *English Drama and Theatre* 1800–1900: *A Guide to Information Sources*, ed. Leonard W. Conolly and J. P. Wearing (Detroit: Gale, 1978). The emphasis is more on the drama than the theatre, and there are entries for 110 dramatists, with sections on history, criticism, and aspects of the theatre as well.

Information about Fitzball is contained in his own autobiography, *Thirty-Five Years of a Dramatic Author's Life* (London: Newby, 1859), 2 vols. For Coyne, the *Dictionary of National Biography* is really the only useful source. Edgar W. Hirschberg, *George Henry Lewes* (New York: Twayne, 1970) is the principal source of information about Lewes, as is Sims's autobiography, *My Life* (London: Eveleigh Nash, 1916) for his career. The standard biography of Jones is his daughter's: Doris Arthur Jones, *The Life and Letters of Henry Arthur Jones* (London: Gollancz, 1930). R. A. Cordell, *Henry Arthur Jones and the Modern Drama* (New York:

Long and Smith, 1932) is the sole book-length critical study, now somewhat dated but still authoritative.

Given the paucity of critical work on individual nineteenth-century dramatists before Shaw and Wilde, there is no body of writing on any author in this volume except for Jones. It is, indeed, not really possible to separate studies of nineteenth-century drama from studies of nineteenth-century theatre, since the drama and theatre of the period are so closely related that one cannot consider the one satisfactorily without the other. Several writers, however, emphasize the play more than the stage. Volumes iv and v (1800–50, 1850–1900) of Allardyce Nicoll, *A History of English Drama*, 2nd edn. (Cambridge: Cambridge University Press, 1955–9), 6 vols., are part of a major general history, especially valuable for the theatre and play lists at the end of each volume. The introductions to the five volumes of *English Plays of the Nineteenth Century*—which deal with tragedy, melodrama, comedy, farce, pantomime, extravaganza, and burlesque—have been reprinted as *Prefaces to English Nineteenth-Century Theatre* (Manchester: Manchester University Press, 1981). Vol. vi (1975) of *The Revels History of Drama in English* (London: Methuen) covers the period 1750–1886, with a long section on the drama, chronologically arranged, by Robertson Davies. There are also sections on the social and literary context (Michael R. Booth), theatres (Richard Southern), and actors (Frederick and Lise-Lone Marker). Victor Emeljanow, *Victorian Popular Dramatists* (Boston: Twayne, 1987) is a thoughtful and well-documented examination of Jerrold, Taylor, Robertson, and Jones. Michael R. Booth, *English Melodrama* (London: Herbert Jenkins, 1965) is a standard work on this subject. Paul Ranger, *'Terror and Pity Reign in Every Breast': Gothic Drama in the London Patent Theatres, 1750–1820* (London: Society for Theatre Research, 1991), is a recent survey of the kind of melodrama of which *The Inchcape Bell* is a notable representative.

Such studies can be supplemented by those more specifically about theatre practice, although discussions of the drama can also be found here. Although 'Victorian' is treated with some latitude, an excellent introduction to the period is George Rowell, *The Victorian Theatre, 1792–1914*, 2nd edn. (Cambridge: Cambridge University Press, 1978). A more recent book, Michael R. Booth, *Theatre in the Victorian Age* (Cambridge: Cambridge University Press, 1991), contains one chapter on the drama; the others discuss theatre and society, management, theatre architecture, production methods, and acting. A most useful collection of contemporary documents relating to theatres, audiences, production, management, and play-writing is *Victorian Theatre*, ed. Russell Jackson (London: A. and C. Black, 1989). Two books in Blackwell's Drama and Theatre Studies series, Joseph Donohue, *Theatre in the Age of Kean* (Oxford, 1975) and George Rowell, *Theatre in the Age of Irving* (Oxford, 1981), focus on the work of two great actors (in Irving's case, a great manager as well) at approximately opposite ends of the century. Alan Hughes, *Henry Irving, Shakespearean* (Cambridge, Cambridge University Press, 1981), is a thorough examination of the acting and production of Irving's sizeable Shakespearian repertory. Good illustrations of Victorian theatres appear in Richard Southern, *The Victorian Theatre* (Newton Abbot: David & Charles, 1970), and Victor Glasstone, *Victorian and Edwardian Theatres* (London: Thames and Hudson, 1975); the Southern book also contains information on production practices. Michael R. Booth, *Victorian Spectacular Theatre, 1850–1914* (London: Routledge and Kegan Paul, 1981), considers the dominant pictorial, archaeological, and spectacle modes of production, including their relationship to Shakespeare, melodrama, and pantomime. Terence Rees, *Theatre Lighting in the Age of Gas* (London: Society for Theatre Research, 1978), is by far the best account of nineteenth-century stage and auditorium lighting, and is fully illustrated. George Taylor, *Players and Performances in the Victorian Theatre* (Manchester: Manchester University Press, 1989), is the only general study of nineteenth-century acting published since the last century; Tracy Davis, *Actresses as Working Women* (London: Routledge, 1991), is valuable as a social and economic study rather than an analysis of performance.

Finally, an ample selection of the best dramatic criticism of the day has been selected and edited by George Rowell in *Victorian Dramatic Criticism* (London: Methuen, 1971); there are well over 100 essays here, on topics ranging from acting and the drama itself to audiences and the music hall. It is hardly necessary to add that many of the books cited in this bibliography contain extensive bibliographies helpful as guides to further investigation.

CHRONOLOGY

Edward Fitzball (*1792–1873*)

1822   *The Fortunes of Nigel, or King James I and His Times*. Melodrama. Surrey.

1824   *The Floating Beacon, or The Norwegian Wreckers*. Melodrama. Surrey.

1825   *The Pilot, or A Tale of the Sea*. Melodrama. Adelphi.

1827   *The Flying Dutchman, or The Phantom Ship*. Melodrama. Adelphi.

1828   *The Inchcape Bell, or The Dumb Sailor Boy*. Melodrama. Surrey.

1829   *The Red Rover, or The Mutiny of the Dolphin*. Melodrama. Adelphi.

1833   *Jonathan Bradford, or The Murder at the Roadside Inn*. Melodrama. Surrey.

1851   *Azael, or The Prodigal of Memphis*. Spectacle melodrama. Astley's.

1855   *Nitocris, Queen of Egypt*. Tragedy. Drury Lane.

Joseph Stirling Coyne (*1803–68*)

1842   *Dobson and Company, or My Turn Next*. Farce. Adelphi.

1843   *Binks the Bagman*. Farce. Adelphi.

1846   *Did You Ever Send Your Wife to Camberwell?* Farce. Adelphi.

1847   *How to Settle Accounts with Your Laundress*. Farce. Adelphi.

1850   *My Wife's Daughter*. Comedy. Olympic.

1852   *Box and Cox Married and Settled*. Farce. Haymarket.

1861   *A Terrible Secret*. Farce. Drury Lane.

1868   *The Woman of the World*. Comedy. Olympic.

George Henry Lewes (*1817–78*)

1850   *The Noble Heart*. Tragedy. Theatre Royal, Manchester.

1851   *The Game of Speculation*. Comedy. Lyceum.

1852   *A Chain of Events*. Drama. Lyceum.

1853   *The Lawyers*. Comedy. Lyceum.

1854   *A Cozy Couple*. Farce. Lyceum.

George Robert Sims (*1847–1922*)

1881   *The Lights o' London*. Drama. Princess's.

1882   *Romany Rye*. Drama. Princess's.

1883   *In the Ranks*. Drama. Adelphi. (With Henry Pettitt)

1885   *The Harbour Lights*. Drama. Adelphi. (With Henry Pettitt)

1889   *London Day by Day*. Drama. Adelphi. (With Henry Pettitt)

1891   *The Trumpet Call*. Drama. Adelphi. (With Robert Buchanan)

Henry Arthur Jones (*1851–1929*)

1882   *The Silver King*. Drama. Princess's. (With Henry Herman)

1884   *Breaking a Butterfly*. Drama. Princess's. (With Henry Herman. A version of *A Doll's House*)

1889   *The Middleman*. Drama. Shaftesbury.

1890   *Judah*. Drama. Shaftesbury.

1891   *The Dancing Girl*. Drama. Haymarket.

1894   *The Masqueraders*. Drama. St James's.

1894   *The Case of Rebellious Susan*. Comedy. Criterion.

1896   *Michael and His Lost Angel*. Drama. Lyceum.

1897   *The Liars*. Comedy. Criterion.

1900   *Mrs Dane's Defence*. Drama. Wyndham's.

THE INCHCAPE BELL, OR THE DUMB SAILOR BOY

A Nautical Burletta

In Two Acts

BY

EDWARD FITZBALL

CAST

SIR JOHN TREVANLY, a retired sea officer	Mr Bromley
CAPTAIN TAFFRAIL, of the Preventive Service	Mr Kirk
HANS HATTOCK, the rover	Mr Osbaldiston
GUY RUTHVEN, the outcast	Mr Rayner
THE DUMB SAILOR BOY	Miss Scott
SAMPSON SAWDUST, a ship's carpenter	Mr Vale
JUPITER SEABREEZE, a marine	Mr Rogers
AMELIA	Mrs Smith
BECKEY BUTTERFLY, her attendant	Mrs Vale
MRS TAPPS, the landlady	Madame Simon

Sailors, Marines, Smugglers, &c.

First performed at the Surrey Theatre
26 May 1828

1.1

*Exterior of an old-fashioned public-house on the sea-coast, L
Inscription over the door, 'The Inchcape Bell'—an ancient castle
on distant cliffs—vessels mooring, R a tree, under which Mrs
Tapps is spreading a table.*

*Seamen discovered mending nets, &c. They come forward, and
sing*

CHORUS

> Over the green and curling wave,
> Warning the seaman from his grave,
> When rocks disappear, and billows swell,
> Ding, dong, rings the Inchcape Bell.°
>> Ding, dong, &c. (Bell heard)   5

> Oft, through the stilly midnight gloom,
> Knelling the drowned wretch to his tomb,
> Through sullen rock, and tempest yell,
> Ding, dong, rings the Inchcape Bell.
>> Ding, dong, &c. (Exeunt seamen R)   10

Enter Jupiter from the Inn, L

JUPITER Here comes Captain Taffrail, my master; hurrah! Lend a
hand there boys, to tow in the boat; yo ho, your honour!

TAFFRAIL (*without, RUE*) What cheer? what cheer? yo ho!
*Enter Taffrail, landing from a boat, out of which Jupiter takes
a portmanteau, and carries it into the house, L*

MRS TAPPS (*LC*) Welcome, your honour, to the Inchcape Bell:
thanks to the previous arrival of your servant, Mr Jupiter, every   15
thing is in ship-shape. Won't your honour walk in, and take
refreshment after your honour's fatigue?

TAFFRAIL (*C*) No, I thank you, my good lady. If this table be not
better engaged, I'll take it; this seat commands a fine sea view—and
yonder old castle—   20

MRS TAPPS Belongs to Sir John Trevanly, your honour.

TAFFRAIL Who has been lately travelling on the Continent.

MRS TAPPS Yes, with his young and beautiful niece, Miss
Amelia.

TAFFRAIL (*aside*) She *is* here, then. I must and will obtain another   25
interview; she'll relent—I'm sure she will. Much as I disliked my
new appointment to this Preventive Service,° since it has conducted me to Amelia's feet—(*bell heard*) What bell is that?

MRS TAPPS That's the Inchcape Bell, your honour.

TAFFRAIL Still I don't understand.   30

MRS TAPPS It's a bell constructed by Sir John's orders, which, being
attached to a raft, is rung by the rising of the sea itself, and serves
as a warning to mariners to keep off the dangerous Inchcape Rock
when it is concealed by the water, your honour.

TAFFRAIL A benevolent man, this Sir John Trevanly, though an   35
unfortunate one, as I'm sorry to understand.

MRS TAPPS Yes, it's now some years agone, during Sir John's
absence in town, to wait on His Majesty, that the smugglers
pillaged the castle, and carried away Lady Trevanly and her
infant son: many people are of opinion that both mother and son   40
were murdered in the very cavern where the Inchcape Bell
hangs.

TAFFRAIL And the assassins never discovered?

MRS TAPPS Never, to my knowledge; but your honour stands in
need of something better than sad stories—we have excellent wine.   45

TAFFRAIL (*sits at table*) I'll trouble you for some.

MRS TAPPS Trouble! It's a pleasure. (*Exit into the inn, L*)

TAFFRAIL Poor Sir John; I don't wonder at his reluctance to separate
from his niece.

    Enter Jupiter from the inn, L

Well, Jupiter, how do you like the house?   50

JUPITER A mud-hole! a mere mud-hole, your honour.

TAFFRAIL Well, but a mud-hole, touched by the necromantic shaft
of love, becomes a golden palace; what ecstasy to be so near my
Amelia!

JUPITER Ah, sir! but I've better news than that: my old flame Beckey   55
Butterfly, whom, when I last quitted England, I left barmaid at the
Crab in Boots, has come somehow to live at the castle here, and is
now principal soubrette° to your Amelia.

TAFFRAIL Have you seen Beckey?

JUPITER Yes, for a few minutes only: the false-hearted hussy! She   60
had the assurance to tell me she'd gotten a new sweetheart, one
Sampson Sawdust, a carpenter. Think of a carpenter, after a smart
little handsome marine like me; a tar-bucket to a bottle of
burgundy. Ha, ha! I say, captain, if we could but press these

women aboard our schooner, what a splice the chaplain would   65
make of it.

TAFFRAIL Egad, I wish it were possible! (*Sampson sings without,*
RUE) But who's that?

SAMPSON (*without*) 'A sawyer's° the man, with his hammer and nails;
His spirits are stout, and his heart never fails.'   70
Holla! Inchcape Bell! Mother Tapps! ho! soho!
Enter Sampson Sawdust, RUE, who crosses to the inn, L,
meeting Mrs Tapps, who re-enters from the house, with wine and
bread in a basket

MRS TAPPS Your servant, Mr Sawdust, your servant. (*Goes to the*
table with wine)

JUPITER Mr Sawdust! oh ho! 'tis the very man—how I should like
to strangle him!   75

SAMPSON (*putting down his basket of tools*) Take care, little fellow;
don't tumble into my basket.

JUPITER I—little fellow—what a rhinoceros!

SAMPSON Boo! (*Jupiter retires up*) And you, Mother Tapps, you are
a nice woman!   80

MRS TAPPS (*C*) Dear me, Mr Sawdust, what are you going to say?
No harm, I hope, before customers. (*Taffrail comes down, R*)

SAMPSON I begs pardon, your honour, but on my way from the next
village, through the short cuts among the rocks there, I just met
with a poor body that's a-starving—and that's a shame I makes free   85
to nail on the back of the first housekeeper I meets with; that's
you, Mother Tapps—do you know anything of a famished boy?

MRS TAPPS Ah! then you've seen the dumb sailor-boy of the rocks,
whom every body is talking about so.

TAFFRAIL (*R*) What dumb sailor-boy?   90

MRS TAPPS A poor outcast cretur, your honour, who of late has been
seen wandering amongst the almost inaccessible recesses once so
haunted by the smugglers.

TAFFRAIL But who is he?

MRS TAPPS Nobody can tell that; all attempts to detain him have   95
been in vain. He speaks by action, and never quits his retreat,
except impelled by hunger.

SAMPSON Then he's hungry enough now, for here he comes—no,
he's afraid.

MRS TAPPS Come here, boy; we'll give you something to eat.   100

TAFFRAIL Show him something to eat. Here, boy, here; we'll do you
no harm.

5

Music. As he holds up the basket, the Boy rushes wildly on R, sinks on his knees, and begins to eat voraciously. Jupiter comes down R

JUPITER Well, I declare he runs and eats like a greyhound: if you can't speak, boy, what's your name?

SAMPSON Numbskull!   105

JUPITER Well, I'm sure, that's a very odd name indeed; I'm glad it doesn't apply to me. (*Goes up*)

TAFFRAIL What a picture of misery! Boy, do you understand when you are spoken to? Can you hear?

Music. The Boy kisses his hands, and implies that he can hear

TAFFRAIL You perceive he does understand me; I must endeavour to   110
understand him.

HANS (*in the house, L*) Landlady! where are you? ho!

The Boy utters an exclamation of terror, and suddenly starts up, trembling—drops the basket

TAFFRAIL He's terrified! Whose voice was that in the house?

MRS TAPPS That? Oh! Hans Hattock's, an honest trader, who comes here from foreign parts once in a while; his ship is just off the   115
coast. Never fear him, boy—he's a kind-hearted—I may say a charitable cretur; why, his stay now is to pay a visit to an old comrade of his in distress—poor crazy Guy Ruthven, who, for the matter of that, is as indigent and friendless as this boy.

The door opens; and, as Hans presents himself, the Boy, with a cry of terror, rushes out, R

HANS 'Tis he!   120

TAFFRAIL You know that boy?

HANS I—ugh—no, no (*eagerly*)—do you?

TAFFRAIL We know that he is unfortunate—that he is perishing for want; but you and he seemed to recognize each other.

HANS Yes; it struck me that he was a deserter from my ship—I must   125
follow him. (*Exit hastily R*)

SAMPSON (*having observed Hans*) If that man's fissygognomy doesn't mean no good, I don't know a mopnail° from a tin-tack.

JUPITER Well said, Sawdust; what think you, your honour?

TAFFRAIL I'm of the same opinion; besides, Hans Hattock's ship   130
bears no good name. (*Musing*) Jupiter!

JUPITER Your honour?

TAFFRAIL Call back the boatmen—I may require their assistance.

JUPITER Ay, ay, your honour. (*Exit, RUE*)

6

TAFFRAIL Friend carpenter, you are acquainted with this neigh- 135
bourhood; you must become my pilot to the dumb boy's retreat.

SAMPSON Why, your honour, I'd do anything in a charitable way;
but really them there caverns are so cold, and my constitution so
delicate, that— 140

TAFFRAIL Nay, no remonstrance, sir: I have an imperfect knowledge
of this Hans Hattock; for aught I know, the life of one of His
Majesty's subjects may be at stake here. I charge you, in the king's
name, to attend me—refuse at your peril.

SAMPSON Well, your honour, I'm ready at all times to sarve his most 145
gracious majesty; but surely His Majesty's generosity wouldn't
object to my taking a little small tiny drop of brandy with me, just
to keep up my courage. Excuse my modesty; but mine's a poor
constitution.

TAFFRAIL By all means, the brandy! (*Exit, R*) 150

SAMPSON Here's my pocket vial; fill it, Mother Tapps; it is but a
little one, but it sarves a purpose. (*Gives a large bottle to Mrs Tapps,
who goes into the inn, L*) Lead the way, your honour—I'll not fail.
Come, Mother Tapps, make haste. (*Re-enter Mrs Tapps*) You take
care of my basket—my hatchet I takes with me; I never travels 155
without my hatchet—with that and brandy I never fears cutting
my way through the world. (*Exit Mrs Tapps into the inn, L*) I likes
brandy—it makes one brave and loving; I always drinks it when I
goes a-courting.

SONG—Sampson
Air—'Blue Bonnets'°

Drink, drink, lovers of every sort; 160
    Then, my boys, boldly you Cupid may throttle.
Drink, drink, while you can get a drop;
    Often man's courage lies hid in a bottle.
        Many a Captain Bluff
        Feels his pulse low enough, 165
    Nor dares the question pop, though e'er so handy.
        Prime and make ready, then,
        Boys, when you kiss again,
    Smacks for the lasses, and bravos for brandy.
Drink, drink, else you may shut up shop; 170
    All know that love is an awkward disorder;
Drink, drink, while you can get a drop,

7

> Then march to love's battle straight forward in order.
> > (Staggers)
> Come, carpenters all, whose hammers are thumping—
> Tailors enamoured, and trembling with fears—   175
> Come, and get groggy, while Cupid is bumping—
> Come with the thimble, the bodkin, and shears.
> > Lasses hates bashful men;
> > Here's lignum wity,° then—
> Brandy, the balsam of ev'ry disorder.   180
> > You that, like me, am shy,
> > Drink, and 'tis all my eye,—
> March to love's battle straight forward in order.

Staggers out, R

1.2

A Gothic room in the castle, a window in CF. The portraits of a lady and child hanging up, R

Enter Sir John Trevanly, L

SIR JOHN Ever, on the anniversary of this fatal day—a day of woe, of misery, to the wretched, heirless Trevanly—my soul turns with new yearning to yon sad lineaments. Oh! my sainted wife—my lost, lost boy, worse than dead, torn from me in a fatal unguarded hour! Oh! when will my torn, lacerated heart have ceased to   5
remember, to deplore ye! Must I still live, live on, despairing? Hear me, Heaven!

Enter Amelia with caution, L, regarding him as he gazes at the picture

AMELIA My uncle! my dear, loved, unhappy uncle!

He starts—she throws herself into his arms

SIR JOHN My only, only child!

AMELIA Oh sir! if you love me, why continue to yield yourself to this   10
despondency! Your health, your life, is rapidly declining beneath accumulating sorrow. I knew, I was sure, your return to this melancholy scene of early misery must increase the gloom which too fully occupies your heart: for your poor Amelia's sake, I entreat you, dear sir, study to abandon these too vain regrets.   15

SIR JOHN Yes, I will, my child—my good, obedient Amelia. Truly, as thou sayest, my once peaceful home does indeed more fully

8

remind me of all I have lost, while it leads me to forget the remaining gem which I ought most to estimate. We'll not tarry long here, Amelia, for your sake; no, no—yet I'm glad that I have 20 this roof to screen me from the world on the anniversary of the distracting day on which I was deprived of my wife! My poor boy! But I'll be firm, Amelia; yet a father's, a husband's feelings will have way.

AMELIA Tears; ah! come with me dear uncle, I'll take my harp, and 25 sing to you; you know that always consoles you.

SIR JOHN Presently, presently, Amelia: I'll retire an instant; after a moment of solitude, of devotion, and tears, I shall be better. Come presently—presently, good girl.

Hurries out, R

AMELIA Ah, woe is me! If my hand were not already promised to 30 another, how could I add to the sufferings of my uncle, by acceding to an union, which, as yet, his voice has not sanctioned.

Enter Beckey, L

BECKEY Not marry Captain Taffrail, Miss; not see him!

AMELIA How can I, Beckey? Long ere I beheld Captain Taffrail, my uncle had promised my hand to another, and has he not kindly 35 consented to leave me to my own choice, on condition that I accede to the suit of no one till the completion of a year? That year will soon have expired, and how dishonourable, undutiful in me, not to keep my word with my uncle. His sufferings—

BECKEY Consider the captain's sufferings, Miss. 40

AMELIA I do; but, if Captain Taffrail truly loves me, as he professes, the present delay will but enable him, by his patience, to prove that affection. What letter is that in your hand?

BECKEY A love-letter, Miss.

AMELIA A love-letter! Indeed—from whom? 45

BECKEY From my new sweetheart, Sampson Sawdust: I loves love-letters, so I always make Sampson send me one every morning by the carrier. Here's a pistol, Miss, all charged with oaths and detestations,° that go quite through your heart, so they do—only listen. (*Reads*) 'Dearest and most beautifullest Beckey—I love you 50 a great deal'—a great deal,° you know Sampson's a carpenter, Miss—'a great deal better than I do good nails. Your heart is the sawpit of my affection; and the gimlet of your eye has bored such a hole right through my brist, that if you don't shortly consent to plug it up with Hymenses torch, I shall be dead and useless as a 55 rusty saw.—Yours inaffectionately,—Sampson Sawdust.'

AMELIA Ha, ha! if you love Sampson, why not marry him?

BECKEY Why, that's true; and Sampson has offered to make an honest woman of me, as you perceive, Miss; but I fear the thing's impossible.   60

AMELIA How?

BECKEY Why, you must know, Miss, I've gotten another sweetheart, Jupiter Seabreeze, the captain's little man, and he's wanting to make an honest woman of me, too.

AMELIA You astonish me.   65

BECKEY Ah, Miss! I've astonished many in my time, I promise you. Jupiter's more genteeler, and writes finer love-letters than Sawdust; but then, again, you know he's such a morsel of a man, not bigger than one's thimble.

AMELIA I don't think you are likely to break your heart for either,   70
Beckey, if I may judge by your discourse.

BECKEY Why, you see, Miss, as for heart-breaking, we servants have to pay for breakages, and that always makes me very careful; and hearts, you know, are neither to be bought nor mended, like cups and saucers. But won't you write a line to the captain, Miss, just   75
to welcome him ashore. Jupiter assured me that his master would be at the Inchcape Bell by this time; I'm just going down to the village, and I could leave the letter, you know.

AMELIA I'm afraid it would be very wrong.

BECKEY I'm sure it would be very charitable; and, as parson says   80
at church, charity covers a multitude of sins—and the captain's so uneasy for a line; you'll break his heart if you don't write, Miss.

AMELIA Well, Beckey, sooner than do that—

BECKEY Ah, you'll write. Well, Miss, I'll go and busy myself till the   85
letter's finished.

AMELIA Oh, you needn't do that.

BECKEY Indeed; why not, Miss?

AMELIA Oh, because it's finished already.
          Gives a letter from her pocket

BECKEY Daisy me! I suppose she wrote it in her pocket; sure, how   90
clever some folks be. Ah, Miss, I see you young ladies likes love-letters as well as we poor servant girls—I'm sure it's very pretty amusement; so I'm off: how pleased the captain will be. I'll bring you an answer, Miss: the captain will give me half-a-crown; and, Jupiter, he'll give me a kiss. Daisy me! I wish he was a little   95
taller—he can scarcely reach my lips. (*Exit, L*)

AMELIA Happy Beckey! What innocent insensibility! Heigho! I'm
afraid, by these palpitations, that my tenderness on Taffrail's
account is even more deeply rooted than I believed; but my
uncle—yonder he sits, so sad, so mournful, (*looking off, R*) I   100
must not forget him. Ah! how assuasive is the voice of those we
love!

SONG—Amelia

> *Let us wander through the meadows,*
>   *Where the water-lilies bloom,*
> *And the honey-bee is drinking*   105
>   *From the cups of golden broom.*
> *In my bow'r full of beauty,*
>   *While the tear is in your eye,*
> *I'll take my harp, and sing the song*
>   *Of happy days gone by.*   110
>
> *Let us wander through the forest,*
> *Under leaf and under bough,*
> *Where the merry birds are singing,*
> *And the briar-roses blow.*   115
>   *In my bow'r, &c. (Exit, L)*

Re-enter Sir John, approaching the picture

SIR JOHN In the absence of Amelia, a moment of contemplation;
and—(*knocking at window*)—still fresh interruption! Who knocks?
> *Music. The window is hastily opened by the Boy, who enters,
> and, throwing himself at Sir John's feet, indicates that he is
> pursued, and that he is dumb*

SIR JOHN Dumb, and pursued. Ah! Captain Taffrail here; is it of him
you are afraid?
> *Music. Enter Taffrail, and two sailors. The Boy runs towards
> Taffrail, embraces him, places his hand on his heart, and
> indicates that he is his friend*

SIR JOHN What am I to understand? Captain Taffrail, what seek ye?   120
TAFFRAIL Protection for this poor boy, who is pursued by a
smuggler.
SIR JOHN By a smuggler! Boy, can you describe your wrongs; can
you point out your enemy?
> *Music. The window suddenly opens, and Hans Hattock looks in.
> Boy screams, and runs towards Sir John. Hans disappears*

TAFFRAIL Behold the oppressor, Hans Hattock!   125

SIR JOHN Let him be pursued. (*Exit sailors, L*) Boy, you remain here
in safety.

> *Music. Boy expresses joy and gratitude, embraces Taffrail,
> points to the window, then exit with Sir John, R. Taffrail
> hurries out, L*

1.3

> *A miserable hut, composed of two boats, and rudely
> thatched—window and door—the back scene dark—knotted
> rocks on the flats.*°

> *Enter Hans, hastily, L*

HANS 'Tis the place: luckily, I have discovered it just ere nightfall,
which has screened me, also, from further pursuit. Old comrade,
ho! Guy Ruthven—come forth, I say!

> *Knocking violently. Guy, with a lamp in his hand, opens the
> window*

GUY What want ye? Is it Guy Ruthven you seek? No violence! I'll
not be taken—no—I'll fire the thatch—burn the cabin—burn it,   5
with myself, to ashes. Ha, ha, ha, ha! (*Wildly*)

HANS Ugh! don't you know me, Guy Ruthven? Why, man, I'm an
old friend; look at me: I'm Hans Hattock, your old captain, come
here on purpose to shake you by the hand.

GUY Hans Hattock, the rover,° here again; it can't be—mortal men,   10
laden with crimes like his, live not through such storms as I have
heard. Demon of darkness, even in that form I know thee; tempt
me no more to the edge of yonder dreadful precipice—leave
me—go, go, go!

HANS Nonsense! how you talk: is this your hospitality to a comrade   15
who brings you aid and comfort?

GUY Comfort to me—ha, ha! mocking devil! leave me! (*Shuts the
window violently*)

HANS Ah, dog! come forth, come forth! Or my fury—you know
me—(*shaking the door*)—Guy Ruthven, ho!   20

> *Enter Guy Ruthven, abruptly, wielding a staff*

GUY Horrible tormentor, fly! Or—death!

HANS How's this, Guy Ruthven? how's this? I'm not to be cajoled;
be mad to all the world, but not to me: the blood that you have
sold, do I not know the price—tremble!

GUY (*dropping the staff*) Blood, innocent blood: my secret—oh yes!   25
Then you are indeed Hans Hattock. Oh, these hands—how often and
vainly have I plunged them into the sea-wave to wash away the guilt
which enstained them, which enstains them still. (*Shuddering*)

HANS Bah! what is all this? When first I knew you, you had the
courage of a man.   30

GUY Yes, yes, yes; for then I felt like a man conscious of his own
integrity. The sky shone on me, then, all blue and lovely, though
in sorrow. The sea of my life was smooth, dangerless to what it
became afterwards—dreadful was the tempest that ensued—all
wreck'd: hope, peace, innocence. (*Wildly*)   35

HANS Psha! hadn't you the revenge you coveted so?

GUY Revenge, on a poor defenceless boy.

HANS What if I tell you that the boy lives?

GUY Lives! Said you not at our last interview that he was drowned?

HANS Yes, that was because you were always talking of confessing—I   40
did it to mislead you; but I tell you now, he lives, and on this very
shore too, and is this moment in the castle, and under the
protection of Sir John Trevanly. They have taken him there for
safety; I listened, and overheard.

GUY Then all has been discovered.   45

HANS No, no; the boy was happy enough in the ship, clever and
active as the best man aboard, till a dying fool, stung with what he
called conscience, revealed the whole story of the lad's being forced
away while an infant; but, as luck would have it, I cut short the
disclosure just time enough to prevent the discovery, not of the   50
mother's fate, but of the father's name. The boy was never happy
from that moment; and at length found means to elude even my
vigilance, and quit the ship.

GUY And knows that Sir John Trevanly is—

HANS Have I not said—no; that secret is still our own; but the urchin   55
must not be suffered to escape, even though they detain him at the
castle. You, who know the subterranean passes so well, must
conduct me, and some of my crew, at midnight—

GUY Not through those fearful vaults again—no, no, never again—do
not ask it. (*Recoiling*)   60

HANS Better there than to the gallows, where you and I must soon
be swinging, if that boy's evidence—

GUY I will not—I dare not—

HANS (*fiercely*) You shall! Coward-hearted slave! Will it content you
to walk tamely to the scaffold, while that boy laughs at the ruin he   65

has wrought? Have you ceased to remember the mother that bore
you, over whose grave you swore—

GUY Oh! do not, do not, I implore you, rekindle flames which have
already raged too long; do not add new life to the misery which
gnaws, and has well nigh eaten, its way to my brain. (*Pressing his*   70
brow) O—h! for you, seek your ship again; leave every ill here to
me.

HANS I can't go without my cargo: I won't go without the boy. Will
you do as I require?

GUY No.   75

HANS The night thickens. I'm not to be trifled with: it were as easy
to carry out that boy by the means I have suggested, and that
without suspicion too, as it is to run before the wind. Who
amongst the few inmates of the castle is to thwart us? You are still
obstinate? Force, then, must compel you. (*Blows a whistle—several*   80
pirates enter, L) You see, I'm not quite defenceless; seize that
deserter from our ship.

GUY Hold! I'm no deserter from your ship.

HANS You left us without my permission; and, though years are gone
since then, you know the rules which bind us, bind us all. And, if   85
you refuse to become our pilot this night, expect the resentment
you merit. Forward: if he hesitates, do your duty. (*They seize him*)

GUY Nay, hear me; what should urge me on?

HANS Your father's infamy! Your mother's wrongs!

GUY Spare me, spare me! Brain, brain! (*They force him out, L*)   90

1.4

*A back view of the castle, composed of a turret occupying half
the stage, beyond which, over a rampart of rocks, the sea, by
moonlight. A verandah and window, practicable° in the turret,
beneath which is a skylight; on the R, a rampart overhung by a
tree; near the rampart, a ladder.*

Amelia discovered in the verandah. Taffrail beneath

TAFFRAIL Stay, dearest Amelia, why thus hasten my departure?
Think what I have endured since last we met. Ah! you little
imagine what fond and faithful emotions swell the breast of a
sailor, while ploughing the green sea-billows. He turns to the
recollection of the far-distant maid of his heart, his brightest hope   5

and solace. Let me, then, still continue to gaze on those dear eyes:
'tis early yet—the moon is scarcely up.

SAMPSON (*peeping over rampart, R*) Captain, captain, you'll excuse
me, but I hear a boat—we may chance to get a clincher° if we don't
peg off.°   10

TAFFRAIL At this hour! who can it be?

AMELIA My uncle; in his wildness, of late, he paces the ramparts.
Adieu.

TAFFRAIL Till when, Amelia?

AMELIA Soon, very soon: your generosity in behalf of the poor dumb   15
boy today has induced my uncle to speak of you with less reserve.
He perceives the regard which we entertain for each other, and, I
am quite sure, will not long withhold his consent. Let us not, then,
by stolen interviews, appear to doubt his goodness, but part at
once. Adieu. (*Exit, L*)   20

TAFFRAIL Adieu, loved Amelia!

SAMPSON Captain, captain, look sharp, or you'll have a chisel thrust
into your ribs—I hear them coming.

TAFFRAIL The ladder! quick. (*Exit by ladder*)

BECKEY (*entering by verandah*) I'm sure I thought my young lady   25
never meant to leave off courting; these gentlefolks never considers
any folks' wants, but their own. I wonder what Sampson would
say, if he knowed I'd consented to meet little Mister Jupiter
tonight. What a while he is a-coming—I don't hear him whistle.
Yet I told him how he might climb the wall there, by means of the   30
old tree, as easy, as easy—any body below there? (*Coughs*)

SAMPSON (*peeping over the wall*) That's Beckey's hem! It's as musical
to my ear as the notes of my hammer; how hammerous I am of
Beckey, to be sure. (*Enters by ladder*) So, all still again—Beckey,
ah Beckey!   35

BECKEY Who is it?

SAMPSON Your own dear Sampson Sawdust, love! I wants to kiss
your beautiful red hand, Beckey.

BECKEY Sampson, as I live! I'm sure you be vastly perlite,° Mr
Sampson, and if you were tall enough to reach my hand, as the   40
night's dark enough to hide one's blushes, mayhaps I might
consent, for once—so you would go home and go to bed sober, like
an honest man.

SAMPSON Tall enough! Oh, I've got a ladder here, Beckey, and a
strong one, too—made it myself, on purpose to come a-courting   45
with.

BECKEY A ladder! (*Aside*) Dearest me, if Mister Jupiter should arrive, what a dickament° I should be in, surely.

>*He places the ladder under the window*

SAMPSON (*on ladder*) Oh, Beckey! this is the most suspicious° moment of my life. Oh, Beckey! all other women, compared in beauty to you, are but as common white deal compared to Spanish mahogany. This night, Beckey, this celestral night, I swears, by my adze and my plane, you've excited such a locomotion here, as makes my heart all curl up like a new shaving, and my lips as dry as sawdust itself.

BECKEY I hopes, Mr Sampson, you don't mean to take any ungentle-man-like vantage, sich as trying to get up here, because, you see, nobody would hear me if I were to scream ever so loud.

SAMPSON What, not nobody at all, Beckey?

>*A part of one of the ramparts is opened, and Hans appears, listening*

BECKEY No, Miss Amelia is gone to her chamber. Sir John sleeps at the other end of the castle; nobody rests on this side, except the stranger boy, whom the captain brought here today—he's put into that room (*pointing up*) but he can't hear, you know, because he's dumb.

HANS In that room! (*Retires*)

SAMPSON What the devil was that?

BECKEY When? (*Hears a whistle. Aside*) Mercy on us! it's Mr Jupiter's signal: how shall I manage?

>*Jupiter, behind the verandah, puts up his head, and disappears*

SAMPSON There, again! (*Whistle*) Don't you hear it?

BECKEY No.

SAMPSON Then here's deaf and dumb near enough each other for once. I hope, Beckey, you've not been playing me false; my blood boils at the idea, like a glue-kettle over a slow fire. See! see there! That's very like a man's head bobbing up and down behind that apple tree; and very like little hop-o'-my-thumb's head,° too. Ah, Beckey, I'm afraid you're perfiderous. I'm afraid you are.

BECKEY Sure and sartain, the man's not in his right mind.

SAMPSON You knows well enough who's a-coming; this is a point-ment unbeknown to me, Beckey. You are perfiderous, I say. I'm an undone carpenter, but I'll give your gallant a welcome he little dreams on. I'll make him look as contemptible as a one-eared donkey, I will; only admit me into that there chamber.

BECKEY What the deuce does the man mean? I'll cry murder, so I will.   85

SAMPSON Do: nobody will hear, you know; so, if you expects me to be your wife—no, no, if you expects to be my husband—bah! lend me your cap, and not a word—in I come. (*Enters the window, by the verandah*)

>   *Music. Enter Jupiter by the tree. He whistles*

JUPITER Nobody answers yet; that must be the window—how   90 cunning in me to pretend to the captain I was ill, and must go to bed. He little thinks where I am; no, no—he's fast asleep by this time. Ha, ha! Poor Sampson, I wonder how his head feels? He, he! Beckey's in the right on't—we marines are devils of fellows. So, so, here's a ladder! Well done, Beckey—I know what a ladder   95 placed under a pretty woman's window means. Poor devil, Sampson, how I pity him; I wonder how his horns° are? Ha, ha, ha, ha! (*Sampson looks out at the window, with Beckey's cap on*) Beckey! hist, Beckey dear.

SAMPSON Heigho! did you speak?   100

JUPITER Yes, it's I, your own cunning little Jupiter.°

SAMPSON You may come up in a minute. Oh!

JUPITER Only just suffer me to feel the ends of your fairy fingers.

SAMPSON Yes—there! (*Strikes him and closes the window*)

JUPITER Oh, murder! (*Falls through skylight*)   105

SAMPSON Immortal Jupiter fallen into the coal-cellar; and Beckey gone squalling into the castle like an alarm-bell. I shall be taken up for murder and housebreaking, and hanged, without judge or jury. Oh! somebody else.

>   *Music. Comes down and conceals himself, as Hans and smugglers enter—he perceives the ladder, and enters the castle, as they disappear. Re-enter Sampson—he removes ladder, and places it against the opposite rampart*

SAMPSON There's a gang of 'em—Jupiter, I say! So! the little man's   110 safe enough; more frightened than hurt. Jupiter, I say, are you there?

JUPITER Yes, I'm here, safe as a mouse in a trap—lend me a hand. Oh!

>   *Music. A loud cry—the Dumb Boy appears at the upper window, through which he escapes, and lets himself down to the verandah—noise—Sampson runs up the ladder, and escapes over the rampart*

SAMPSON So, more alarms! Heels befriend me.° I—oh! I'm afraid I'm a coward as well as a carpenter; I'm afraid I am.   115

17

Music. The Dumb Boy escapes by climbing over the verandah—he is pursued by Hans and the smugglers. The Boy is half way up the ladder, which Sampson has left standing against the rampart. Hans is about to seize him, as Guy Ruthven, from the secret opening, rushes in, and, snatching up a fragment of rock, stands in an attitude of defiance at the foot of the ladder, and cuts off the pursuit

GUY Fly, boy, fly, and save yourself; and he amongst ye that dares to advance a single step to harm one hair of his defenceless head dies instantly! (*Picture*)°

2.1

Deck of the smuggler's ship, by moonlight.

Hans Hattock, Guy Ruthven, and crew discovered, seated and lying about, carousing°

CHORUS

> *Here's a health and success to the free-trader,°*
> *Wherever the breezes blow—*
> *May prosperous gales*
> *Fill our bonny white sails,*
> *As over the billows we go,*   5
> *Merrily,*
> *Merrily—*
> *A health! A health to the free-trader, &c.*

HORNPIPE°

Enter Hans, from the hold

HANS (*C*) Ha, ha, ha! That scoundrel, Guy, thought to betray us, but, thanks to the defenceless state of the castle, and the lateness   10 of the hour, we brought off all safe; they must have sharp wits indeed who think to outwit me. Master there, turn the boy off to his duty again, and haul up the other prisoners before the mast. So, here comes the runaway.

> *Music. Enter the Dumb Boy, R, with two buckets in his hands, beneath the weight of which he appears sinking; he puts them down in despair, and throws himself at Hans' feet*

HANS Come, come, none of your palaver here, youngster. You   15 thought to elude my craftiness, did you, by flying to the old cave? But it wouldn't do: I knew the haunt too well. Only you do your duty, and you'll find me, as usual, a most indulgent master. Recollect, I could have better spared any of the crew than yourself; you, with your slim figure, climbing about the rigging like a cat,   20 in here and out there, above and below, where no grown man could stow himself. To your duty, to your duty, and you and I'll be better friends than ever.

> *Music. The Boy starts up, throws down the buckets; stretches out his hand, in token of Heaven's vengeance, and his own resolution still to effect his escape*

HANS So, you threaten me: refractory, eh? Aloft, I say—still obstinate! Seize and lash him to the bows; let him threaten there till the   25
cold waves wash away his fury.
> *Music. The Boy is forced out, R, by two of the crew*

GUY Hear me, Hans: by our old acquaintanceship, by the fidelity
with which, for many years, I served you, I pray of you, on my
knees, let that boy go free. He knows nothing that can harm you,
out of this country; and, for myself, though I have been dragged   30
hither like a dog, I'll stay with you for ever, through fair weather
and through foul, as I have stayed, and serve you till I die.

HANS No, no, Guy Ruthven! You stay not here; it was only in the
hurry of the moment that I brought you off; you would have
betrayed us ashore. You are an old comrade, and I will not take   35
your life: a boat there, ho! a boat.
> *One of the crew hauls the boat alongside, L;° and the two who
> forced off the Boy re-enter, R*

GUY I'll not quit the vessel without the boy; if he remain, so do I.

HANS Hadn't you better take command of the ship at once, ha, ha,
ha! Away with him to the boat; we shall have it morning else. (*Two
of the crew advance to seize him*)   40

GUY Sailors, if you are men, as you hope to be pardoned your
offences hereafter, hear me, hear me.

HANS What! would you excite a mutiny, too? The manacles, I say.
(*Two of the crew fetch the manacles, and put them on*) I'll not
leave you till you are fairly rid of, and the first man that dares to   45
open his lips in reply to your appeals—he!—they know me; to the
boat!
> *Music. The Dumb Boy rushes in and throws himself into the
> arms of Guy; he is torn away by some of the crew, and carried
> out, R, sobbing violently. Smugglers return directly, R*

GUY (*as they carry out the Boy*) Boy, boy, you and I will meet again.
> *Guy is dragged into the boat, and followed by some of the crew,
> as Jupiter, in great disorder, runs in, R*

JUPITER Good Mr Hans, sweet gentlemen! If you are going ashore,
pray take me with you—I assure you I'm a wronged individual; I   50
don't like my berth. If you would but just take me from whence I
came, I should feel so much obliged.

HANS No, no, a detected spy stands little chance of liberation here.
You must be sneaking about to watch our actions, must you, out
of windows and skylights; you shall see enough of us, I warrant   55
you.

JUPITER Indeed, Mr Hans, that was all a mistake; I'm no spy, upon my word and honour.

HANS Can you deny that you belong to Captain Taffrail's vessel, which would be down upon us with a broadside in less than five 60 minutes, if we would suffer you to quit this. Down with him into the hold till my return; then to decide whether we take him to work through the voyage, or toss him over to the fishes.

    Hans and another get into the boat, and exit, L

JUPITER Toss me over to the fishes! Oh! Jupiter, Jupiter, a most inauspicious star art thou to thy namesake and representative 65 this night. Fishes' meat! This comely and interesting person food for sharks and lobsters. Ah, Beckey, Beckey, this comes of going a-courting by moonlight; beware, ye lovers all—beware, I say—(*two of the crew seize him, while the rest open a trap°*) Oh—o—h dear! sweet gentlemen, if ever your feelings was 70 touched, I—oh!

    They force him down, shut the trap, and exeunt, laughing, R

2.2

    A cavern opening to the sea, near the Inchcape Rock—still moonlight. Across a projecting timber, and directly over a clump of rocks, hangs the Inchcape Bell. This bell is attached by a chain to a floating raft, which lies on the other side of the cave, at the water's edge—an upright mast is embedded in the sand near it. As the scene opens, Sampson appears, descending hastily, but cautiously, RUE. The raft is lifted up and down by the rising and receding of the tide, and the Bell rings softly

SAMPSON Oh dear, oh dear, oh dear! What a run I've had! Thanks to the bell's clapper, I know exactly where I am now. I wish every bell's clapper were half as useful—fooh! If them rascals should have robbed the castle! If I don't hang myself before morning, I shall be taken up as an accomplish; and, if the smugglers happen 5 to catch hold of me tonight, they'll be laying an embargo on me, to prevent my 'peaching.° A sober man like me in such a quandary: where am I to go—what am I to do? I hear a boat—the smugglers, by all that's horrible—I'm pressed,° and sent to sea. Luckily, I seldom travel without my hatchet, stuck into my belt; and, if they 10 comes any nonsense, why—but I'm afraid I'm a coward—I'm afraid I am—so I'll creep in amongst this clump of rocks, just under the old Inchcape Bell, and lay there as still as a gimlet in a nail-box, till I can summon up courage to run away. Oh!

> *Music. He creeps in amongst the rocks immediately under the bell. Enter Guy Ruthven, Hans, and the smugglers, through the cave, RUE*

HANS Here we part, Guy Ruthven, and for ever. It was on this spot   15
we first met, the old bell ringing as now. You recollect that crazy mast.

GUY Recollect it! Oh yes—yes. It was there she fell, the unhappy Lady Trevanly—it was there these hands scooped out her unhal-lowed grave. Why have you brought me hither?   20

HANS Merely because our boat happened to get aground here somehow; I can't account for it. The tide sweeps up against this old cavern stronger tonight than ever. I can't say I should have entered here by choice; but as it is, bring the rope from the boat.

SMUGGLER You gave no orders for one.   25

HANS Here; you tear the rope off the Inchcape Bell—make haste—that rope will do exactly for my purpose.

GUY What act of impiety are you about? Would you silence that bell, whose friendly voice has saved so many human beings from perishing? Have a care, Hans, lest your own ship, as a judgement   30
on you, in the darkness of this very night—

HANS Bah! The rope, the rope, I say: we have no other means of securing him to the mast. See, now, your rough grappling has made those crazy old timbers give way, and the bell is coming down with its own weight. No matter; ease it to the rock, and off   35
with the rope—quick! quick!

> *They sever the rope, and the timbers break—they let down the Bell, which falls directly over the crevice where Sampson lies concealed*

GUY Mercy, Hans, mercy; if you leave me here, here, in this place, more dreadful and distorting to me than a living tomb, ere morning, the waters, which have already covered the Inchcape Rock, may rise and overwhelm me.   40

HANS Not so—the waters never rise above the summit of that mast, to which we'll leave you length of rope enough to climb; and you need not fear but at sunrise the hue and cry at the castle will send Taffrail and all his men on the look-out through every creek of these rocks. As for the bell there, I'm not sorry 'tis down. I never   45
liked the sound on't pealing out of this place—it was like—bah—

farewell, Guy; look to our next meeting. Aboard there, aboard—
the sky's as dark o' the sudden as though we should have a
squall—to the ship, ho!

    Music. Hans enters the boat, followed by the crew who have tied
    Guy to the mast. Exeunt, RUE

GUY Hans! Hans! Pity me, pity me: gone, all. The echoes of these   50
terrific° rocks yell in mine ear, like the accusing groans of the gone
for ever. In my wild, mad fancy, I see again the white form of her,
who, sleeping or waking, has ever haunted me—midnight, too—
hour of all hours to the guilty most terrific.

    The moon disappears, and the waves become more agitated.
    Music. Guy attempts to climb the mast, but falls strengthless

SAMPSON (*under the Bell*) Hillio! ho! Where am I? (*He breaks away*   55
one side of the Bell with his hatchet,° and peeps out) Where the deuce
am I? As I live, while I have been poking about to no purpose, to
find another way out, if the old bell hasn't fallen over the door of
my berth, and extinguished me. (*Comes out of the Bell*) Lucky I
had my hatchet, or I should never have been able to cut this bell.   60
What do I see? Mr Boreous° coming to invade these territories;
then I must decamp, or—

GUY A friendly voice. Help! help!

SAMPSON O dear! Here's a dead man calling for help. Who are you?

GUY A wretch.   65

SAMPSON Wretches must be saved, as well as other folks. Here's
another job for my hatchet. (*Chops the rope and releases Guy*)

GUY Kind fellow, I'm bound to you for ever.

SAMPSON Fiddlededee! You were bound to the post, you mean; but
we must think of going—this way. I know another track. Oh dear!   70
(*Sees Taffrail and marines*) Here's another knot in the wood.

    Enter Taffrail and marines, with torches, R

TAFFRAIL Hold! We have watched you from the heights above; we
have noticed your communion with the suspected boat, which just
now left the cave. You are our prisoners, and must attend us.

GUY Whither?   75

TAFFRAIL To the castle.

GUY Willingly.

SAMPSON Dear me, captain, don't you recollect me? I'm honest
sober Sampson, at your honour's service.

TAFFRAIL I know you well enough, Sampson; but your presence   80
here, and your recent separation from yonder men—these matters
surprise me.

SAMPSON What men, your honour? I'm a ruined carpenter, your honour, as sure as deals is deals, and brandy is brandy.

TAFFRAIL I have no doubt you are an excellent judge of the one, as   85
well as the other. Do you think you could tell smuggled brandy by the taste?

SAMPSON Oh, to be sure—that is (*they laugh*)—I'm afraid I've got into a kind of a sort of a hobble° here. Don't hang me, your honour. Oh dear!   90

TAFFRAIL Hang you—no! If you merit a rope's end, and if it be left for me to decide, why then—

SAMPSON What then, captain? Noble captain, what then?

TAFFRAIL Why, then, I am afraid you'll come off with the worst on't. For let me tell you, Master Sampson, there is nothing so agreeable   95
to me in life, as to punish the rascal who is base and mean enough, for his own paltry ends, to rob his native country of its dues, or the equitable tradesman of his just rights, and the lawful earnings of his honest industry.

Exeunt, R

2.3

A chamber in the castle. A window, through which lightning is seen at intervals.

Enter Beckey, sobbing, followed by Amelia, L

BECKEY O dear! O dear! I will break my heart at last, so I will.

AMELIA Don't take on so, Beckey: all will be right yet, depend on it.

BECKEY Ah, Miss, it's all very well for you to be tranquil, and calm, and easy; your sweetheart is to be found safe and well—but   5
what's become of mine? Both on 'em; poor Sampson—poor little Jewpeter—both carried off by the nasty wicked smugglers. If they had left *one*, it wouldn't have been so bad; but to take away every bit of 'em—mine's a hard case, so it is.

AMELIA Well, but Beckey, isn't Captain Taffrail gone in quest of   10
him? How fortunate for me this circumstance, which has introduced the captain to the castle, to protect us, as he says. I'm quite sure my uncle is grateful, and doesn't dislike the captain.

BECKEY No, no, Miss: you'll get a husband by last night's adventure, while I shall lose two. But suppose the smugglers should   15 carry away the captain too, Miss. (*Aside*) I wonder how she likes that.

AMELIA Heavens, Beckey! how you frighten me.

BECKEY (*aside*) I thought so! If she would grieve for the captain, what must I do with double her loss? Hah! didn't you think you heard the great gate flap to, Miss? (*As Beckey runs to the window behind, Amelia crosses to R*) Yes, it's the captain and his men, and I do really believe I hear my Sampson's musical voice—if it should be he, I'll not lose any more time, and so I'm determined. (*Runs out, L*)

AMELIA (*RC*) I hope they may have rescued the poor dumb boy—so amiable—so interesting.

    Enter Sir John Trevanly, R

SIR JOHN (*C*) So unfortunate, too—his image haunts my recollection like the bright spirit of a happy dream. (*Enter Beckey, L*) Well, Beckey, is he safe? (*Crosses to Beckey*)

BECKEY (*L*) Oh yes, Sir John, quite safe, and quite well, heaven be praised; and looking—

SIR JOHN The sweet picture of innocence.

BECKEY As innocent as a little lambkin.

SIR JOHN His looks have in them such a forcible appeal to the heart. Where is he? I long to behold him again; I would almost gladly adopt him as my son.

BECKEY (*aside*) As his son? Here's luck! You needn't be afraid—you may come in.

SIR JOHN Come in! Oh yes, these arms shall be to him an asylum. Lovely and unfortunate child, advance.

    Enter Sampson, sheepishly, L

SAMPSON May I come in?

BECKEY Yes, yes, your peace is finely made, I promise you—here he is, your honour.

SIR JOHN Who?

BECKEY Sampson Sawdust.

SAMPSON Sober Sampson, at your honour's service. (*Crosses to Sir John*) The best hand at a hammer for twenty miles around.

SIR JOHN But I was speaking of the dumb boy.

AMELIA And I.

SAMPSON That makes all the difference.

    Enter Taffrail, L

SAMPSON Oh, Beckey, Beckey, you are the very turnscrew° of my affections. (*Goes up the stage with Beckey*)

TAFFRAIL Here's one without, Sir John, who, by his discourse, could, I think, tender some information respecting the object of   55
our mutual anxiety.

SIR JOHN Pray admit him. (*Marines and Taffrail go over to R*)
Enter Guy Ruthven, led in by marines, L

AMELIA Heavens! 'tis the strange and solitary being whom we have so often observed from the battlements, wandering on the sea-beach, and gazing so intently at the castle.   60

GUY How my heart trembles!

SIR JOHN Fear not me—I am misfortune's friend.

GUY Misfortune's friend!—he—oh!

SIR JOHN That groan of desolation—perhaps I may assuage your sorrows.   65

GUY You—yet hear me; for Providence has conducted me hither to speak a tale of woe—a tale to which no ear but thine and mine should listen. (*Sir John waves his hand for the others to retire*)

AMELIA Dearest uncle, you surely will not trust yourself alone with—   70

GUY If I am feared, cover me with fetters; bind me—I'll not resist.

SIR JOHN No, no; go, all.
Exeunt Amelia and Taffrail, RSE, Beckey and Sampson, LSE, marines, R

SIR JOHN Now, friend, speak boldly.

GUY (*starting from abstraction*) Ah! we *are* together, and by ourselves; I thought to have found myself more courageous. I—Sir John—   75
Tre—van—ly; you must hear me patiently.

SIR JOHN Willingly, proceed.

GUY (*turning up the sleeve of his coat and showing a miniature clasped to his arm*) Do you know that portrait?

SIR JOHN Heavens!   80

GUY (*kissing the miniature*) It was my mother!

SIR JOHN You, then, are—?

GUY Your son! that is, your natural son. My mother, as you know, was beautiful as she was poor and humble. You sought her dwelling with all the glitter of wealth and power blazing around   85
you; you swore what she, poor confiding victim, believed; she was lost—you deserted her—and—she died. (*Bursting into tears*)

SIR JOHN I will not hear thee—

GUY Yes, for the sake of the true son, the lawful heir of these proud domains, whose destiny hangs on my lips—mine, you will, you   90
must hear me.

SIR JOHN Ah! say'st thou—speak—speak.

GUY I was, indeed, but a mere infant when my unhappy mother, stung to the soul by your marriage with another, first gave way to the despondency which at length, happily for herself, destroyed 95 her. Oh, Heaven! can I ever forget that death-bed scene, the annihilation of all that I loved—of all that ever loved me? Too young to be conscious that she was dying, I saw the last tear gleaming in her eye unmoved; it was only when I felt her prayer-clasped hands frozen round mine own, and shuddered 100 beneath the wintry coldness of those late affectionate lips, which, as I kissed them, no longer impressed mine, that the terrible conviction rushed like a thunderbolt to my brain, and I was assured—I knew, that she was dead. (*Crosses to R*)

SIR JOHN (*trembling*) Well—well—well? 105

GUY (*R*) Enough that an aged relative sustained me—one who, amid the struggles of bitter poverty, disdained appealing to my unnatural father; I myself would have starved ere I had implored his charity. Cruel man, where is now thy lady wife? Seek her in the grave dug by these despised, but not inhuman hands. Where is now the 110 proud heir, whose high and honourable name was to fall like a mildew on the hopes of the recreant bastard? Seek him in beggary, even more abject than mine—in calamity still more poignant. (*Crosses to L*)

SIR JOHN Horror! Has hate made thee an assassin? 115

GUY (*L*) Who is he that asks it? Is it less merciful to stab with the poniard, which, at a blow, destroys all misery, than to wound with the seducer's arts, which entail unceasing anguish? But no, no, I am no murderer—thank Heaven! I am no murderer! Robbed by thee, ere I was born, of fame, marked by adversity for its own, 120 what refuge had I but with the very humble—the destitute? No paternal voice stilled my sea of passions; no friend shielded me from insult. Pressed into the service of Hans Hattock, I heard a plan to rob this castle. By a letter from yourself to my mother, I had discovered the secret staircase to the ramparts; revenge almost 125 changed my nature to that of a demon. I led the ruffian band— thou wast absent—thy wealth—thy wife—thine honourable son— all, all, all were torn away, ha, ha, ha, ha! (*Laughs wildly and crosses to R*)

SIR JOHN Their fate, in pity? 130

GUY The lady, I know not how, for the night was dark and stormy as my wits, in the pursuit of her child—it might be, impelled by frenzy, rushed over the edge of a precipice, and was dashed to death.

SIR JOHN Ah! woe is me! and the boy?   135

GUY He was my prize, mine alone. Many years I fostered him in our ship; kind was I to him—how much kinder than thou to me! I meant to hate him, but my hate changed all to love, and the poor thing loved me, too. He was dumb, I know not why; and, when my unsettled reason compelled me to quit the ship, I left him   140 behind me, happy, and brave, and good.

SIR JOHN And does he live? (*Lightning is seen at the window*)

GUY Yes, and you have seen him, the dumb boy. Alas, for this crazy night—he lives in the vessel of Hans Hattock. (*Wind and guns heard*) Hark! signals of distress; how the wind roars. (*Going—gun*   145 *heard at a distance°*) The sea-mist gathering all around; the Inchcape Bell, too, no longer warns the vessel to avoid yon fatal rocks: but I'll go—I'll warn them in an open boat, alone. Oh, spirit of my sainted mother, look down upon me, this night; where I shall be struggling with the dark deep waters, aid me to save   150 yonder innocent boy—to place him once again in the arms of his now penitent father. Then, mother, and not till then, thy wrongs and mine will nobly be avenged. (*Rushes out, L. Storm*)

SIR JOHN Help, help, who waits? (*Enter Amelia, Taffrail, &c.*) Amelia, I have found my son!   155

AMELIA Oh, where?

SIR JOHN The dumb boy; in the storm, in yonder ship!

TAFFRAIL Ah, let us fly—fly all, to save him. (*Crosses to L. Storm*)

SIR JOHN That done, Amelia shall be yours; farewell, my child, fear not thou. Heaven pardon and preserve us well; remember us in   160 your prayers.

> *Music. Exeunt hastily, L, all but Taffrail and Amelia. Storm*

TAFFRAIL Dearest Amelia, farewell. Inspired by love and pity at the same time, 'tis impossible I should do otherwise than succeed; and, depend on it, Amelia, our union will not prove the less happy, because we purchased its consummation by previously subscribing   165 to the rescue of an unfortunate fellow-creature. (*Exit, L*)

AMELIA Nay, leave me not. I'll follow. (*Exit, L*)

> *Enter Beckey and Sampson, R.*

BECKEY And will you leave me again, Mr Sampson?

SAMPSON Yes, Beckey—enterprise calls, and your valour pints the way. Bless you, I swims as naturally as any goose; don't alarm   170 yourself about me. And, when I've lent a hand i' the storm yinder, and the worst is passed, back I'll fly with a wedding-ring, and I expects to find a quiet dromedary in your arms.

BECKEY Dromedary, indeed—dromitory,° you means.

SAMPSON Do I? What a scholard she is. How the sea is a-hammering! Up and down, like a saw at work. Good bye, Beckey; and, above all things, stick to your larning; oh! oh! 175

BECKEY Oh! (*He embraces her, and exit L*) If he should be drowned, it might be a week, or perhaps a fortnight, before I could find another. (*Exit, L*) 180

2.4

The wreck of the rover's vessel on the Inchcape Rock, during a storm. As the scene changes,° a dreadful crash is heard. Sailors clinging to the shrouds, &c. Some of the rigging falls

CREW Help! help us, heaven! the ship has struck on the Inchcape Rock!

HANS On the Inchcape Rock! Oh, horror! The vessel lies wedged in between these accursed masses of stone, still and motionless as a drowned man in his last berth. Withered be this hand which sunk 5 the warning bell—that bell whose kindly voice would have cautioned us from these wild shallows. Retribution, it comes—it comes!

CREW The leak gains rapidly upon us—five feet of water in the hold—the pumps are choked already.° 10

HANS The jolly-boat° washed away, too—we are lost—all, all must perish. Methinks, struggling with the din of the elements, already I hear the strokes of the accusing bell, knelling me to perdition. Mercy! mercy! (*Tears his hair*)

CREW A boat! a boat! A man alongside! A rope! a rope! 15

HANS What unearthly being, what unhallowed boat, could exist in such a storm? Yet, as I live, and feel, by the fast sinking of the ship, approaching death, true, as ye say, a boat has reached us from the land. That desperate man, who is he?

Enter Guy Ruthven, R. He forces his way through the sailors, who are thronging to the side of the ship

GUY 'Tis I, Guy Ruthven! The dumb boy! Where is he? Speak, Hans 20 Hattock, as you would rescue yourself, me, and all these men from perdition—speak, speak!

HANS (*aside*) Ah, blessed thought! the dumb boy! there! there!
(*Pointing to the cabin. Exit Guy Ruthven hastily into the cabin. To
the crew*) Now then, while he remains, into his boat, and save   25
yourselves!
     *The crew shout, and hurry into the boat,° R, while Hans goes
     to the cabin-door, and fastens it with a chain*
HANS Ha, ha, ha! You that would betray Hans Hattock, stay there,
and perish, (*going to the ship's side*) while I—(*groans, L.*) The boat
has sunk with the weight of the crew, and I here—madness—ah!
     Enter the Dumb Boy, from another cabin
HANS Thou the cause of all my despair and misery—revenge! (*He   30
seizes the Dumb Boy, and drags him forward—the Dumb Boy sinks on
his knees, L, while Hans draws a knife from his belt, and observes him
maliciously*)
GUY (*at the window*) Horror! Hans! Hans! let not your last moment
be lost in murder. The ship is sinking. For the sake of your own   35
soul, mercy! mercy!
HANS No, no—revenge! revenge! He dies. (*He brandishes the knife—
the Dumb Boy falls against the rigging*)
JUPITER No; not he, but you. (*He shoots Hans from the hatchway*)
There, rascal, how do you like that? (*Jupiter rushes forward and   40
liberates Guy Ruthven, who receives the Dumb Boy into his arms*)
HANS Oh! I die—revenge—re—Ah! that accursed bell—still, still
knelling—death—terrible—spirit of Lady Trevanly, leave me.
I—sinking—sinking—help—I—(*Falls amongst the rigging*)
GUY The boat gone! The crew escaped! Consternation! We, then, are   45
the only victims doomed to fall. Oh, heaven! is it thus thou
sufferest infamy to triumph—innocence, like this, unheard to die?
All have sunk like a shot in the deep trough of the sea!° Hans
Hattock and his lawless crew, all gone to their long account—pardon them! pardon them! For us, alas! although the storm abates,   50
the waters are breaking upon our decks, we have no hope!
JUPITER (*waving his hat*) Yes, yes, a boat quits the shore. They seek
us. Ho! ho! hillio!
GUY You know not the extent of your danger. The vessel is going
down piece by piece; follow me. (*Guy supports the Dumb Boy with   55
one arm, and with the other he grasps the mast—Jupiter follows him*)
For this poor victim, 'tis well he's unconscious. Help! help! (*A boat
is seen leaving the shore in the background,° R, and crossing to L, just
as Guy Ruthven, the Dumb Boy, and Jupiter are sinking with the
mast, which is struck by a thunderbolt*)   60

Re-enter Sampson, Taffrail, and Sir John, in the boat,° into
which they drag Guy Ruthven, the Dumb Boy, and Jupiter
GUY Mother! mother! it is accomplished! You are avenged. (*Guy*
places the Dumb Boy in Sir John's arms, and sinks exhausted with
fatigue)

DISPOSITION OF THE CHARACTERS AT THE FALL OF THE CURTAIN

Taffrail.   Sampson.   Dumb Boy.   Sir John.   Guy.   Jupiter.
R   L

DID YOU EVER SEND YOUR WIFE TO CAMBERWELL?

An Original Farce

In One Act

BY

JOSEPH STIRLING COYNE

CAST

HONEYBUN	Mr Wright
CRANK	Mr O. Smith
MRS HONEYBUN	Miss Woolgar
MRS CRANK	Mrs Frank Matthews
MRS JEWELL	Mrs Laws

First performed at the Adelphi Theatre
16 March 1846

SCENE *A chamber poorly furnished with practicable lattice, window, opening on the parapet of the house at C back. A closet° with practicable door L, and further back same side a bed with cotton curtains. A fire-place with lighted fire 3 ER. A chest of drawers at back RH1E, door of entrance, R, table with writing materials RC, at which Chesterfield Honeybun is sitting writing, and smoking a clay pipe, in a shabby morning gown and cap. Mrs Honeybun in a plain cotton dress, seated LC darning a stocking and singing 'We may be happy yet'°*

MRS HONEYBUN 'Oh, never name departed years, &c.'°

HONEYBUN Mrs Honeybun, my love, I wish you would cut that dreadful song; it gives me a headache, my dear—

MRS HONEYBUN Oh, very well, Mr Honeybun, I'll be silent—but I remember when that song used not to give you a headache! 5

HONEYBUN When was that, my love?

MRS HONEYBUN Before we were married!

HONEYBUN (*smoking*) Before we were married! Blissful recollection! Bright days of satin waistcoats and lobster suppers! Why did I relinquish ye for—(*puffs*) 10

MRS HONEYBUN For what, sir?

HONEYBUN For love and sheep's trotters,° my dear! (*Puffs*)

MRS HONEYBUN Well, it's all your own fault, look at *me*, your wife, Mr Honeybun—a perfect object of compassion in a paltry cotton gown—four-pence halfpenny a yard, not a farthing more as I live— 15

HONEYBUN And look at me, Mrs Honeybun, a terrible example of matrimony—a dead beggar is entitled to six feet of earth, while I, a living gentleman, am reduced to a miserable 'yard of clay'. (*Holds up his pipe*)°

MRS HONEYBUN Oh! I have been cruelly deceived by you. When I 20
ran away with you from Elm Grove boarding school, you led me to believe you held some high situation—

HONEYBUN So I did—a high situation on a tall stool in an attorney's office.

MRS HONEYBUN Then your dividends that you regularly went to 25
receive—

HONEYBUN Quite right, went every Saturday regularly to receive my weekly dividend of one pound one.°

MRS HONEYBUN And you were never tired talking of your fine prospects!   30

HONEYBUN Well, my love, no man has finer prospects—six church steeples, and no end of chimney pots from that window there—

MRS HONEYBUN And now here we are living up four pair of stairs in miserable chambers, in Clements Inn,° on a paltry guinea a week—   35

HONEYBUN And free stationery—don't forget the stationery, my life!

MRS HONEYBUN What's the use of stationery, when the butcher says 'he won't supply us with any more meat 'til his account is paid?'

HONEYBUN How, no more legs of mutton? Then, as Shakespeare says, 'The times are out of joint.'°   40

MRS HONEYBUN There's the milk account, too—

HONEYBUN I'm afraid there's a serious *chalk* to us in that article°— but where's the use of totting up our misfortunes—something must be done to mend our condition, and I've been thinking of appealing to the feelings of my Aunt Jewell, she, you know, is as   45 rich as—

MRS HONEYBUN Yes, *you've* told me she has ever so many thousands in the bank, or the Thames Tunnel,° and that she hasn't a friend in the world or a relative, except a green parrot and a ring tailed monkey.   50

HONEYBUN And a handsome nephew, my dear. All very true; and though my Aunt and I hasn't been on terms since I married, I have written her a pathetic letter, imploring a little advance in the way of tin:° here's a passage that would move a beadle° to shed tears. (*Reads*) 'It is not for myself I complain—but the sight of my   55 beloved Matilda'—that's you, my dear, 'the uncomplaining sharer of my last of sheep's trotter drives me to distraction and despera- tion—I have purchased a quart of laudanum—the deadly potion is at hand.' I'll trouble you, my dear, for that pint of porter;° (*Mrs Honeybun hands him a pint of porter which has been placed on a chair*)   60 thank you! (*Reads*) 'The deadly potion is at hand—but I shall wait for your answer before I drain the fatal bowl. Should it be unfavourable, consider me as defunct, and bury like a gentleman, your late unfortunate nephew—Chesterfield Honeybun.' (*He drinks the porter with great gusto*)   65

MRS HONEYBUN (*deeply affected*) Beautiful! Never heard anything more cutting° on the stage.

HONEYBUN Ah, my love—but that's not all—I have another grand idea. You shall go to Camberwell° and deliver the letter yourself to my Aunt this evening. Nothing like striking the iron while 'tis hot. 70

MRS HONEYBUN You don't mean that, Chesterfield?

HONEYBUN I do upon my life—and I know you'll not refuse me. (*Aside*) I must contrive to get her out of the way this evening. (*Aloud*) Here's your bonnet, let me put it on, (*puts bonnet on Mrs Honeybun*) there—there's a look of angelic innocence—bless you— you can't think what a heap of suffering virtue there is in a dunstable bonnet° and a pair of blue eyes. 75

MRS HONEYBUN But what's the use of this violent hurry—would not tomorrow do as well? 80

HONEYBUN No—no—no time like the present—you'll catch the Camberwell omnibus at the corner—sixpence all the way. Where's your shawl—ah (*takes a shawl and wraps it round her*) what a charming figure! There! There! Take care of your precious health, my angel—don't forget the letter, (*goes to table for letter—aside*) I hope she don't suspect— 85

MRS HONEYBUN (*aside*) Humph! He wants to get rid of me, it's plain enough. And how do you mean to pass the evening in my absence, Mr Honeybun?

HONEYBUN Oh—I—a—I shall amuse myself by being a—very miserable 'til you return, my love. 90

MRS HONEYBUN (*shakes her finger at him*) No, Chesterfield— Chesterfield, you don't deceive *me*—you're never miserable but in your wife's company.

HONEYBUN There, now, you're at your old jealous fancies again—I see how 'twill be, you'll break my heart and miss the omnibus! 95

MRS HONEYBUN Oh, don't be afraid, I'm going, (*aside*) but I'll be back sooner than you expect, my gentleman.

HONEYBUN Good bye, my love—adieu, my soul's delight—oh! (*Exit Mrs Honeybun, RD*) Gad! she's off at last, (*listening at the door*) pat, pat, pat, down the stone stairs—and across the court. Well, it's a horrid bore to have a jealous wife, always suspecting an innocent husband. (*Clock strikes seven*) Seven o'clock! I shall scarcely have time to make myself adorable and keep my appointment with Fanny Shinners in the park. (*Takes a note out of his pocket which he kisses*) Poor little Fanny! 'Pon my life, we good looking fellows should never marry. (*Goes into closet, L*) 100 105

    Isaac Crank puts in his head, RD

CRANK I beg your pardon, sir—hem! (*Enters and taps on the table*) Sir!

HONEYBUN (*in the closet*) Who's there? If it's the milk, put it on the shelf where the cat can't get at it.

CRANK I beg your pardon, sir, I'm not the milk.

HONEYBUN (*inside*) If you're the taxes then, you may call tomorrow.

CRANK Sir, I assure you I'm not the taxes; my name is Crank, and I live in the chambers opposite.

HONEYBUN (*enters without his coat, mixing up a lather in a shaving box*) Oh, excuse me, how d'ye do, Crank. (*Aside*) This is the new tenant of the chambers. (*To him*) Happy to have so handsome a neighbour on the same floor.

CRANK (*bows*) Oh, sir! I have intruded to beg the loan of a pair of bellows for a few minutes; my fire's gone out.

HONEYBUN Bellows? Bellows? Well I don't think I have one; but there's a coal scuttle, if it will answer you.

CRANK Oh, you're particularly kind, but never mind—I should beg pardon for troubling—

HONEYBUN Don't mention it my dear fellow, (*takes his arm*) I hate ceremony. By the bye, Crank, you've not been long in London?

CRANK No; only four days; I have lived all my life in the village of Stoke Poges.°

HONEYBUN Stoke Poges! I know that sweet spot well. (*Aside*) Never heard of it in my life. (*To him*) The romantic pump—the gothic ruins of the market-house—the ancient pound—

CRANK (*delighted*) Yes, that's it! that's it!

HONEYBUN And the magnificent church clock!

CRANK Do you know the clock?

HONEYBUN Do I? I've travelled fifty miles to set my watch by that clock.

CRANK My dear sir, allow me to shake your hand, (*shakes Honeybun's hand*) I have regulated that clock for the last five and twenty years.

HONEYBUN You amaze me.

CRANK Yes, sir, I'm the principal, and only clock and watch maker in Stoke Poges.

HONEYBUN The parochial time-keeper! What then brings you to London?

CRANK (*mysteriously*) Hush! that's a secret—but I don't mind telling *you*; you must know I'm come up to take out a patent for a

hydro-galvanic° locomotive steam engine on a new principle—I'm 150
constructing the model in my room there. (*Points to door*)

HONEYBUN You don't tell me so?

CRANK I do, and the best of the matter is my wife knows nothing
about it.

HONEYBUN My dear sir, there are some matters that our wives
should know nothing about. 155

CRANK Why—the fact is—I once blew the roof off the wash-house
making experiments with my new safety gas apparatus, and nearly
burnt the whole family in their beds, proving the efficacy of my
novel fire extinguisher. In consequence of which Mrs Crank won't
permit any more of my inventions on the premises: so one morning 160
before she was awake I got into the first train, ran up to London,
and took these chambers, where I can work away at my model
without interruption.

HONEYBUN (*aside*) Pleasant neighbour this, a fellow that blew up his
own wash-house. (*To him*) Excuse me, Crank, (*lathering his face*) 165
proceeding with my toilet—I have to shave for the Countess of
Hammersmith's soirée; but I'll be polished off in a few minutes—
meantime make yourself at home in my humble saloon, my dear
fellow.

CRANK Thank you. But a moment—allow me to ask you, which do 170
you prefer, the broad or the narrow gauge?°

HONEYBUN Eh! Broad or narrow gauge? Oh—well—I should say,
taking a wide view of the matter, give me the *broad*; but looking at it
the other way, I should certainly vote for the narrow dodge.°

CRANK Oh! I perceive. One word more, sir. What power do you 175
consider the most effective?

HONEYBUN What power? hem! well, I think you can't have anything
stronger than—a power of attorney. (*Exit into closet*)

CRANK Eh! a power of—bless me, what did he say?—power of
attorney. I'll just take a note of that, and then write to Mrs Crank, 180
to let her know that I am safe and well. (*Sits at table, and writes*)

HONEYBUN (*coming out of the closet half shaved*) I say, Crank, have
you any knowledge of the Terpsichorean art?°

CRANK The what, sir?

HONEYBUN The Terpsichorean art. 185

CRANK Not that I'm aware of—

HONEYBUN What a devilish slow coach you must be, old fellow.
(*Re-enters the closet with a shirt which he takes off a chair near the
fire*)

CRANK Slow coach! (*Honeybun singing the polka° in the closet*) A very 190
odd young man—I'll go and write my letter in the next room.
(*Exit, leaving his hat on table*)

HONEYBUN (*coming out of the closet*) I say, Crank, d'ye think opening
our oysters with a razor improves it much? Hey! gone! Well it
don't much matter. A man who can't dance is no loss to any 195
society. (*Takes a shirt collar from chair, and enters the closet dancing
the polka*)

> *Mrs Crank enters in travelling dress; she carries an infant in her
> arms, and an umbrella in her hand*

MRS CRANK So, a pretty chase I have had of it, after that runaway
husband of mine. However I have traced him out at last—I can't
be mistaken. The guard of the coach knows Crank as well as he 200
knows the statty at Charing Cross°—and he told me confidentially
that he was living up atop of the house here. So I've travelled all
the way from Stoke Poges to catch my old fox at his tricks—for
I'm sure it's no good he can be after, to desert his innocent
babe—and his virtuous wife that any man might be proud of. (*Sees* 205
Crank's hat on table) Oh, I knew I couldn't be mistaken, here's his
hat, and his name 'Isaac Crank' inside it. Soh! Soh! He's pretty
comfortable here too—well I suppose a wife has a right to make
herself at home in her husband's chamber. So I'll just put baby to
bed—bless the dear little fellow, he's fallen asleep in my arms— 210
he's the living picture of his unnatural father, he is! (*Kisses the child
which she places in bed and throws her cloak over him*) And now I'll
sit down and rest myself, for I'm tired to death. (*Sees a woman's
cap on the chair and utters a scream of horror*) Oh! What's this? A
cap—a cap—a woman's cap! Oh Crank, you old reprobate—I see 215
it all now—real lace, too—and his lawful wife obliged to put up
with bobbinet°—that's an aggravation no woman couldn't stand,
and I won't stand it—real lace! (*Tearing the cap to shreds*) There,
there, and there! Oh dear, I'm a wretched insulted woman. I don't
care what becomes of me now. I'll put an end to myself—I'll throw 220
myself into the river—*real* lace! Oh I could forgive anything but
that. Where is the villain? I'll leave my death on him, and have
him hanged for it I will. (*Rushes out and in her exit snatches a plate
from the table and dashes it on the floor*)

HONEYBUN (*in closet*) Ha, puss, ha! (*Flings a brush into the room*) 225
Hush, cat, hush! That d—d cat is breaking all my Dresden
china—hunting for her dinner, I suppose. I only hope she may get
it! Ecod, a cat's quite a superfluous animal in this establishment.

Re-enter Crank

CRANK I must have forgotten my hat in this room. (*Perceiving it, and taking it*) Yes, yes, here it is; and now to pop my letter to Mrs Crank 230 into the post. (*The child cries in bed*) Oh! there's a child here—poor little creature! How it cries—I wonder where's its nurse? (*Goes to bed and looks at the child*) Eh! bless me—am I dreaming? No, as I'm a christian clock maker—'tis my own blessed little cherub, my precious Tommy. (*Snatches the child out of the bed and kisses it rapturously*) Bless 235 his little heart, how like his father—the roman nose—the grecian mouth—the roguish eye—hah! the feelings of a paternal parent overcome me; but lord, now I think of it, how did it come here? I left it in Stoke Poges with its mother, and now I find it in this stranger's apartment. (*Sees the umbrella which Mrs Crank has left*) Ha! the family 240 umbrella, too, and that cloak—my wife's! I'll swear to it—phew, she's been here! Oh, I see it all—took advantage of my absence—came to London—oh, a horrid thought strikes me—that handsome fellow— she's a pretty woman, and I—oh, Crank! (*Child cries*) Go, you juvenile imposter—now that I look at you, you're not a bit like me—there. 245 (*Throws child into bed*) Oh! the mainspring of my peace is broken, and my happiness wound up for ever. But I'll be revenged upon the vampire of my domestic hearth-stone—I'll do for him. (*Rushes out*)

Honeybun enters from closet polishing a boot

HONEYBUN Somebody has been blackleading the stove with the polishing brush, or else Warren disdains to shine° today. (*Child* 250 *cries*) Hollo, that vagabond cat has got into the bed! (*Throws the brush and runs to the bed*) What's this! Ecod, it's a live baby! (*Takes child up*) What the devil brought it here—I wonder who owns it, or where it came from! I hope nobody means to leave this little responsibility on my hands. (*Child cries*) Hush—h—h—ha! They'll 255 hear it all over the chambers and my character will be completely destroyed. (*Sings and dandles child*) A pretty rabbit I've caught! Hush—a—a—a! Cock a doodle doo! Hold your tongue you young vampire, or I'll strangle you. (*Sings*) Hey diddle diddle, the cat and the fiddle, the cow jump'd over the moon. The poor little wretch 260 is hungry—it's no use your looking for anything there my little dear—bye, bye—we'll have the third floor running up to see what's the matter with the attic. But what am I to do with it? I must get rid of it some way before Mrs Honeybun returns, or there'll be a royal row in the buildings! (*Knock at the door*) Now who the devil 265 is this? I shall be discovered in an interesting situation. I've a great mind to throw it into the next yard—the man there has

twelve children, this will make a baker's dozen. (*Goes to window*)
Ecod tho' if I do, I may kill the child, and be hanged for it! (*Knock
again*) Stop, I have it, I'll pop it behind this chest of drawers and 270
get into the closet myself. (*He lays a pillow behind the drawers,
wraps the child up in the counterpane and places it on the pillow. Exit
into closet*)

    Enter Mrs Jewell, RD

MRS JEWELL Dear me, a body might knock their knuckles off at this
door before they'd get an answer—careful housekeeping this, doors 275
open and nobody at home. That ride from Camberwell has tired
me. (*Sits*) Soh! Well, I wonder where that graceless nephew of
mine is, and his young wife? They don't expect a visit from old
Aunt Jewell—but I think they have been sufficiently punished for
their imprudence, so now I'm come to make the undutiful pair 280
happy by my forgiveness. What a surprise it will be to the poor
things, who don't seem a bit too well off here. But it's always the
way with young folks—they fall in love and marry without ever
thinking of—(*child cries*) Bless me, I didn't know there had been a
child already—well, well, but where is the little innocent, eh? 285
Good gracious! If they haven't thrust it like a bundle of old clothes
behind the chest of drawers—what barbarity! (*Takes up the child*)
A sweet little creature too—and the wretch of a mother to leave it
so. Bless its dear little heart! It shan't want a mother while I live,
that it shan't. I'll take it away with me and get a nurse for it 290
directly. They shall never have it again, never—or my name's not
Jewell. (*Exit RD carrying the child which she has wrapped up in her
shawl. Chesterfield Honeybun peeps out of the closet*)

HONEYBUN (*entering*) Soh! The coast is clear—I thought I heard
some one moving about here, but I was afraid to look out and see 295
who it was—very likely the laundress or the baker, or perhaps the
green grocer expecting to be paid—what a very green° grocer he
must be. (*Goes up*)

    Crank enters, RD. He appears greatly agitated

CRANK I can't wait, I must see this destroyer of my happiness! (*Sees
Honeybun*) Oh, sir, Mr Boneyhum— 300

HONEYBUN Honeybun—Chesterfield Honeybun—rather a picturesque name; though as Shakespeare says 'What's in a name° if
it's no good on a sixpenny stamp.'

CRANK Sir—Mr—wretch! Look at me, behold your victim, the
injured Crank! 305

HONEYBUN What the devil's the matter with the man! Has the Gal-hydro-locofogo biler bust?

CRANK Matter! How can you look me in the face—villain! Seducer! (*Seizes him by the collar*) Where's my wife—my Mary Anne?

HONEYBUN Your Mary Anne! How the devil should I know! There, what are you about—let me go—would you destroy my character and my shirt front? (*Shakes Crank off, who again seizes him—they struggle towards the chest of drawers*)

CRANK No, I'll never leave you, 'til I have satisfaction°—never! (*A struggle, in which the chest of drawers is thrown back—Crank holding Honeybun down on the drawers*)

HONEYBUN Hollo! Do you mean to murder me? Let me up—if you want satisfaction, take it like a gentleman, and don't break my back bone—

CRANK Get up then, I have pistols in the next room. I'll go for them—you must fight me—one of us must fall. (*Rushes out RD*)

HONEYBUN Well I hope it will be you, down four flights of stairs. Ecod, that's a lunatic. I might have known it when he talked of his gallows hydro-loco-moco-foga-tive steam engine. (*Suddenly perceives the end of the counterpane appearing from beneath the chest of drawers*) Oh! Oh! Here's a horrid business! I've squashed the baby—oh! I daren't look at it—it's as flat a pancake—what shall I do! (*Comes down*) There'll be an inquest—and twelve gentlemen will sit upon that small child's body,° and I shall be hanged as a public example—where shall I fly? If I try to escape by the door, I shall meet the lunatic—I'll get on the roof, and take refuge on the tiles. (*Gets through the window on the roof and disappears as Crank opens the door. Rain heard*)

    Enter Crank, RD, with a very large and a very small pistol

CRANK Now sir, here they are, take your choice—are you ready? Where is the wretch—what, hiding! (*Goes to closet*) Come out and meet your doom! (*Looks in*) Not here! But he shan't escape me—I'll follow him to the world's end, and from there to Stoke Poges. (*Exit, RD*)

    Rain heavy. Honeybun is seen peeping in at the window as if afraid to enter. He manages to reach to a bonnet which he puts on, and afterwards a woman's cloak hanging near the window

HONEYBUN (*sneezes*) I shall take my death of cold here in the rain. I wish I could get at the umbrella. (*Gets partly in at window, when*

43

footsteps are heard outside the door) Lord! here's somebody coming!
(*Gets out on the roof*)

    *Enter Mrs Crank, RD. During this scene the evening closes, and
the stage becomes dark*

MRS CRANK So he's not here yet—well, second thoughts are best. I
had quite made up my mind to drown myself, but the water was
so damp I didn't like it, and after all I may have been wrong. I'll   345
stop and see how he'll account for himself. Dear me, how tired and
sleepy I am, and it's raining as if it never meant to give over.
(*Shivers*) Baby's fast asleep, so I'll lie down without disturbing it,
and make myself comfortable until he comes home. (*Gets into bed
and draws curtains*)   350

    *Rain. Honeybun appears at the window and listens
anxiously—he is thoroughly wet with the rain which is falling
heavily. He enters cautiously, and listens at RD*

HONEYBUN (*in a low voice*) All's quiet—that lunatic's gone to
sleep—when shall I sleep again? Never! Who could sleep with a
squashed baby beside their pillow? (*Mrs Crank snores*) What horrid
sound is that? Again! (*Snore*) Oh—h—h—horror! (*Snore—
approaches bed*) I thought it was the groan of crushed innocence,   355
but 'tis only a gentle snore—I know it. Matilda has returned—ah!
She little dreams that her cherished Chesterfield is a murderer. I
cannot bear this horrid darkness—where are the matches? (*Lights
a candle with matches*) Talking of matches—I shall be hanged, and
Matilda will then be looking for another match. (*Approaches the bed*   360
with lighted candle, and starts) Eh! Who's this? Ecod that's not my
Matilda—this is not the legitimate Mrs Honeybun. Who *is* the
female that has taken this remarkable liberty with me? It's rather
a delicate situation though.

MRS HONEYBUN (*outside*) Chesterfield! Chesterfield! Hold a light,   365
will you?

HONEYBUN My wife! What the devil's to be done now? Nothing will
convince that jealous woman that I am innocent, if she finds this
anonymous female in her place. (*Pulls the curtains round the
bed—puts on his dressing gown hastily—places chair at table, and sits*   370
*with his back towards bed, in a disconsolate attitude, as Mrs Honeybun
enters*)

MRS HONEYBUN Well, I think you might have lighted me up stairs,°
Mr Honeybun.

HONEYBUN (*affects to start*) Hah! Is it you, my angel? I hadn't an idea   375
that you could be back from Camberwell so soon!

MRS HONEYBUN Why, I haven't been at all. I missed the seven o'clock omnibus, and as I knew you would be so miserable in my absence, I returned home.

HONEYBUN And so it came back to its own solitary Honeybun—dear soul! Sit down—sit down—for, as the song says, 'We may be happy yet.'

MRS HONEYBUN No, I shall go to bed, I'm dreadfully fatigued. (*Takes off her bonnet and goes toward bed; Honeybun jumps up and takes the bonnet*)

HONEYBUN Allow me, my dear—allow me—there, never mind going to bed yet—in fact, my love, I have come to the conclusion that going to bed is a very unnecessary practice.

MRS HONEYBUN Chesterfield, what nonsense you do talk. There—hang up my shawl.

HONEYBUN (*aside*) Hang up! Hah! I shall be hung up myself some of these days. (*Hangs it up—to her*) Matilda, my love! sit down—I have an important observation to make—you haven't had your supper yet. (*She sits at table—aside*) If I could only get her out of the way for five minutes—(*to her*) what do you think if you were to step to the cook shop round the corner for a knuckle of ham?

MRS HONEYBUN I don't want ham, and I hate knuckles, Chesterfield!

HONEYBUN Well then a little cold beef and pickles—I know you love pickles?

MRS HONEYBUN No, I'd rather have a sleep than all the pickles in the world. (*She rises*) If you wish—*you* can sit up. I shall go to bed.

HONEYBUN (*starts up and pushes her back in the chair*) To bed! No, no—oblige me, stay up a little longer.

MRS HONEYBUN How tiresome you are, Chesterfield. Well, I'll just get my nightcap out of the drawers. (*Rises*)

HONEYBUN (*aside*) The drawers! Excuse me, Matilda, I hate you in your nightcap, it makes you quite a fright.

MRS HONEYBUN (*seeing drawers*) Good heavens! What have you been about—the drawers overturned, and I dare say my best cap crushed to atoms!

HONEYBUN (*holding her*) Matilda, forbear! There's something more than a cap crushed beneath those drawers!

MRS HONEYBUN What is it? I shall, and will know, that's flat.

HONEYBUN Flat! Hah! That's the word—flat as the ace of spades.

MRS HONEYBUN What do you mean? I—I insist upon knowing, sir! (*Mrs Crank sneezes in the bed*) What was that! A sneeze!

HONEYBUN A sneeze—very likely—our cat has been out and 420 brought home a remarkably bad cold in her head. (*Aside*) How the devil am I to get out of this scrape!

MRS HONEYBUN A cat indeed! (*Mrs Crank in bed as if awaking, yawns, and says 'Oh dear me!'*) I suppose that's the cat too, sir! (*Rushes to bed, draws back curtains and discovers Mrs Crank, screams*) 425 A woman!

MRS CRANK Yes, mum!°

HONEYBUN Well—it really is very like one.

MRS CRANK (*getting out of bed*) Good heavens—where am I! Where's my child? 430

HONEYBUN (*aside*) Her child—then that's the mother of the victim.

MRS CRANK Where's my child?

HONEYBUN How should I know—let everybody mind their own children.

MRS HONEYBUN What, there's a child too! Oh you reprobate! But 435 I'll leave you—the same roof shan't cover us another hour. I'll be separated—I'll be divorced—I'll—I'll—I'll go home to my mother. (*Sinks into chair sobbing hysterically*)

MRS CRANK Where's my precious babe—tell me what you have done with it? 440

HONEYBUN Have patience ma'am, have patience—'pon my life I didn't mean it, do forgive me. (*Drops on his knees, and takes her hand as Crank enters*)

CRANK Ha! Then my worst fears are confirmed—my faithless wife here with the destroyer of my happiness. (*Rushes at him*) Now 445 villain, you shan't escape me!

HONEYBUN (*retreating*) Zounds, it's the lunatic again—(*brandishing a chair*) keep off—don't come near me! (*Gets behind the chair*)

MRS CRANK A lunatic! No, no, 'tis my husband, 'tis my runaway Crank. (*About to embrace him*) 450

CRANK Stand off, woman! Go to your paramour there!

HONEYBUN Mrs Honeybun, will you sit there and hear your hand-some husband called a paramour?

MRS HONEYBUN Wretch, don't speak to me—

CRANK Scoundrel! 455

HONEYBUN Come, come, I'll stand this no longer—every English-man's house is his castle. Get out of my attic, Crank! (*Flourishes chair*)

MRS CRANK Why, Crank, isn't this *your* room?

HONEYBUN Certainly not, madam, it's *my* boudoir! 460

MRS CRANK Why, the guard at the coach told me you lived here!

HONEYBUN Then that guard must have been a blackguard ma'am.

CRANK I *do* live here, but in the opposite chambers. But pray, what brought you here?

MRS CRANK When I heard where you were, I followed you to town, 465
with our dear baby, and finding your hat on the table there, I
naturally thought this was your apartment, so being fatigued I lay
down to rest, but I protest—I never set eyes upon this gentleman
until I just now awoke—

CRANK Oh! That sets matters in a new light. (*Crank and Mrs Crank* 470
retire up and converse earnestly apart)

HONEYBUN There, Mrs Honeybun, you heard that—now how can
you look your injured husband in the face.

MRS HONEYBUN (*throwing herself into his arms*) Dear Chesterfield,
forgive me! I'll never suspect you again. 475

HONEYBUN Don't Matilda—don't! It wounds my feelings. (*They*
embrace)

CRANK (*coming down*) But where is the child?

MRS CRANK I left it asleep in this bed. (*To Honeybun*) Please, sir,
where is my dear baby? 480

CRANK Aye, where is our child?

HONEYBUN (*in a hollow voice and pointing to the drawers*) There—
under that chest of drawers.

MRS HONEYBUN, CRANK, and MRS CRANK Under the drawers!

HONEYBUN Yes, flattened, and I fear it will never come round 485
again. (*All utter an exclamation of horror—Crank and Mrs Crank*
endeavour to raise the chest of drawers which slips from their hold;
both call 'Police'. Mrs Crank sinks on bed. At this moment Mrs Jewell
enters)

MRS JEWELL Don't be alarmed. I found this baby there this 490
evening;° isn't it yours?

    Enter Nurse, RD carrying child

HONEYBUN No! I repudiate the allotment!

CRANK It's mine! It's mine! (*Snatches it from Nurse*) My little
Tommy! Ain't it like me? There's my roman nose—plain
enough— 495

HONEYBUN Of course it's plain enough if it's like you—

MRS CRANK Now Crank, my dear, let's go back to Stoke Poges; all
the clocks there have run down since you left.

CRANK Never mind, Mrs Crank, I'll wind them all up when I get home. 500

HONEYBUN Aunt Jewell—hem—you have taken pity upon one little innocent today, (*takes his wife's hand*) here are two more thrown upon your humanity.

MRS JEWELL Ah, naughty pair, I ought not to forgive you, for you have both acted very foolishly. 505

HONEYBUN We know it, Aunt—it was wrong of us to get married—but we've been very sorry for it ever since—

MRS JEWELL Well, well I won't be obdurate. I forgive you—you shall both come home and live with me. (*Embrace*)

HONEYBUN Well, upon my life, this kindness deeply affects me. 510
Matilda, my love, we've been snatched by our aunt from the jaws of our uncle.°

MRS HONEYBUN Then, Chesterfield, we may indeed 'be happy yet'!
It shan't be my fault if we're not—for from this moment, I give up all my jealous ways. 515

HONEYBUN Do you, then Matilda—I—a—yes—(*takes note out of his pocket which he looks at for a moment and then tears up*) I promise to give up all my other ways. (*To audience*) Are there any married men in the house? Yes! I think that gentleman there looks very like one. I beg your pardon, sir—did you ever send your wife to 520
Camberwell? I'm not inquisitive—but if you ever should do so—mind and see her off in the omnibus; or she may return unexpectedly as mine did—and make herself remarkably jealous and particularly disagreeable. However, as we are all friends here—I'll tell you confidentially that—with your approbation it is 525
my intention to send my wife to Camberwell every evening till further notice.°

DISPOSITION OF THE CHARACTERS AT THE FALL OF THE CURTAIN°

	Mr Honeybun	
Mrs Crank		Mrs Honeybun
Mr Crank		Mrs Jewell
R		L

THE GAME OF SPECULATION

A Comedy

In Three Acts

BY

GEORGE HENRY LEWES

CAST

MR AFFABLE HAWK	Mr Charles Mathews
SIR HARRY LESTER	Mr Robert Roxby
EARTHWORM	Mr Frank Matthews
PROSPECTUS	Mr Basil Baker
GROSSMARK	Mr Suter
HARDCORE	Mr H. Horncastle
FREDERICK NOBLE	Mr H. Butler
THOMAS	Mr Oxberry
GRAVES	Mr Clifford
MRS HAWK	Mrs Horn
JULIA	Miss M. Oliver
DIMITY	Miss Grove
MRS MASON	Miss Ellis

First performed at the Lyceum Theatre
2 October 1851

1.

Drawing room in Mr Affable Hawk's house, handsomely furnished; table and two chairs, R; table and two chairs, L; doors, R and L; window, L; sofa, R, at back. Mrs Dimity, Thomas, and Mrs Mason discovered

THOMAS (*RC, seated*) Yes, my dears, our respectable and respected master, Mr Affable Hawk, may swim well, but he'll be drowned this time.

MRS MASON Lor! do you really think so?

THOMAS Burnt his fingers, I can tell you; and although there is always pretty pickings in a house where the master is in debt, still, you know he owes us all a year's wages, and it is time now to be turned out of doors. 5

MRS MASON It ain't so easy with some missusses! I have already been impertinent two or three times to our'n, but she always pretends not to hear. 10

DIMITY As for me, I have been lady's maid in a great many families, but never in such as this. One has to become quite an actress! A creditor arrives—you have to throw astonishment into your eyebrows, and exclaim—'What! you don't know, sir?' 'Know what?' 'Mr Affable Hawk is gone to Manchester, about some new speculation.' 'Oh! gone to Manchester, is he?' 'Yes, sir, a splendid affair, I hear—discovery of a copper mine.' 'So much the better! When does he come back?' 'Really, sir, we don't know.' 15

OMNES Ha, ha, ha! 20

DIMITY He's settled!° But what a countenance it requires to lie with that superiority! And my wages are none the higher for it.

THOMAS Besides, these are all such coarse-minded creatures; they bully as if *we* owed the money.

DIMITY It must end. I shall formally demand my wages, because the tradesmen absolutely refuse to serve us any longer. 25

THOMAS AND MRS MASON Yes, let's have our wages and go.

DIMITY A pretty family to pretend to gentility, indeed!

MRS MASON Genteel people are those who spend liberally in eating and drinking! 30

THOMAS And become attached to their servants.

DIMITY To whom they leave little annuities—that's what a gentleman *ought* to do.

MRS MASON Well, for my part, I most pity poor Miss Julia, and her
lover, Mr Noble.   35

THOMAS Her lover! Do you suppose that a man like Mr Affable
Hawk would give his daughter to his clerk, with one hundred and
fifty pounds a year salary? No! He has better than that in his eye.

MRS MASON Oh, do tell us!

THOMAS You remember the two gentlemen who came yesterday in   40
their cab? The groom tells me that they are going to marry Miss
Julia.

MRS MASON Lor! What, are those gentlemen who came in white kid
gloves and flowered waistcoats going to marry Miss Julia?

THOMAS Not both, you simple creature! We don't allow bigamy in   45
England. It's only in France that women have two husbands.

DIMITY And do you believe that a rich man will be brought to marry
Mr Hawk's daughter, now his ruin must be suspected?

THOMAS If you knew Mr Affable Hawk half as well as I do, you
would believe anything of him. I have seen him with creditors   50
around him like hornets, till I have said to myself—'Well, at last
he's done for!' Not a bit of it! He has received reams of writs, tons
of protested bills°—Basinghall Street° has gasped for him—when,
hey presto! he bounds up again, triumphant, rich! Then his
invention—was there ever such invention! Every day a new   55
speculation; every day a new committee formed! Wood pavement—quilted pavement—salt marshes—railways—waterworks—
and yet always in debt!

MRS MASON But he don't seem to care for creditors.

THOMAS He! To see him cajole and caress them—how he wheedles   60
them, and diddles them, and sends them away delighted with his
affable manner and magnificent promises. I have often seen them
come with arrest written in every line of their faces; but they have
gone away smiling, shaking him by the hand, the best friends in
the world. We hear of men who tame lions and tigers, but he does   65
more; he pacifies a creditor! I call him the Van Amburgh° of the
City.

MRS MASON There is one I especially hate—Mr Grossmark.

THOMAS A shark that feeds on post obits.° Then there is old
Earthworm.   70

MRS MASON Ha, ha! a begging creditor—I always feel that I ought
to offer him some broken victuals.

DIMITY Then there's Hardcore—

MRS MASON And no end of 'em! But here's missus!

Enter Mrs Hawk, LD

MRS HAWK Thomas, have you bought the things I ordered? (*Sits, R*) 75

THOMAS Bought them, ma'am, but not *got* them. The tradespeople refuse to send things home.

MRS MASON And the butcher, ma'am—and the baker, ma'am—and them all, refuse to send the things.

MRS HAWK I understand. It is useless to conceal from you my   80
anxiety about my husband's affairs. We shall need your discretion; and we may count upon you; may we not?

OMNES To the last, ma'am!

DIMITY We were saying, but now, that we had a most excellent master and mistress.   85

THOMAS And that we would go through fire and water to serve them.
Hawk appears at back, C

MRS HAWK Thanks! You are good creatures! (*Hawk shrugs his shoulders contemptuously*) Mr Hawk only wants to gain time; he has so many plans—a rich husband is in view for our daughter—

HAWK (*advancing and interrupting*) My dear Caroline! (*The servants*   90
draw aside—Hawk, speaking to her aside, says) That is the way you speak to your servants! Tomorrow they will be impertinent. (*Aloud*) Thomas, go at once to Mr Prospectus, and tell him to come here immediately, about an affair which admits of no delay. Be mysterious, for he must come—I want him. You, Mrs Mason,   95
go back to the tradespeople, and tell them, indignantly, to send the things ordered by your mistress. They shall be paid—yes, cash down—go! And stop! if those—gentlemen call again, admit them.

THOMAS Those—gentlemen? What! the creditors?

HAWK Precisely.   100

MRS HAWK Are you serious?

HAWK (*throwing himself into a chair*) I'm sick of solitude, and I want to see them. (*To Thomas and Dimity*) Go! (*Exeunt Thomas and Dimity, CD*) Mrs Mason, has your mistress ordered dinner?

MRS MASON No, sir; besides, the tradespeople—   105

HAWK Today you must surpass yourself—you must make Soyer° pale with envy. We have four persons to dinner, besides our-selves—Prospectus and his wife, Sir Harry Lester, and Mr Graves. Let me see—there must be all the delicacies of the season.

MRS MASON But the tradespeople won't—   110

HAWK Don't talk to me of my tradespeople, the day my daughter is to see her future husband!

MRS MASON But I must, for they won't send in the orders.

HAWK Nonsense! What are tradesmen for, but to serve their custo-   115
mers?

MRS MASON But they are creditors.

HAWK Well, what are creditors, but to give credit to their customers?
We're their customers! If they are obstinate, go to others—their
rivals—promise them my custom, and they will give you Christmas-boxes.°   120

MRS MASON And how am I to pay those whom I leave?

HAWK That's their business and mine—leave that to me!

MRS MASON They mustn't look to me for money, that's all!

HAWK (*aside*) Holloa! Mrs Mason has saved money! (*Aloud*) Mrs
Mason, in these days credit is everything—credit is the wealth of   125
commerce, the foundation of the State! If my tradesmen refuse
credit, it is a proof that they have no respect for the British
Constitution, our safeguard and our pride! They are radicals and
chartists° of the worst description! The man who would refuse
credit, would erect a barricade! Don't distract me any more about   130
people who are in open revolt against the vital principles of
Government! Mrs Mason, you look after the dinner—I depend
upon you for it; (*rising*) and if Mrs Hawk, in settling with you on
the day of Julia's marriage, finds herself a trifle in debt to you, I'll
take care you are no loser.   135

MRS MASON Oh, sir! (*Aside*) I'll buy the things myself, if the
tradesmen refuse.

HAWK And I will put you in the way of getting your ten shillings
interest for every five pounds, twice a year—that's a little better
than the Savings' Bank,° eh?   140

MRS MASON I should think so—the interest there is next to nothing!

HAWK (*aside to his wife*) I told you that she had money. (*Aloud*) Then
I may rely upon you, Mrs Mason?

MRS MASON That you may, sir! Come what will, the dinner shall do
you credit. (*Exit, CL*)   145

HAWK That woman has fifty pounds or more in the Savings'
Bank—all pilfered from us: it is but right she should pay for dinner
on the occasion.

MRS HAWK How can you descend so low?

HAWK My dear Caroline, do not attempt to judge my means of   150
action. In this world, nothing is trifling—nothing too insignificant.
Just now, you were trying to win over the servants by gentleness.
Error, my dear—complete error! You should be firm as the Iron
Duke,° and as brief.

MRS HAWK And why issue commands, when you cannot pay?   155

HAWK My love, the principle of social existence is extremely simple.
   Pay with gold, when you can—when you can't, pay with brass.°

MRS HAWK But we often obtain, through affection, services, which
   are refused to—

HAWK Through affection! How little you know the present age.   160
   Now, nothing but selfishness exists. Every one places his future in
   the Three-per cents.° There lies our paradise. The wife knows her
   husband is insured; the son insures his father's life. All our morals
   lie in dividends! As to servants, we change them every day.
   Attachment, indeed! Pay them their wages regularly, and they   165
   leave you without regret; but owe them money, and you keep them
   devoted to the last.

MRS HAWK Oh! You, so honourable, you to utter such things?

HAWK I utter what we all feel, but what few have the boldness to
   avow. Here lies modern honour. (Holding up half-a-crown)   170
   Chivalry has shrivelled into that! Shall I tell you why plays succeed
   which have scoundrels for their heroes? It is because the spectator
   is flattered, and says to himself as he goes away, 'Come, come,
   hang it, after all I'm not such a scamp as he is.'

MRS HAWK No, no!   175

HAWK My dear Caroline, I see my levity wounds you, but consider
   our positions. Are we not suffering for the crime of our partner,
   Sparrow, who decamped with all our funds? You know the honour
   and integrity with which I raised our house to wealth—a house
   untainted in reputation till that fatal act reduced us all to beggary.   180
   The fault was not mine, but what was to be done! A coward would
   have destroyed himself. Not I. Die! never. I had not lived so long
   in the world, my dear, without discovering its weakness. I had not
   mixed so much with monied men, without reading their inmost
   souls—and so, like a man of that world in which I had studied, I   185
   gaily accepted the new position forced upon me. Necessity, mark
   me, not choice, compelled me to it—and I thenceforth determined
   to give the world the benefit of the lessons it had taught me, and
   turn my very ruin into an amusement.

MRS HAWK Your elasticity of mind was commendable, no doubt, but   190
   is the line you have taken justifiable?

HAWK Perfectly. The speculators who enriched themselves quietly
   under the shadow of my former successes, are now the toys and
   puppets with which I divert my leisure and dispel my melancholy.
   When I am dull I pull their strings, (imitates the action of pulling   195

the strings of a puppet) and they dance till I am merry again. The game of speculation, which I formerly played for love, I now play for money, that's all.

MRS HAWK Aye, but your former worshippers are now turned into ravenous creditors. 200

HAWK Creditors? Not at all. They are my bankers. If I did not use their money they would be miserable. Besides, after all, where is the dishonour of debt? Is it not national? Every man dies in debt to his father, to whom he owes his life, which he can't repay. What is life, Caroline, but one enormous loan? A perpetual borrow, 205 borrow, borrow. Moreover, there is some skill required to get handsomely in debt—it is not every one that can get trusted. Am I not greatly superior to my creditors? I have their money—they must wait for mine. I ask nothing from them—they pester my life out with importunities. Think, my dear—a man who owes noth- 210 ing, what a solitary, miserably incomplete being! Nobody cares for him; nobody asks about him; nobody knocks at his door. Whilst I am an object of intense and incessant interest to all my creditors. They think of me in going to bed; they think of me in rising every day—their lips grow familiar with my name; their hands love my 215 knocker.

MRS HAWK Yes; but remember that we owe their money to their confidence in your probity.

HAWK Well, isn't that an agreeable reflection? But the truth is, that we owe it more to their avidity than to their confidence. The 220 speculator is no worse than the shareholders. They are both moved by the desire of becoming rich, without trouble, and without much care for the means. All my creditors have been enriched by me, and they still hope to gain something more. Were it not for my knowledge of their interests, I should be lost; as it is, you will see 225 how I make each of them show their cards, and play their little game before me. I have given orders to have them admitted.

MRS HAWK For what? To pay them?

HAWK Pay them, my love! no; to make them lend me more money. Don't be astonished. The marriage of our daughter is our last 230 hope, our last resource. I must have money for the jewels, for the trousseau, the wedding breakfast, and the many exigencies of the hour. Sir Harry Lester, who is to marry Julia, must have no suspicion of our being in difficulties; so that ready money is indispensable just now. By-the-bye, what amount of jewels will she 235 require, with a fortune of twenty thousand pounds?

MRS HAWK But you can't give her twenty thousand pounds.

HAWK The greater reason for giving her the jewels. How much? Eh?
Eight hundred—nine hundred?

MRS HAWK And you count upon your creditors?   240

HAWK Of course! Who should I count upon? Are they not, so to
speak, all of my family? Find me a relation who desires to see me
rich, as much as they do. Were I to die tomorrow, I should have
more creditors than relations inconsolable. Relations feel grief in
their hearts, and put crape on their hats; creditors feel the loss in   245
their pockets. The heart forgets, the crape wears out, but the
unpaid debt is ineffaceable—the blank is never filled up.

 Enter Thomas, C

THOMAS Mr Hardcore wishes to know if it really be true that you
desire to see him, sir.

HAWK That amazes him. Beg him to walk in. (*Exit Thomas, C*)   250
Hardcore, the most inexorable of all—a walking writ; but withal,
a greedy speculator, and timid as a fawn, venturing on the wildest
schemes, and trembling the moment he has set them going.

 Thomas announces Hardcore, who enters, C

HARDCORE (*angry*) So, sir, you are to be found when it pleases you.

MRS HAWK Mr Hardcore, this tone—   255

HAWK (*C, calming her*) My dear, Mr Hardcore is a creditor.

HARDCORE (*L*) And one that will not stir from here till he is paid.

 Hawk motions Hardcore to take off his hat

HAWK (*aside*) One that will not stir from here till he has given me
some money. (*Aloud*) Ah! you have not behaved handsomely to
me, Hardcore, to have a writ out against the man with whom you   260
had so many transactions.

HARDCORE Transactions which have not been all profit.

HAWK Otherwise, where would be the merit? If all affairs brought
profit, all the world would be speculators.

HARDCORE You have not sent for me, sir, I presume, to give me   265
proof of your wit—I know you are cleverer than me, for you have
got my money.

HAWK Money, my dear Hardcore, must be *somewhere*. Yes, Caroline,
strange as it may appear to you, Mr Hardcore has hunted me like
a hare. In my place some people would avenge themselves—for I   270
have him in my power, and can make him lose an enormous sum.

HARDCORE If you don't pay me I shall; but you will pay me—the
writ is in the hands of the sheriff's officer.

MRS HAWK Heavens!

HAWK Sheriff's officer! Are you entirely losing your sagacity? Poor 275
devil! You don't know what you are doing—you ruin me and
yourself at one blow!

HARDCORE Eh! *You* I understand, but me—how me?

HAWK Both, I tell you—both, you stupid fellow! There, sit down and
write at once—delay is frightful! (*Hardcore crosses to L*) Moments 280
are precious!

HARDCORE (*taking the pen, alarmed—sits LC*) Write! What?

HAWK (*C*) To your head clerk, to stop proceedings—and to send me
two hundred pounds I want.

HARDCORE (*throwing down the pen*) I dare say indeed! 285

HAWK You hesitate? You, when I am about to marry my daughter to
a man immensely rich? You have me arrested? You lock up your
debt, not me. You ruin your debtor. Your brain is softening!

HARDCORE Oh! you are about to marry Julia to—

HAWK Sir Harry Lester—as many thousands as years! 290

HARDCORE As many thousands as years? How old is he, though? All
depends upon that. If he is a middle-aged man, that is a reason for
suspending proceedings. But two hundred pounds—two hundred
pounds? No, no—I can't stand it—I'm off! (*Crosses up C, with hat
on. Every time Hardcore puts on his hat, Hawk motions him to take* 295
it off)

HAWK (*with vehemence*) Go, then—go, you dolt—your blood be upon
your own head!

HARDCORE (*stops*) Eh—my blood?

HAWK In your ruin, remember that I offered to save you! 300

HARDCORE Save me—from what?

HAWK From what? Simply from utter ruin!

HARDCORE From ruin! Impossible! (*Hawk motions him to take off his
hat*)

HAWK (*seating himself, L*) What, you! An adroit, intelligent man, 305
thoroughly up to all the knowledge of the humbug of speculation—for he is, Caroline, perfectly wide-awake in general—you
dabble in such schemes? (*Mysteriously*)

HARDCORE (*C, getting more fidgety*) To which do you refer?

HAWK I was quite angry when I heard you had been duped so—not 310
out of love to you, observe. No, out of pure selfishness; for, in
some sort, I looked upon your fortune as my own: I said to myself,
'I owe him too much, not to be certain but that he will aid me on
great occasions'—such as the present, for instance: and you are
about to risk all, to lose all, in one scheme. 315

HARDCORE (*in agony*) Hawk, my dear friend, is it then true? Is that Indian Emerald Mine Company really a flam?°

HAWK (*aside*) Oh, you have shares there have you. I knew I should make him betray himself. (*Aloud*) A flam! You, the knowing Hardcore, ask me if it is a flam?   320

HARDCORE But it is considered such a splendid scheme. Shares are at three per cent. above par already.

HAWK Oh, yes, a splendid scheme for those who sold yesterday.

HARDCORE They sold yesterday?

HAWK Yes, in secret—hush!   325

HARDCORE Adieu. Mrs Hawk, good morning.

HAWK Hardcore?

HARDCORE Well?

HAWK And your note to the chief clerk—

HARDCORE I'll speak to him.   330

HAWK No; write. When a man says he'll write, he means to forget. Write! Meanwhile, I may tell you of some who will buy your Emerald shares.

HARDCORE All my shares? (*Reseats himself, L, and takes pen*) And who, pray?   335

HAWK (*aside*) There's an honest fellow, now; eager to rob some one else, as a cat to pounce upon a mouse. (*To Hardcore*) A promise of three months delay?

HARDCORE There—it's done! (*Comes down, L*)

HAWK My friend, who is buying in secret, believing the scheme as   340
splendid as you believed it, wants three hundred shares. Have you as many?

HARDCORE Three hundred and fifty!

HAWK Fifty more—well, I have no doubt he'll take them. (*Looking upon what Hardcore has written*) Have you mentioned the two   345
hundred pounds?

HARDCORE And what's your friend's name?

HAWK His name is—but you have not written two hundred pounds.

HARDCORE His name?

HAWK The money!   350

HARDCORE (*crosses to L and sits at table*) What a man you are! (*Writes*) There it is.

HAWK His name is Grossmark.

HARDCORE (*rising*) Grossmark?

HAWK At least, Grossmark is the man commissioned to buy. Go   355
home, and I'll send them to you.

HARDCORE I'll go myself. (*Crosses to C*)

HAWK If you run after the buyer, he'll lower his terms.

HARDCORE True! You are my preserver. Adieu, my dear friend— 360
you are my friend, my very dear friend. (*Hardcore retires, and
returns to bow very obsequiously to Mrs Hawk, shakes hands with
Hawk, turns, and exit, C*)

HAWK Yes, dearer to you than you imagine. (*Imitates the action of
pulling the strings of a puppet*)

MRS HAWK (*R*) But is that true, what you told about the Emerald 365
Company?

HAWK (*L*) There *is* truth in it. My friend Prospectus is anxious to
get up a panic in these shares, which will eventually turn out a
magnificent property. Ah, if I had but a thousand pounds to
purchase with, my fortune would be—but no, I must first marry 370
Julia.

MRS HAWK Do you know this Sir Harry Lester well?

HAWK Intimately! I have dined with him.

MRS HAWK Oh!

HAWK Charming house, splendid plate, everything in the first style. 375
Our child will make a famous match. And as to him—bah! in
marriage, it is devilish lucky if one of the happy pair is satisfied.
     Enter Julia, LD

MRS HAWK Here comes Julia. (*Crosses to C*) My dear, your papa and
I have just been talking of you; and apropos to a subject young
ladies always like to hear of—marriage. 380

JULIA (*L*) Has Frederick Noble, then, been talking to papa? (*Crosses
to C*)

HAWK (*R*) Noble! (*Crosses to C*) Mrs Hawk, were you prepared to
find that gentleman comfortably established in your daughter's
affections? What! my clerk? 385

JULIA (*R*) Yes, papa.

HAWK You love him?

JULIA Yes, papa.

MRS HAWK Does he love you?

JULIA Oh, dearly! 390

HAWK (*C*) What proofs have you?

JULIA His wish to marry me.

HAWK How sharp these chits are with their answers. Miss Julia
Hawk, permit me to inform you that a clerk, with one hundred
and fifty pounds a year, does not know how to love. He has not 395
the time—'tis too luxurious—he can't afford it.

JULIA But Frederick loves me, and I love him.

HAWK In that case, you shall marry him. (*Julia is overjoyed*) Wait a
bit. I said in that case: the case isn't yet proved. You know that
you will not have a penny. How are you to live after you're   400
married? Have you thought of that?

JULIA (*overjoyed*) Yes, papa!

MRS HAWK She's out of her senses.

HAWK Well, my child, tell me your plans. Confide in me, as your
best friend. How will you live?   405

JULIA Live upon love, papa!

HAWK Pleasant and cheap. But will love from his quiver wing his
arrows with bank-notes?

JULIA Yes, for it will give us both courage. Oh! I will work for him.
Frederick has ambition—he will get on.   410

HAWK An ambitious bachelor may get on: but, married, he has no
chance. The great Bacon said—'The man who has a wife and
children has given hostages to fortune.'° In other words, has
pawned his whole existence. But a thought occurs to me—your
Frederick believes me rich?   415

JULIA He has never spoken of money.

HAWK Exactly. I see it all. Julia, you may write to him at once to
come and speak to me.

JULIA (*throwing her arms around his neck*) Oh, you darling papa!

HAWK But you will marry Sir Harry Lester. Instead of being the wife 420
of a poor clerk, you will be Lady Lester—rich, flattered, and
courted. I'm sorry that I've nothing better to offer you.

JULIA But Frederick—

HAWK Oh, he will give you up of his own accord.

JULIA Never, never!   425

MRS HAWK Suppose Frederick really loves her?

HAWK Suppose he loves her fortune? (*A knock is heard, LUE*)

MRS HAWK A knock! And no one to open the door.

HAWK (*sits, R*) Let them knock again.

MRS HAWK It's very strange, but I can't help fancying that every   430
knock must be Sparrow returned.

HAWK Sparrow? I think you said Sparrow—did you not? Ha, ha!
Well, that is good! What! After running away with our funds—
after eight years' absence, and no hint of his existence—you believe
in Sparrow's return? Why, you are like the old French soldiers,   435
who still live in hope of Napoleon's returning to them. (*A knock*)

MRS HAWK Another knock!

HAWK Go, Julia, and say we are out. None but a creditor can have the indecency to disbelieve a young girl—and, in that case, let him enter. (*Exit Julia, C*)   440

MRS HAWK (*L*) That child's love—sincere, at any rate, on her part—has quite moved me!

HAWK (*R*) You women are all so romantic! We shall see what Mr Noble says.

      Enter Julia, C, comes down, L

JULIA It is Mr Grossmark, papa.   445

HAWK (*R*) Grossmark—the laughing hyena—coarse in speech as in mind. His bantering is like the badinage of a young elephant; but he is civil to me, because he thinks I have still resources. I tame him as we tame wild beasts—by audacity, and an unflinching eye. If he thought I feared him, he would swallow me up whole!   450 (*Going to door*) Come in—you can come in, Grossmark. (*Ladies cross to L*)

      Enter Grossmark, C

GROSSMARK (*LC*) Ha, ha! I've come to compliment you. I know that Miss Julia is going to be married to a millionaire; the rumour has already got abroad.   455

HAWK Millionaire! no. Some hundred thousands—that's all.

GROSSMARK That magnificent dodge will make many of your creditors patient—ha, ha! And even I—

HAWK Thought of arresting me.

JULIA Arresting you, papa?   460

MRS HAWK Oh, Mr Grossmark!

GROSSMARK Hear me. The money has been owing two years; but this marriage is a superb invention, and—

MRS HAWK An invention, Mr Grossmark!

HAWK My son-in-law is Sir Harry Lester, a young man of—   465

GROSSMARK What! really a young man? Ha, ha! How much do you pay him? Oh, come now—

MRS HAWK Oh!

HAWK Enough of this impertinence; or else, my dear Grossmark, I shall insist upon settling accounts; and at the price you sell me   470 money, I rather imagine you would be something the loser by that.

GROSSMARK But, my dear—

HAWK (*haughtily*) Mr Grossmark, I am about to become rich enough to permit no longer the vulgar jests of any one—not even a creditor.   475

GROSSMARK But—

HAWK Not another word, or—I pay you. Enter my private room, and
we will settle the affair about which I sent for you.

GROSSMARK (*humbly, and crossing to R*) At your service, Mr Hawk.
(*Aside*) What an imposing chap he is. (*Exit, RD 2E*)   480

HAWK (*following him, and speaking to them*) The wild beast is
tamed—I will have his skin ere long. (*Exit, RD 2E*)

JULIA Oh, mamma, I shall never be able to marry this baronet.

MRS HAWK (*R*) But he is rich.

JULIA (*L*) Yet I prefer poverty and happiness.   485

MRS HAWK My child, there is no happiness possible in poverty. Let
our experience be a lesson to you. We are at this moment going
through a terrible crisis. Marry well, my child, while you can.

    Enter Thomas, followed by Dimity, C

THOMAS (*C*) All your orders are executed, ma'am.

DIMITY The tradesmen are civil again, and Mrs Mason says the   490
dinner will be superb.

THOMAS As to Mr Prospectus—

    Enter Hawk with papers in his hand, RD 2E. Exit Dimity, C

HAWK What of Mr Prospectus?

THOMAS He is coming at once; he had to take some money to Mr
Johnson, who lives next door.   495

HAWK You keep at the door, and manage that he speaks to me *before*
he sees Johnson. Tell him 'tis a case of immense importance,
admitting of no delay. (*Exit Thomas, C*)

MRS HAWK (*C*) And Grossmark?

HAWK That is all I could extract from him—delay, and these bills of   500
exchange for some shares. Bills on a certain Bradshaw, a man of
fashion, very insolvent, but who has a rich old aunt in the environs
of Dublin. Sir Harry comes from Dublin—he will tell me, perhaps,
whether the bills are worth anything.

MRS HAWK But the tradespeople will be here immediately.   505

HAWK And I shall be here to pay them. Never fear, Caroline, the
money will be ready. But leave me to myself. (*Mrs Hawk and Julia
cross, and exeunt, 1EL*) They are coming! Everything now rests
upon the doubtful friendship of Prospectus—a man whose fortune
I made. But the world is so ungrateful; where the benevolent   510
people are, I know not. Prospectus and I like each other very well.
He owes me gratitude, and I owe him money—neither of us pay.

THOMAS (*without, CD*) Yes, sir, master is at home.

HAWK 'Tis he—my friend! (*Rushes to the door—Earthworm appears*)
Oh, it's Mr Earthworm!   515

EARTHWORM (*L*) I have been eleven times during the last week, my dear Mr Affable Hawk; and want obliged me to wait for you three hours in the street yesterday; and I saw that they told me the truth, in saying you were in the country, so I came today.

HAWK (*R*) My dear Earthworm, we are equally miserable.   520

EARTHWORM Um, um! I am in a wretched plight—everything I have pawned!

HAWK Pretty nearly my case.

EARTHWORM I never reproached you with my ruin, for I believed it was your intention to make us rich; but, after all, fine words pay   525
no baker, and I am come to beg the smallest instalment of interest, to keep my family from starvation. Starvation! Imagine what a fearful thing starvation must be!

HAWK Earthworm, you unman me! Be reasonable—I will share with you what I have. (*In a low voice*) There is but five pounds in the   530
house, and that is my daughter's money.

EARTHWORM Is it possible? You, whom I have seen so rich!

HAWK I have nothing to hide from you.

EARTHWORM Between those who are wretched, truth is a sacred debt!   535

HAWK Ah! if *that* was all we owed, how promptly it might be paid! But mind you keep my secret. I am on the point of securing a husband for my daughter.

EARTHWORM I have two daughters, and they must work, work, work, without hope of marriage! In the circumstances in which you   540
are placed, I would not importune you, but my wife and children await my return in anguish and anxiety.

HAWK You move me deeply. Come, I'll give you three pounds. (*Exit, RD*)

EARTHWORM My wife and children will for ever bless you! You have   545
saved them from starvation—starvation! (*Aside, during Hawk's brief absence in another room*) The others who pester him get nothing; but by my doleful and modest complaints, I gradually get from him all the interest due to me. Ah, ah! starvation is a fine ferret! (*Taps his pocket*)   550

HAWK (*who has observed the latter part of Earthworm's pantomime,° aside*) Eh? Oh, the old miser! Ten instalments on account, each of three pounds—that makes thirty pounds. I have sown abundantly—now I must reap. (*Aloud*) Here is the money.

EARTHWORM (*L*) Three sovereigns°—three golden sovereigns?   555
Eh, eh! What a time it is since these fingers have touched

gold! Adieu! My whole family will pray for the happiness of
Miss Julia.

HAWK (*R*) Good bye! (*Holding him back*) Poor fellow! when I look at
you, I fancy myself rich. Your misery so affects me, that I can't   560
express it. And to think of my being only yesterday on the point
of repaying you all—capital and interest!

EARTHWORM (*eagerly*) To repay me?

HAWK It hung upon a thread.

EARTHWORM Tell, tell me all about it!   565

HAWK Imagine the most brilliant invention—a speculation so
grand—which appealed to all interests—which was certain to
realize gigantic profits—and a stupid banker refused me the paltry
sum of two hundred and fifty pounds, when perhaps there was a
million to be gained.   570

EARTHWORM A million?

HAWK A million to begin with—for no one can tell the limits to
which commercial vogue might not push the 'Conservative Pavement'.

EARTHWORM Pavement?   575

HAWK Conservative—a pavement upon which and with which barricades are impossible!°

EARTHWORM Really!

HAWK You see, all the Governments interested in the maintenance
of order° become at once our shareholders. Kings, princes, minis-   580
ters, form our committee, supported by the banker lords, the
cotton lords, and all the commercial world. Even the very Repub-
licans themselves, finding their chance ruined, will be forced to
take my shares, in order to live!

EARTHWORM (*eagerly*) Ah, yes! That is grandiose—colossal!   585

HAWK And so philanthropic! And to think of my being refused three
hundred pounds to advertise and start this magnificent scheme.

EARTHWORM Three hundred. I thought it was only—

HAWK Three hundred; not a sixpence more; and I would have had
half the profits, that is to say ten fortunes!   590

EARTHWORM Wait a bit—I will see—I will speak to some one who,
perhaps, will be glad.

HAWK Hush! not a word. Above all things, don't speak of it—they
might steal the idea; or, perhaps, they might not see at once
the enormous fortune certain to be realized, as your sagacity   595
has seen it. Capitalists are so stupid; besides, I am expecting
Prospectus.

EARTHWORM Prospectus—but it is quite possible that I may know
some one.

HAWK Lucky dog, that Prospectus! He's speculative too. If he only   600
has the wit to see how easily he may make his fortune—five
hundred pounds is all that are required.

EARTHWORM Five hundred? Just now, you said three hundred.

HAWK Three, yes, exactly. It was three hundred I was refused; but
it is five hundred I must have. And Prospectus, whom I have so   605
often enriched, will become a millionaire through me now. After
all, he's a good fellow, Prospectus.

EARTHWORM Hawk, if I were to find the sum.

HAWK You? No, no, my friend, think nothing of what I told you.
Besides, Prospectus is coming, and he is certain to give me the   610
money; and then I shall soon pay you the two thousand pounds I
owe you.

EARTHWORM But you won't listen to me.

    Enter Mrs Hawk, L

MRS HAWK Mr Prospectus has arrived, dear.

HAWK (*aside*) Bravo! (*Aloud*) Detain him one instant. (*Exit Mrs*   615
Hawk, L) Now, my dear Earthworm, I must say good bye to you.
Prospectus is here, and my money is secure. I needn't appeal to
your gallantry. (*Forcing him*)
      All things, you know, my friend, give place,
        When there's a little money in the case.   620

EARTHWORM Stay, stay, I have the sum by me, and I will give it
you. (*Takes out his pocketbook*)

HAWK You! Earthworm! Five hundred pounds!

EARTHWORM It—it—some one—a friend commissioned me to invest
it for him; and I don't think I could do better than invest it in your   625
hands.

HAWK Oh! For an investment, I defy you to find a better. (*Taking
the notes*) So much the worse for Prospectus—he ought to have
come before.

EARTHWORM Then you will prepare the agreement. (*Crosses to R*)   630

HAWK At once! Good bye! Go out through my private room. (*Shows
him out, 2ER*)

EARTHWORM You have got the money safe?

HAWK Safe. (*Putting it in his pocket*)

EARTHWORM Oh, Mr Hawk. Oh! oh! (*Exit, R*)   635

    Enter Mrs Hawk, 1EL

MRS HAWK My dear, Prospectus says, if you're engaged, he'll look in again, as he must call on Johnson, next door.

HAWK I'm with him directly. Oh, my dear Caroline, I ought to blow my brains out.

MRS HAWK (*L*) Heavens! What has occurred?   640

HAWK (*R*) Not five minutes ago, I asked Earthworm, the old miser, to lend me five hundred pounds.

MRS HAWK And he refused you?

HAWK On the contrary, he gave them!

MRS HAWK Well?   645

HAWK I'm miserable to think that he gave me the money so readily—it might have been a thousand, had I been adroit!

MRS HAWK What a man you are!
  Enter Thomas, CD

THOMAS Please, sir, the tradesmen are waiting in the hall.

HAWK Have they their little bills with them?   650

THOMAS Yes, sir.

HAWK Then show them into my study.

THOMAS What! all of them, sir? And what in the world am I to do with them there? They would eat me up!

HAWK Do with them? Why pay them, of course! What should you 655
do with them?

THOMAS Pay them? What! with money?

HAWK With gold!

THOMAS Oh! (*Exit, CD*)

MRS HAWK Come and see Mr Prospectus—don't keep him—he's in 660
a dreadful hurry!

HAWK True! Send him to me, while I'm in the vein. I've sufficient already for the jewels; and a few hundreds now, for the tradesmen and sundries, will carry me through.

MRS HAWK You must succeed with Mr Prospectus—he is such an 665
old friend! (*Exit, L*)

HAWK An old friend! How comfortable that sounds! What a crutch to lean upon! And what a delusive reed it really is! Prospectus is an old friend; but I'm afraid that he's more the friend of money than of myself.   670
  Enter Prospectus, L2E

PROSPECTUS Good morning, Hawk! What is it you have to say to me? Quick! Thomas stopped me on my way to Johnson's.

HAWK What! Do you visit such a fellow as Johnson?

PROSPECTUS My dear Hawk, if we only visited those whom we   675
esteem, we should never pay visits at all, for hang me if I know a
door I could knock at!

HAWK (*R, laughing, and taking his hand*) No, not even your own—
not even your own.

PROSPECTUS Well, what is it you want of me?

HAWK You leave me no time to gild the pill. I see you have guessed.   680

PROSPECTUS Money? My dear fellow, I have none; and, frankly, if
I had, I couldn't lend it to you. I have already lent you all that my
means permitted. I have not dunned you for it—between friends,
you know. But if my heart was not filled with gratitude; if I were
as other men are, the creditor would long since have absorbed the   685
friend. If I had money enough to save you altogether, I'd do it: but
you are done up. All your recent speculations, though ingenious,
have failed. When ruin comes, you will always find a home, and a
knife and fork, in my house; but for the present, depend upon it,
your game is up. It is the duty of friendship not to conceal   690
unpleasant truths.

HAWK A duty friendship very steadfastly avails itself of. You may
always trust to your friends for that. What would friendship be,
without the luxury of complimenting oneself while saying dis-
agreeables to one's friend? So, I am a lost man in public opinion,   695
am I?

PROSPECTUS Well, I don't say that. There is no man for whom the
public has a greater admiration than yourself, but it is thought that
necessity, the mother of all evil, has forced you to have recourse
to expedients.   700

HAWK Which are not justified, because they are not successful.
Success, success! What an idol it is! And of how many infamies is
it not frequently composed! I'll give you a proof of it. I have this
very morning brought about that fall in Indian Emeralds so
necessary for your operations, that you may buy largely before the   705
news is published of its—

PROSPECTUS Hush! (*Taking him by the waist*) My dear Hawk, is that
true? Ah, how like you that is now! There's no one has your genius
after all.

HAWK That will show you that I don't want advice, but money. Nor   710
do I ask that for myself; I ask it for my daughter, whose marriage
depends on it. We are at the last pinch. Poverty reigns in this
house, though under the form of plenty—and, unless I have a little
ready money, Julia's chance is lost. In a word, I want a week's

opulence here, as you want four-and-twenty hours' untruth on   715
'Change.° To be frank with you, my wife and daughter have not
the wherewithal to provide the wedding dresses.

PROSPECTUS (*aside*) Is he humbugging me?

HAWK This very day my future son-in-law is to dine here, and all
my plate is—having my crest engraved on it!° All I ask is to   720
lend me three hundred pounds—and your service of plate—for
a day.

PROSPECTUS Three hundred pounds! No one has three hundred
pounds to lend. Lucky he who has the sum for himself; (*crosses to
R, and sits upon sofa, R*) and if he lent it continually he would never   725
have it. (*Goes to the fire-place*)

HAWK (*following*) Look here, my dear fellow. I love my wife and
child; their love is my only consolation amidst my present troubles;
and they have been so patient, so resigned! My greatest anxiety is
to see them safe from misfortune. (*Coming down the stage arm-in-*   730
arm with him) I have suffered much of late. I have seen my best
hopes frustrated—my best schemes fail—but all these are nothing
compared with the pain of being refused by you.

PROSPECTUS Well, I'll step home and see if I have as much at my
banker's, and I will drop you a line. I will write to you.   735

HAWK No. When a man says he will write, he means to refuse. I have
promised to pay dressmakers and other tradesmen on the certainty
of your aiding me. You will not suffer Julia, your god-daughter, to
miss a splendid marriage.

PROSPECTUS My dear Hawk, I haven't the money. I will lend you   740
the plate with pleasure. (*Goes R, and sits at table*)

HAWK (*sinking into chair, L of table*) Enough! All is over. My child
must suffer for her father.

     Enter Mrs Hawk and Julia, L

MRS HAWK What is the matter?

HAWK (*drawing them both to him*) Look here, Prospectus—here are   745
my anxieties! Oh, the sight of them unmans me! I could implore
you on my knees.

JULIA Papa, I will implore for you. Oh, sir, whatever his request,
grant it! (*Crosses to R*)

PROSPECTUS Do you know what the request is?   750

JULIA No.

PROSPECTUS Three hundred pounds for your marriage.

JULIA (*RC*) Oh, sir; then *forget* what I have said! My marriage must
not be bought with the humiliation of my father. (*Hawk kisses her*)

PROSPECTUS (*moved*) Julia, you are a good girl—and my god-   755
daughter—and—and—I'll go and fetch the money.°

Prospectus goes quickly up stage, towards CD. Hawk towards
door, R. Julia and Mrs Hawk towards L

2.

*Hawk's Office. Doors R and L1E; window, L; a large desk,
with drawers and compartments for letters, deeds, papers, &c.,
R; two chairs and table, L; writing materials at back; bookcases,
tin cases, &c.; doors 1 and 3ER, 1 and 3EL; window, 2EL;
fire-place, 2ER*

Enter Thomas, followed by Frederick Noble, L1E

NOBLE You say Mr Hawk wishes to speak with me?

THOMAS Yes, sir; but Miss Julia begs you to wait here for her, before
you see her father.

NOBLE *(aside)* Her father wishes to see me—she wishes to speak with
me before the interview: something has happened!　　　　　　　5

THOMAS Here is Miss Julia.

NOBLE Julia!

　　　　Enter Julia, R1E

JULIA Thomas, inform papa that Mr Noble has arrived. (*Exit
Thomas, UER*) Frederick, if you wish our love to shine as
brilliantly in the eyes of others as it does in our hearts, you must　　10
summon all your courage.

NOBLE *(L)* What has happened?

JULIA *(R)* I am threatened with a husband—young, rich, titled. My
father is evidently eager for the match.

NOBLE A rival! And you ask me if I want courage? Tell me his name,　　15
and you shall soon—

JULIA Frederick! You terrify me; is it thus you hope to persuade my
papa!

NOBLE He is here.

　　　　Enter Hawk, UER

HAWK *(C)* So you love my daughter?　　　　　　　　　　　　20

NOBLE *(L)* I do, sir.

HAWK At any rate, she believes as much. You have had the clever-
ness to persuade her of that.

NOBLE Sir, these insinuations, from another, would be unpardonable
insults; from Julia's father I will let them pass. Not love her? How　　25
could I help loving her? The friendless orphan has no one in the
world to love; none but her, and she has been a world to me. She
has smiled upon me in my darkness; and yet you ask me if I love
her.

JULIA (*R*) Ought I not to leave the room, papa?   30

HAWK Oh! Your modesty suffers from these praises? Mr Noble, I
happen to entertain those ideas on love, which usually accompany
age and experience. My doubts are all the more rational in this
case; as I am not one of those parents who believe their goslings
are cygnets, I see Julia as she is—without being plain—she wants   35
that beauty which arrests the eye.

NOBLE (*L*) You are mistaken. I venture to assure you that you do not
know your daughter.

HAWK I don't?

NOBLE You do not know her.   40

HAWK On the contrary, I know her perfectly. I know her as well as
if—in fact, I know her.

NOBLE No, no! You know the Julia seen by all the world, but love
has transformed her. Tenderness, devotion, gentleness, invest her
with a beauty which love alone creates.   45

JULIA Oh! Let me leave the room; I am all confusion!

HAWK (*C*) You are all gratitude and delight, hussy! (*To him*) And if
you say such things to her—

NOBLE I can say nothing else!

HAWK (*aside*) Who can wonder that lovers are such bores to other   50
people, if that is the staple of their talk? (*To him*) I fancied I was
Julia's father, but you are the parent of a Julia so charming, that I
should be glad to make her acquaintance.

NOBLE Have you ever loved then?

HAWK Considerably—and often. Like most men, I have been a fool   55
and a dupe.

NOBLE Is it to be a dupe, to feel that exalted passion, which attaches
us to the ideal? Which charms every hour of life?

HAWK Yes, every hour, except the dinner hour.

JULIA Ah! Now you are laughing at us; we love each other truly—our   60
love is pure and holy, founded on our knowledge of each other;
and on the conviction that, together, we could battle through life
bravely and cheerily.

NOBLE What an angel she is!

HAWK (*aside*) Yes, yes—we shall see what you say to the angel   65
without wings! (*Aloud*) So, you love each other desperately? What
a charming romance! You will marry her?

NOBLE It is my highest ambition.

HAWK In spite of every obstacle?

NOBLE In spite of everything!   70

HAWK Julia, my dear, you may leave us. I have to mention a few details not quite so romantic, but quite as necessary, as those we have just had.

JULIA (*going*) Remember, I shall never love any one but Frederick! (*Exit, R1E*)   75

NOBLE (*aside, L*) I feel certain of his consent.

HAWK (*R*) Young man, I am ruined!

NOBLE Mr Hawk!

HAWK Totally, irretrievably ruined! Now, if you still claim my daughter's hand, it is yours. I feel bound in honour to be explicit   80
with you. She will be at least saved from want, as your wife; whereas she must, at home, share worse than poverty.

NOBLE Worse?

HAWK I have enormous debts—ruin stares me in the face!

NOBLE Impossible!   85

HAWK You don't believe me? (*Aside*) He's obstinate. (*Taking out book from desk*) Look here—our property is here reckoned. Here are the protested bills—the mortgages—the lawyers' threats. You see how imminent the ruin is. Look at them—they are all in order—all classed. For, my young friend, bear this in mind—it is, above all   90
things, in disorder that order is necessary. In a well ordered disorder you are at your ease—you are master of the field. What can a creditor say, when he sees his debt methodically inscribed in due order? It gives bankruptcy a business-like air—makes it quite respectable; and nothing goes down so well with men of business,   95
as business-like appearances. Order, my dear young friend, methodical order, is the hypocrisy of commerce! They ought to make me librarian to the British Museum—I'd make them a catalogue. (*Replaces book in desk*)

NOBLE And you have paid nothing?   100

HAWK Little more. I pay alphabetically, and have not come to *A* yet. My debts amount to seventeen thousand pounds and odd shillings.

NOBLE (*absorbed in thought*) Ruined! Ruined! No help!

HAWK (*observing him—aside*) I was sure of it—I knew how a douche of reality would cool the ardour of the ideal. (*Aloud*) Well, my   105
young friend?

NOBLE I have to thank you sincerely for the frankness of this confession.

HAWK And the ideal? And your love for my daughter?

NOBLE You have opened my eyes.   110

HAWK I knew I should.

NOBLE I fancied that I loved her to extremity—

HAWK And now?

NOBLE Now I feel that I love her ten times more.

HAWK What?   115

NOBLE You have opened my eyes to the sacred responsibility of my
love—to the need of all my courage, of all my devotion; and with
that increased demand has come increased love to meet it! I give
my life to labour for her, and she will love me the dearer for my
toil!   120

HAWK What! You still think of marriage?

NOBLE Still! More than ever. I believed you rich—it was a draw-
back. With trembling and shame, and fear lest my motive
should be misinterpreted, I asked for your daughter. Now, I can
hold my head erect; and ask you, without shame, to give me her   125
hand.

HAWK (*aside*) Um! I did not think there was so much goodness in
the world. (*Aloud*) Forgive me the opinion I had formed—I had
wronged you: and, above all, forgive me the pain I must cause
you—Julia cannot be your wife.   130

NOBLE No! What, in spite of our affection, and your ruin?

HAWK Precisely on account of my ruin. I have told you all; and
thereby discovered what a generous spirit lives in your breast. To
that generosity I must now appeal. I have a brilliant marriage in
view. That marriage will give me money; and, that which is more   135
than money—*time*. By its aid, I can reconquer my position—pay
off my debts, and save my family from ruin. Thus, the marriage
of my daughter is my last hope—my last resource—the plank that
floats past the shipwrecked family: without it, I lose all, even my
honour—with it, I save all. Now, since you so truly and disinter-   140
estedly love my daughter, I appeal to the very generosity of your
love; do not condemn her to poverty.

NOBLE (*with emotion*) But what—what is it you ask? What would you
have me do?

HAWK (*taking his hand*) I would have you seek in your affection a   145
courage, which I should not have—

NOBLE *What* is it? There is nothing I would not do for her.

HAWK Brave and generous fellow! Listen to me. If I refused you her
hand, she would refuse the man I intend her to marry: so that it
is necessary that I should give my consent, and the refusal come   150
from you.

NOBLE From me? She wouldn't credit it.

HAWK She will believe it, if you tell her that you fear poverty for her.

NOBLE She will think my love is mercenary.   155

HAWK But she will owe to you her happiness.

NOBLE (*with pathos*) But she will despise me.

HAWK She will.

NOBLE And can I bear that?

HAWK If I have read your heart aright, you would bear that, or worse   160
than that, to secure her happiness. What is love but self-sacrifice?
I ask you to do what I could not do myself—I confess it: what
thousands could not do, because the thousands are selfish. But you
will do it, because your heart is high-placed, and your love
unselfish. Am I not right? May I not count on you?   165

NOBLE (*after a struggle*) Yes, you may.

HAWK I knew it. (*Shakes his hand warmly*)
      Enter Mrs Hawk and Julia, 1 ER

MRS HAWK Julia is so impatient to hear the result of your conversation, that she has found me to come with her.

HAWK I have laid before Mr Noble a frank statement of our position,   170
and it remains with him to decide.

NOBLE (*aside*) How shall I tell her? My heart will break.

JULIA Well, Frederick? (*crosses to RC*)

NOBLE Oh! Julia, I—

JULIA Speak! Quick! All is settled, is it not?   175

NOBLE Your father has placed confidence in me—he has shown me
his position.

JULIA Well, well?

HAWK (*C*) I have told him that we are ruined.

JULIA But that has not altered his intentions—that has not affected   180
your love, Frederick.

NOBLE My love! (*Crosses to C. Hawk, unobserved, seizes him by the
hand*) I—I—I should deceive you, Julia, if I were to say my
intentions—remained the same.

JULIA I cannot believe it! It is not you who say this!   185

NOBLE (*with animation*) There are men to whom poverty gives fresh
energy—men whose happiness would be intensified by the devotion of each day, by the toil of each day; and would hold
themselves as a thousandfold repaid by the smile of a loved wife.
(*Restraining himself*) I—I—am not one of those. The thought of   190
poverty subdues me. I could not sustain the idea of your being in
want.

JULIA (*throws herself, sobbing, into her mother's arms*) Oh! mother—
mother—mother!

MRS HAWK (*R*) My child!—my darling Julia!   195

NOBLE (*aside to Hawk*) Have I said enough?

JULIA I should have had courage for both. I would have slaved for
him! Poverty would have been light to bear with his love! But oh!
he never—never—never loved me!

NOBLE In pity, sir, let me go away at once!   200

HAWK Come!

NOBLE Julia, farewell! You know not what is beating in my heart at
this moment! You despise me! The love which would drag you
into want is madness! My love is that which sacrifices itself for you
and your happiness!   205

JULIA Go—I no longer believe in you! (*To her mother*) He was my
happiness!
       *Enter Thomas, L1E, who announces 'Sir Harry Lester and Mr
       Graves'*

HAWK Caroline, my dear, take Julia to her room. (*To Noble*) Follow
me. (*To Thomas*) Ask the gentlemen to wait here a minute. (*Exeunt
Hawk and Noble, UER; Mrs Hawk and Julia, 1ER*)   210
       Enter Sir Harry Lester and Graves, L1E

THOMAS Master will be here in a minute, gentlemen. (*Exit, L*)

GRAVES (*L*) Well, my boy, you have entered the citadel at last. Have
a care, though, Hawk is deuced keen!

LESTER (*R*) Yes, I'm rather afraid he won't be gulled.°

GRAVES Tut! never fear, if you play boldly. There is no man more   215
easily duped than he who is always duping. He relies too much on
his own sagacity. Hawk is a speculator—rich today, tomorrow he
may be a beggar. To guard against this, my belief is that he wants
to place a fortune of his money in the shape of a dowry for his
daughter, so as to be secure against a rainy day. He wants a   220
son-in-law who will aid him in his plans.

LESTER (*R*) I've no objection, provided he does not look too closely
into my affairs.

GRAVES (*L*) I have primed him.

LESTER Well, fortune assist, for I'm in a sad plight! If I had not,   225
luckily, two names—one for the usurers and bailiffs, the other for
the fashionable world—I should be on my last legs. The only
chance I have lived upon for some time, has been that of meeting
with an heiress or a rich widow; but the race seems almost
extinct—like the pug-dogs.   230

GRAVES It's very sad.

LESTER Then the money-lenders are such scoundrels. Grossmark sends me to old Earthworm, after having emptied my pockets himself. My tailor refuses to understand my prospects—the brute! The horse lives on tick.° As to my tiger,° I don't know a damn how he breathes, nor where he feeds; that is a mystery I dare not fathom. So, you see, I must do something. Besides, I'm sick of idleness. I see that the shortest way to get wealthy is, after all, to work for it: but the devil of it is, that we gentlemen feel ourselves fitted for everything, and so, in reality, are fitted for nothing. A man, with such whiskers as mine, what is he to do? Society has created no employment for us.

GRAVES Join Hawk, and become a speculator.

LESTER And you are positive he won't give less than twenty thousand pounds with his daughter?

GRAVES That was the sum he named to me. And from the magnitude of his affairs, the elegance in which he lives—

LESTER Oh, as to elegance, damn it, look at me!

GRAVES Ah! but look around, and observe that the opulence here is that of a merchant.

LESTER That's true.

GRAVES Besides, Hawk is a great city name.

LESTER Yes, but it suggests uncomfortable ideas to the *pigeons*!° However, he can't hurt me, so I'm all safe.

GRAVES Not counting me, how much do you owe?

LESTER Oh, a mere nothing! Some five thousand pounds, which my father-in-law will pay. I always said I should never become rich till I was penniless; that critical moment is arrived.

GRAVES Have you prepared yourself to answer Hawk's questions?

LESTER Yes; I have the Lester estates. Three thousand acres of the finest land in Ireland—several houses in Dublin—two salt marshes—and powerful political connections, the more useful, as I am resolved upon playing a political part.

GRAVES A good idea!

LESTER I shall commence with journalism; do as they do in France—make the newspapers carry me into the Cabinet.

GRAVES But you never wrote a line in your life.

LESTER Innocent gentleman! Why do you suppose that it is necessary for the editor of a newspaper to know how to write? He leaves that to some poor devil who is paid for it, and whom nobody hears of. I shall shave my whiskers, and assume a dignified demeanour.

(*Speaks with emphasis*) 'The question before us has still to be understood; it lies deep, sir, deep; I shall expose it altogether, very shortly.' To another—'Russia, sir, is a bugbear nobody understands.' Or I may do something in the grandiose and prophetic style—'We are   275
rolling down the abyss; we have not yet evolved all the evolutions of the revolutionary phasis.'° A man establishes a high character upon such pedestals as these: especially if he publish a bulky volume of statistics, which no one opens, and everyone pretends to have read—that settles him as a serious thinker, a solid politician.   280

GRAVES Ha, ha! I believe you are right.

LESTER The moment I am married I put on the air of a man of principles! I can take my choice of principles, for we have them of all colours. Stay! I shall be a Protectionist. The word tickles me. In every age, there is some word which is the latch-key to the   285
Cabinet—and Protection sounds so kind, so generous, so fatherly! Decidedly, I shall go in for the farmers' friend!° (*Crosses to L*)

GRAVES Here comes your father-in-law.

    Enter Hawk, RDUE

HAWK (*crosses to C*) How do you do? Delighted to see you. Sorry to have kept you waiting, but I was occupied with——I may as well tell   290
you, as you are to be one of the family. Poor fellow—an admirer of Julia's. I'm afraid I was rather stern with him—but what could I say to an offer of marriage from a man with only a miserable five hundred a year, and no great prospects?

LESTER Five hundred a year—poor devil!   295

HAWK (*C*) People may vegetate upon that sum.

LESTER (*L*) Not live on it, assuredly.

HAWK The ladies will be here immediately. Meanwhile, shall we talk business?

LESTER (*aside*) The crisis is come. (*They sit down*)   300

HAWK (*L*) You love my daughter?

LESTER (*C*) Passionately!

HAWK Passionately?

GRAVES (*R, aside to Lester*) You are going too far.

LESTER I am ambitious—very: and, in Miss Julia Hawk, I see a lady   305
so distingué in manner and appearance, that, as my wife, she would not only adorn any position I might attain, but assist me onwards by her influence.

HAWK I understand. A wife is easily found; but to find a wife for a Minister, or an Ambassador, is not quite so easy. I see, Sir Harry,   310
you are a man of capacity.

LESTER (*with emphasis*) Sir, I am a Protectionist!

HAWK Um! I don't know what to say to that speculation. I doubt whether it will pay a dividend. However—to our affairs.

GRAVES Should they not be left to the lawyers?   315

LESTER No, no! let us settle amicably. Don't let the lawyers have anything to do with the affair.

HAWK No—damn the lawyers—they confuse everything.

LESTER Frankly then, my fortune is limited to the Lester estates, which have been in our family for a century, and will, I trust, never   320 quit it.

HAWK Perhaps, now-a-days, hard cash would be better; it is always at hand. However, a slice of the good fat earth is not to be despised: what's its extent?

LESTER Three thousand acres—Lester Hall—some houses in   325 Dublin—a salt marsh of considerable extent, which might be worked by a company, and give enormous dividends.

HAWK (*rising, and shaking his hand*) A salt marsh? My dear sir, why were we not sooner acquainted? We can form a company for the working of the Lester salt. I see a million of money there.   330

LESTER I am sure of it—the only difficulty is to get it.

HAWK But you have debts, of course? Is it mortgaged?

GRAVES You would have a poor opinion of Sir Harry, if he had not a few debts.

LESTER Frankness is the order of the day. I will confess that there is   335 a mortgage of about two thousand pounds on it.

HAWK (*aside*) Innocent youth! Only two thousand pounds, when he might have got—(*aloud*) Sir Harry, you shall be my son-in-law. I feel proud of such a man's belonging to me. You don't know the fortune that awaits you.   340

LESTER (*aside, to Graves*) I say—he's too easy. That looks suspicious.

GRAVES (*to Lester*) Pooh! He is dazzled with the salt marsh. You can always lure him with a speculation.

HAWK (*aside*) The Lester salt company! The shares will go like wildfire—I'm a made man! (*Aloud*) We shall get on together, I   345 foresee.

LESTER And now, Mr Hawk, perhaps, you will allow me to ask—

HAWK What is the dowry I give my daughter? I am not so rich as it is generally imagined, and I cannot put down now more than twenty thousand pounds; but Julia is our only child, and will   350 inherit all.

LESTER Twenty thousand pounds!

HAWK   You expected more? But that is the last farthing I can afford. On my honour! You shall receive the interest until we can find a safe and profitable investment—for I can promise you we shall not   355 live idle. You wish to distinguish yourself?

LESTER   I do.

HAWK   I sympathize with you. Together, we shall be able to make superb speculations.

LESTER   We shall—I feel we shall succeed.   360

HAWK   (*aside*) I begin to feel uncomfortable—he is too easy.

LESTER   (*aside*) He has plunged into my salt marsh, head-foremost.

HAWK   (*aside*) He accepts the interest.

GRAVES   (*aside to Lester*) Are you satisfied?

LESTER   (*to Graves*) Well, I don't see the money to pay my debts   365 with, just yet.

GRAVES   Wait a bit. (*Aloud*) My friend, Sir Harry, is too frank a man to hide from you that he has a few debts.

HAWK   Debts! Who has not? How much? A couple of thousand?

GRAVES   About that.   370

LESTER   More or less.

HAWK   Mere nothings!

LESTER   A bagatelle!

HAWK   It will be the subject of a little comedy between you and your wife—but I will pay them—(*aside*) with shares in the salt marsh!   375 (*Aloud*) As you say, a mere bagatelle. So all's settled, I think.

LESTER   All's settled—all's settled—and without the lawyers.

HAWK   (*aside*) I'm saved! (*Rising*)

LESTER   (*aside*) My debts are paid—I'm a rich man.
      Enter Thomas, 1EL

THOMAS   (*aside to Hawk*) Mr Grossmark wishes to speak to you,   380 sir—he says it is a very important affair.

HAWK   (*aside*) What the devil can he want? (*Aloud*) My dear Sir Harry, you'll stay and dine with us, I hope—and you too, Graves? (*They bow*) That's right! Well, then, I'll ask you to step upstairs and see my pictures, while I see a gentleman who has just called   385 upon me. (*Graves goes to RD*)

LESTER   Stand on no ceremony, I beg. Come, Graves—I adore pictures! (*Aside*) All right, eh?

GRAVES   (*aside*) I told you it would be. (*Exeunt Graves and Lester, UER*)   390

HAWK   Show up Mr Grossmark. (*Exit Thomas, L*) Well, at last I think that fortune is in my hand. Julia's happiness—our happiness—everybody's happiness—lies in that salt-marsh. What a prospectus I will issue!

Enter Grossmark, L

GROSSMARK (*L*) Good morning, Mr Hawk! I am come about those 395 bills which I gave you this morning, drawn on Bradshaw of Dublin. They are waste-paper almost, as I told you at the time.

HAWK (*R*) I know you did.

GROSSMARK I'll give you one hundred and fifty pounds for them.

HAWK That's too much to be enough. If you offer one hundred and 400 fifty pounds for them, they must be worth infinitely more—good day! (*Goes up to desk*)

GROSSMARK Two hundred pounds.

HAWK Thank you!

GROSSMARK Three hundred pounds. 405

HAWK Much obliged!

GROSSMARK Four hundred pounds.

HAWK Deal openly with me. What do you want them for?

GROSSMARK Bradshaw has insulted me, and I will have vengeance— I can put him in prison. 410

HAWK Four hundred pounds worth of vengeance? No, my boy—you can't stand such expensive luxuries. Bradshaw has dropped into a fortune, and the two thousand five hundred pounds of accept- ances° are worth two thousand five hundred pounds. Tell me the truth and let's share. 415

GROSSMARK Well, we will share. Bradshaw is about to marry the daughter of some bamboozled nabob,° who gives her an immense fortune.

HAWK Where does Bradshaw live?

GROSSMARK Um! that's not easy to say. He has no fixed residence. 420 In London, all his furniture is in the name of a friend of his—a baronet; but his family lives near Dublin. When I say 'family', I mean he has an aunt living there, who is struggling to exist on fifty pounds a year, and whom he christens°—Lady Balbriggan, in delicate health, with three thousand a year. 425

HAWK I'll find him out. Well, that's settled—we share and share alike.

GROSSMARK Agreed—good day! (*Aside*) Well, I've only got half! I tried to do him—I threw him a bit of meat, but the hawk wouldn't pounce. (*Exit, L*) 430

HAWK That's twelve hundred pounds nicely fallen in! We shall be able to do things in style at Julia's wedding! (*Enter Thomas, L*) Beg

Sir Harry Lester to step this way. (*Exit Thomas, RUE*) I certainly
am in luck today! How the aspect of affairs changes!

Enter Lester and Thomas, RUE

LESTER (*R*) Will you allow me to send your servant with a letter?   435

HAWK By all means. Thomas, take the letter.

LESTER (*giving him a letter and half-a-crown*) There's something for
your trouble.

THOMAS Money begins to circulate again. Welcome, little stranger!
(*Exit, L*)   440

LESTER You wished to speak with me?

HAWK Yes. I assume the family privilege at once with you. Sit down
a moment. I want to ask you something about a gentleman whose
property lies near Dublin. You know most of the people there, I
suppose?   445

LESTER At any rate, my aunt does.

HAWK You have an aunt there?

LESTER Yes, dear old lady—I'm her only nephew; and her health is
very delicate.

HAWK Eh! Health delicate?   450

LESTER She has a nice property there of three thousand a year.

HAWK (*aside*) The very sum.

LESTER So you see, I have every reason to keep well in with the
Lady—

HAWK (*vehemently and rising*) Balbriggan.   455

LESTER You know her name?

HAWK And yours.

LESTER The devil!

HAWK You are over head and ears in debt; your furniture is made
over to a friend—your aunt has fifty pounds a year. Grossmark has   460
acceptances of yours, amounting to two thousand five hundred
pounds; you are Mr Bradshaw, and I am a bamboozled nabob!

LESTER (*stretching himself in his chair*) Egad! You know as much as I
do.

HAWK Sir Harry, your conduct is more than equivocal.   465

LESTER In what? Did I not tell you I had debts?

HAWK Every one has debts, but where is your property?

LESTER In Ireland.

HAWK Of what does it consist?

LESTER Principally of bogs.   470

HAWK And is worth—

LESTER About three thousand pounds.

HAWK And is mortgaged for—

LESTER Five.

HAWK You had talent to do that?   475

LESTER Yes.

HAWK And your salt marsh?

LESTER Is on the coast.

HAWK What, the sea, I presume?

LESTER Well, people were malicious enough to say so, when I wanted   480
to borrow money on it.

HAWK Borrow money on the sea? No—that surpasses even my
faculty! Sir Harry, your morals seem to me—(sits)

LESTER Well, sir.

HAWK Somewhat lax.   485

LESTER Mr Hawk! (Rising, calming himself) We will not quarrel. (Sits)

HAWK Are you aware, sir, that I have in my possession, acceptances
of yours amounting to two thousand five hundred pounds?

LESTER (starts up) What! To Grossmark's order?

HAWK Exactly.   490

LESTER And they came into your possession this morning?

HAWK This morning.

LESTER In exchange for shares of no value.

HAWK (starts up) Sir Harry!

LESTER And Grossmark accorded you a delay of three months for it.   495

HAWK Who told you so?

LESTER Who? Grossmark himself, a little while ago, when I wanted
to arrange with him.

HAWK The devil!

LESTER Oho, Mr Hawk! You give twenty thousand pounds to your   500
daughter on the verge of ruin. Between you and me, it looks very
much as if you wished to entrap a son-in-law.

HAWK Sir Harry!

LESTER You take advantage of my inexperience.

HAWK The inexperience of a man who raises money on Irish bogs,   505
and borrows money on the sea! But let me be calm. At least, do
not divulge the fact of the marriage being broken off.

LESTER I'll swear—except, however, to Grossmark; to whom I have
already written.

HAWK Written to Grossmark!   510

LESTER This moment. You saw the letter. To set his mind at rest.

HAWK And you told him the name of your father-in-law?

LESTER Yes. I believed you were Croesus.°

HAWK All's lost! In half-an-hour, the whole Stock Exchange will
know it. I'm undone! I must write to him at once.   515
    Enter Julia and Prospectus, R

JULIA (*R*) Here's papa.

HAWK (*C*) Ah, Prospectus? It's you, is it? Come to dinner?

PROSPECTUS (*RC*) Dinner be damned!

HAWK (*aside*) He knows all—he's in a fury.

PROSPECTUS This, then, is your son-in-law? (*Bowing*) A superb   520
marriage indeed!

HAWK My dear Prospectus, the marriage is broken off. (*Lester bows
in confusion*)

JULIA Oh, how delightful! (*Exit Julia, RD*)

PROSPECTUS And so it was only another scene of comedy you played   525
this morning to extort money from me; but the affair is blown
upon.° The whole Stock Exchange echoes it.

HAWK Echoes what?

PROSPECTUS That you have your son-in-law's bills in your pocketbook; and Grossmark tells me that all your creditors are assembling   530
at Hardcore's house, to come down upon you, tomorrow, as a
single man.

HAWK Tomorrow! Have I till tomorrow to turn round? Why, I've
hours before me, then: and the world itself only wants twenty-four
to turn round in.   535

PROSPECTUS There is a fixed determination to rid 'Change of all the
speculative humbugs who now infest it.

HAWK The fools! Do they want to convert 'Change into a desert!
And yet to be driven from the scene of my operations, the field of
my glory! Ruin, shame, want!   540

LESTER (*L*) Believe me, my dear Hawk, that I am sincerely sorry for
having been instrumental—

HAWK (*C looking him in the face*) You! (*Aside to him*) You have
hastened my fall—will you assist me to rise?

LESTER On what conditions?   545

HAWK Oh! the easiest. I see consent in your eyes. (*Walks across the
stage*) The idea is bold, novel, and triumphant! They force me to
it—be it on their own heads. My plan is here (*striking his forehead*)
and tomorrow Hawk shall once more flutter over 'Change! (*Takes
stage R and L*)   550

PROSPECTUS What does he say?

HAWK Tomorrow all my debts shall be paid; and the house of Hawk
and Co. shall deal with thousands—I shall be the Napoleon of
Finance!

PROSPECTUS (*R*) But your troops?

HAWK (*L*) Did I not tell you I should pay? What can be said to a
man of business who hands you a cheque? My dear Prospectus, a
moment ago the battle was lost, and now the battle is gained.
Dinner is on the table—come! Tomorrow, I shall have the control
of thousands.

PROSPECTUS The control of thousands! Oh! in that case, I will dine
with pleasure. (*Aside*) What a man it is!

HAWK (*aside, as they approach the door*) Tomorrow I have the
control of thousands,° or I sleep in the wet sheets of the Thames.
(*Exeunt, R*)

3.

Scene same as Act 1.

Enter Thomas, CD, making signs to Dimity, and Mrs Mason;
Thomas steps forward, and looks through keyhole, RD; Thomas,
R—Dimity and Mrs Mason, L

MRS MASON They are not going to hide their situation from us, are they?

DIMITY Oh, I know that master is to be arrested today. He must settle my wages first.

THOMAS (*at keyhole*) I hear nothing; they speak so low—yes, I think   5
I hear.

The door opens, and Hawk appears; Thomas goes to table, R,
pretending to put the things to rights

HAWK (*crosses to LC*) Do not disturb yourself.

THOMAS (*R*) I—I—I was arranging—

HAWK Were you? (*Dimity is going off, C*) Pray stay where you are,
Mrs Dimity; and you too, Thomas. Why did you not come in? We   10
could have talked over my affairs.

THOMAS Master is pleased to be funny.

HAWK Away with you all; and remember that henceforth I am visible
to all the world. Be neither insolent nor humble to whoever calls.
You will only receive paid creditors for the future.   15

THOMAS Oh!

HAWK Now go. (*Exeunt Thomas, Dimity, and Mrs Mason, CD and R*)
Here come my wife and daughter. In such circumstances women
spoil all, they've what they call nerves.

Enter Mrs Hawk, Julia, and Noble, LD

MRS HAWK My dear, you thought that the marriage of Julia was to   20
consolidate your credit, and calm your creditors; whereas the
events of yesterday have only placed you at their mercy.

HAWK You think so? Well, you are altogether deceived. My dear
Noble, may I ask what brings you here?

NOBLE Sir, I—   25

JULIA (*LC interrupting*) Oh, papa, he's come—

HAWK You've not come to demand the hand of my daughter again?

NOBLE Yes, sir.

HAWK Have you not heard of the crisis?

NOBLE I have.   30

HAWK And you would marry the daughter of a beggar?

NOBLE (*crosses to R*) I will. It shall be my pride to work for him.

HAWK You are a fine fellow! (*Aside*) He shall have a share in my first speculation.

NOBLE I told my guardian of my love for your daughter. In return,   35
he told me that I am the possessor of a small fortune.

HAWK A fortune!

NOBLE Yes; he said that he possessed two thousand pounds belonging to me.

HAWK Two thousand pounds!   40

NOBLE As soon as I heard of your misfortune I demanded that sum. Here are the notes. I have brought them to you, my father.

MRS HAWK (*LC*) Excellent creature!

JULIA (*L, with pride*) Well, papa, what do you say now?

HAWK Two thousand pounds! (*Aside*) I could treble that with shares   45
in Grossmark's Gas Company, and afterwards double it with—but no, no! (*Aloud*) Ah, my dear fellow, you're at the age of generosity; I could as soon pay the National Debt as my own, with two thousand pounds. No! Take your money.

NOBLE You refuse?   50

HAWK (*aside*) And yet, if with that I could get a delay of a month—if by some splendid turn I could bring up the value of the shares— no! The money of these children would weigh upon my heart—my calculations would be confused—the figures would be blurred through the tears in my eyes. 'Tis easy enough to play ducks and   55
drakes° with the money of shareholders—but one's children's! (*Aloud*) Frederick, you shall have my daughter.

NOBLE Julia, mine? (*Julia crosses to LC*)

HAWK As soon as she has got ten thousand pounds.

JULIA Oh, papa!   60

NOBLE Oh, sir, when will that be?

HAWK Why in a month—perhaps sooner.

ALL What?

HAWK Yes, with good brains and a little money. (*Noble offers notes*) Pooh, pooh! put it into your pocket. Give my daughter your arm,   65
and take her away—I must be alone. (*Julia and Noble cross to L*)

MRS HAWK (*going L—aside*) What plan has he now? But I shall know. (*Aloud*) Come, Julia. (*Exeunt Mrs Hawk, Julia, and Noble, at door, L*)

HAWK I resisted. It was a good impulse: and yet, perhaps I was   70
wrong to follow it. Those *good impulses* lead one into such

monstrous follies! However, if I do fall, I'll manage that little
capital for the youngsters. I'll speculate with it! Oh! they shall be
rich—rich! What an excellent couple they will make! (*Going
towards door, R*) Now to commence their fortune! Sir Harry is   75
there, waiting for me. I do believe he is sleeping. Sir Harry!
Bradshaw!

  Enter Sir Harry Lester, RD as if just awakened

LESTER Eh, who calls?

HAWK (*L*) Oh, don't be alarmed! I thought Bradshaw was the best
cold pig° for you—it has completely awakened you. The wine   80
hasn't done you any harm?

LESTER Wine? Lord! I refresh my intellects with wine as a gardener
does his flowers with water.

HAWK Yesterday we were interrupted in our conversation.

LESTER I remember perfectly well. We had come to a distinct   85
understanding that our respective houses could no longer keep
their engagements. You've the misfortune to be my creditor. I have
the happiness to be your debtor for two thousand five hundred
pounds, seven shillings, and threepence.

HAWK I see your brain is not heavy.   90

LESTER There is nothing heavy about me—neither purse nor conscience. Yet, who can reproach me? In devouring my own fortune,
I have encouraged commerce. It is a mistake to call us gentlemen
useless. *We* idlers? Not a bit of it! We animate the circulation of
money!   95

HAWK By the money of the circulation. Ah! I see you have all your
intelligence.

LESTER I have nothing else.

HAWK Never mind—intellect is our mint. But to the point. Do you
feel within you a capacity of sustaining yourself in patent leather   100
boots and canary-coloured gloves? Or do you begin to perceive the
Bench° in perspective?

LESTER Why, you are breaking into my conscience like a burglar!
What do you want?

HAWK I want to save you, by launching you upon the sea of   105
speculation.

LESTER I'm ready.

HAWK You must begin by personating the man who is to compromise himself for me.

LESTER I understand—a man of straw. Unfortunately, straw *burns*.   110

HAWK You must be incombustible!

LESTER Oh! If you insure me, I'm prepared.

HAWK Assist me in the desperate situation in which I am now placed, and I will return you the two thousand five hundred pounds, seven shillings, and threepence, that you owe me. To accomplish it, you only require a little address.   115

LESTER What! with the pistol?

HAWK There's nobody to be killed—on the contrary, somebody to be resuscitated.

LESTER That will never do! My dear Hawk, melodramatic situations   120
in real life are no longer taken in good part. There is a very ugly interference of the Police, ever since the abolition of feudal privileges; and, you see, one cannot thrash the Police now—they are gross and muscular.

HAWK But the Bench?   125

LESTER Um! Well, certainly, I don't like the Bench. However, let's hear your plan: all depends on that—because, as yet, my honour is intact; and—and—

HAWK I understand. You consider it to be too good an investment to be lightly placed. So do I. I have as much need of it as you. It's   130
only a Stock Exchange hoax I propose.

LESTER Well, but what is it?

HAWK (*giving paper*) Here are your written instructions. You will be my partner, returned from the Indies.

LESTER Very well.   135

HAWK Go to Long Acre°—buy a travelling carriage—get the horses put to it—and drive here, in a fur pelisse and a long pigtail,° with your teeth chattering like a man who looks upon our summer as a winter. I shall be ready to receive you—to introduce you. You will have interviews with my creditors, not one of whom knows   140
Sparrow; and you will make them suspend operations.

LESTER Long?

HAWK I only want two days—two days, to make the purchases Grossmark and I have arranged—two days, to send the shares up.

LESTER And I shall cease to play the part, as soon as you have   145
realized the two thousand five hundred pounds, seven shillings, and threepence, that I owe you?

HAWK Precisely! But some one comes—it's my wife.
      Enter Mrs Hawk, L

MRS HAWK Here are some letters, dear, to be answered.

HAWK At once. Good bye, my dear Sir Harry! (*Aside*) Not a word   150
to my wife—she won't understand the subject, and might

compromise us. (*Aloud*) Good bye! All luck attend you! And forget nothing.

LESTER Never fear!

    Exit Hawk, R. Lester is going. Mrs Hawk detains him.

MRS HAWK (*L*) I beg your pardon, Sir Harry.   155

LESTER (*R*) Pray excuse me, madam, but I'm in a hurry.

MRS HAWK You will not stir a step!

LESTER But you do not know—

MRS HAWK I know all.

LESTER Eh!   160

MRS HAWK You and my husband have been plotting schemes that will do very well in a comedy. I have employed one that is still older, and, as I think, better. I tell you I know all.

LESTER (*aside*) She was listening!

MRS HAWK The part my husband wishes you to play is a disgraceful   165
one—give it up.

LESTER But, my dear madam—

MRS HAWK Oh! I know to whom I am speaking. It is only a few hours I have had the pleasure of knowing you; and yet I *do* know you.   170

LESTER (*R*) Indeed, I do not know what opinion you may have of me.

MRS HAWK One day was sufficient for me to judge you; and while my husband was seeking, perhaps, for the amount of folly in your breast, which he might turn to his purpose, I discerned that your   175
heart was in the right place, and concealed honourable feelings which might save you.

LESTER Save me? Oh! My dear madam!

MRS HAWK (*L*) Yes, sir, save you—you and my husband—you are going to ruin each other. Do not you understand that debts   180
dishonour no one, when they are avowed? We can but work to pay them. You have before you your whole life; and you have too much intelligence, if not too much heart, to wish to disgrace that life for ever, by a scheme which justice would repudiate, if not punish.

LESTER Why, the truth is, madam, I never should have thought of   185
playing such a dangerous game, if your husband had not my bills.

MRS HAWK He shall return them to you, sir; I will undertake to see it done.

LESTER But, my dear madam, I cannot pay them.

MRS HAWK We will be satisfied with your word, and you will pay   190
them when you have honourably made your fortune.

LESTER Honourably! I'm afraid that will be rather long.

MRS HAWK We will have patience. Now, Sir Harry, go—seek my husband, and persuade him to renounce this scheme, which you can do more easily, now that he will no longer have your assistance. 195

LESTER I am rather afraid of seeing him. I should prefer writing.

MRS HAWK (*pointing to the room from which she entered*) There—in that room you will find writing materials. Remain there until I come to take your letter—I will give it to him myself.

LESTER I obey you, madam. (*Crosses to L*) After all, it appears that I 200 am better than I thought I was. It is to you, madam, that I am indebted for the knowledge (*kissing her hand with respect*)—I shall never forget it. (*Exit, L*)

MRS HAWK I have succeeded. Oh, that I may now succeed with my husband! 205

   Enter Thomas, C

THOMAS Oh, ma'am, here they are all!

MRS HAWK Who?

THOMAS The creditors!

MRS HAWK Already!

THOMAS There are such a number, ma'am! 210

MRS HAWK Ask them to walk in. I'll go and tell my husband.
(*Thomas opens the centre door*)
   *Enter Grossmark, Hardcore, and Earthworm, C from L, talking
   off, as if with other Creditors.*

HARDCORE Well, gentlemen, we are quite decided—are we not?

ALL Yes, yes.

GROSSMARK (*C*) We will have no more dust thrown in our eyes. 215

HARDCORE Believe in no more promises; be moved by no more prayers and supplications!

GROSSMARK Believe no more lies.

HARDCORE Take no more shares!

GROSSMARK Read no more prospectuses! 220

EARTHWORM (*R*) No more of those instalments *on account*, by means of which he always, somehow, dipped his hand deeper in our pockets!

HARDCORE We will be paid.

ALL We will. 225

   Enter Hawk, R

HAWK (*R*) So, gentlemen, you are determined?

HARDCORE (*L*) Unless you pay everything today—

HAWK Today?

GROSSMARK (*CL*) This very day!

HAWK (*sitting in chair, R*) My dear fellows, do you think that I am 230 the Bank of England? Or do you think I have discovered a mine in California?

EARTHWORM (*coaxingly*) Is it possible you have nothing to offer us—not an instalment?

HAWK Absolutely nothing. If you like, incarcerate me at once, but 235 take care who pays the cab, for my assets will not reimburse him.

HARDCORE Don't be uneasy. I'll pay for it, and add it to the rest of my bad debts.

HAWK Thank you; you're a real friend. And you are all quite decided, are you? 240

ALL We are.

HAWK You are only three—but the others?

EARTHWORM We represent all the rest.

HAWK You are all agreed?

ALL Yes, all—all. 245

HAWK Touching unanimity! (*Taking out his watch*) Two o'clock. (*Aside*) Sir Harry has had time enough—he must be en route. (*Aloud*) Upon my life, gentlemen, I must confess that you are devilish clever fellows, and have chosen well your time.

GROSSMARK What does that mean? 250

HAWK For several months—I may say, years—you have allowed yourselves to be played with, in a foolish, idiotic manner! Yes, played with—gulled by stories that would not take in a child— gulled, in fact, by your own cupidity. And this is the day you select to show how implacable you can be. Ha, ha! Egad, it is very 255 amusing! Now, then, let's be off. Send for the cab—I'm ready!

HARDCORE But, my dear sir—

GROSSMARK He laughs—I begin to suspect something.

EARTHWORM There is something in it, gentlemen—I am sure there is something! That manner of his conceals something! 260

GROSSMARK Will you explain yourself?

HARDCORE All we desire to know is—

EARTHWORM Mr Affable Hawk, there is something hid—tell us what it is?

HAWK No, there is nothing—at least, nothing that I shall tell you. I 265 choose to be incarcerated—I shall rather like the change. Besides, I shall be a gainer by it.

GROSSMARK What do you mean?

HAWK I shall rather like to see your physiognomies tomorrow—or
this evening—when you hear of his return.   270

HARDCORE His return?

GROSSMARK Whose return?

EARTHWORM Oh, I knew there was something in it! Do tell us,
whose return?

HAWK The return of—of nobody! Let's go—send for a cab!   275

HARDCORE (*with a change of tone*) But my *dear* Mr Hawk! if you are
awaiting some assistance—

GROSSMARK If you have any hope—

EARTHWORM If you have inherited anything—

HARDCORE If somebody is dead—   280

GROSSMARK Oh, explain!

EARTHWORM Tell us—*do*!

HAWK Take care, take care, gentlemen! You are yielding, you are
yielding—you know you are! And if I chose to give myself the
trouble, I could gull you again—easily, pleasantly, affably, as is my   285
manner. No! Play your parts as creditors! Forget the past—forget
all the brilliant speculations I have helped you to—forget all the
sums I helped you to gain, before the sudden departure of my
worthy, excellent Sparrow!

HARDCORE His worthy and excellent Sparrow!   290

EARTHWORM I have it! Oh! if—yes! Sparrow has returned!

HAWK Yes! forget all the brilliant past, and call a cab!

EARTHWORM Hawk, look me in the face—you are expecting Sparrow!

HAWK (*hesitating*) No—no!   295

EARTHWORM (*as if inspired*) Gentlemen, I know it! He's expecting
Sparrow! Sparrow has returned!

HARDCORE Can it be possible?

GROSSMARK Speak!

ALL Speak—speak!   300

HAWK (*pretending confusion*) No, no! I cannot say that I—certainly,
it's quite possible that, some day or other—in fact, it's very
probable that he will return from the Indies, with an enormous
fortune. (*With assurance*) But I give you my word of honour, that
I do not expect Sparrow today.   305

EARTHWORM Then it's tomorrow! Gentlemen, he expects Sparrow
tomorrow! I am sure of it—I can read it in the wrinkles about his
mouth!

HARDCORE (*in a low tone to the others*) Unless it is another dodge of   310
his, to gain time.

GROSSMARK Do you think so?

HARDCORE It is not impossible!

EARTHWORM (*aloud*) Gentlemen, it must be so! He is laughing at
us! I'll fetch a cab myself!

HAWK (*aside*) The devil! (*Aloud*) Well, gentlemen, shall we go?   315

HARDCORE Yes, at once!
>   *Noise of a carriage is heard—then a loud knock at the street*
>   *door*

HAWK (*aside*) At last! (*Aloud*) Heavens! (*Places his hand upon his*
heart, and sinks into chair)

HARDCORE (*rushing to window, L*) A carriage!

GROSSMARK (*after him, L*) A postchaise!°   320

EARTHWORM (*after him, L*) Gentlemen, it is a postchaise, with the
luggage of a traveller behind it!

HAWK (*aside*) Sir Harry is just in time!

HARDCORE Look—it is covered with dust!

EARTHWORM And is splashed to the roof! It must have come from   325
the Indies, to be splashed like that! He's come overland!

HAWK (*blandly*) My dear Earthworm, you do not know what you
say—people do not come from India by land.

HARDCORE Come and see, Hawk—do look at that man descending
from the postchaise!   330

GROSSMARK Enveloped in a fur pelisse—come!

HAWK No—excuse me!—the joy—the emotion—I—

EARTHWORM He carries a box under his arm—oh, such a large box!
Gentlemen, it's Sparrow! I know him by that box, and the pigtail!
Gentlemen, it's Sparrow! I know him by his tail!   335

HAWK (*rising, R*) Concealment is useless—I expected Sparrow!

HARDCORE Who comes back from Calcutta?

HAWK With an incalculable fortune.

EARTHWORM Did I not say so? (*They all go and shake hands with*
Hawk)   340

HAWK Oh, gentlemen, friends, brothers!
>   *Enter Mrs Hawk, C*

MRS HAWK (*RC*) My dear, such news!

HAWK (*aside*) My wife! The devil! I thought she was gone out. She'll
ruin everything.

MRS HAWK Oh! You do not know the news!   345

HAWK No. Yes—that is, I—

MRS HAWK Mr Sparrow has returned!

HAWK What do you say? (*Aside*) Hollo! does she?

MRS HAWK I have seen him! I have spoken to him; it was I who received him at the door. 350

HAWK (*aside*) Sir Harry has converted her. What a man! (*Aside to her*) Bravo, my dear! You do it capitally!

MRS HAWK I tell you it is Sparrow—he is there!

HAWK (*aside*) Silence! (*Aloud*) I must go and welcome him!

MRS HAWK No—wait a bit! wait a bit! Poor Sparrow had counted 355 too much upon his strength. Scarcely had he entered the parlour, when the fatigue and the exertion produced a nervous crisis.

HAWK Indeed! (*Aside*) How well she does it.

EARTHWORM (*LC*) Poor Mr Sparrow! Poor Mr Sparrow!

MRS HAWK He begged me to see you, and to carry back to him your 360 forgiveness. He says he cannot meet you face to face until he has wiped out the past.

HARDCORE (*L*) How sublime!

GROSSMARK (*LC*) What an excellent man!

EARTHWORM It brings tears into my eyes! Gentlemen, you see the 365 tears!

HAWK (*aside*) Upon my life, I had no conception of what a wife I had! (*Putting his arm round her waist*) My dear Caroline! Excuse me, gentlemen. (*Kisses her*) Bravo! All goes on capitally. You could not do it better. 370

MRS HAWK How lucky; and how much better, than what you contemplated.

HAWK It is indeed! It is ten times as plausible. (*Aloud*) Return to Sparrow, my dear; and you, gentlemen, be kind enough to pass into my study, where we will settle our little accounts. (*Exit Mrs* 375 *Hawk, C*)

HARDCORE At your service, my excellent friend. (*Crosses to R*)

GROSSMARK At your service, our best of friends. (*Crosses to R*)

EARTHWORM If there is one man that I admire and respect above all other, it is you, Mr Hawk. (*Crosses to R*) 380

HAWK And yet they said I was a humbug!

HARDCORE (*at door*) You! a giant in business.

GROSSMARK (*at door*) You! the prince of speculators, a man capable of gaining a million, the moment he has a thousand!

EARTHWORM (*R*) Dear friend, excellent Mr Hawk! We will wait as 385 long as ever you please.

OMNES Certainly! Any time that Mr Hawk likes.

HAWK Gentlemen, I thank you as much as if you had said that this morning—meanwhile, step into my study. (*Exit Earthworm; beckoning Hardcore*) In one hour I'll sell all your shares.   390

HARDCORE Good! (*Exit Hardcore, RD*)

HAWK (*beckons Grossmark*) Stop! Now we are alone. There is not a moment to be lost. There was a fall yesterday, and another this morning, in the shares of the Great Indian Emeralds. Rush to the Stock Exchange—buy up as many as you can—two hundred—   395 three hundred—four hundred! Hardcore, alone, will sell you more than half.

GROSSMARK (*R*) But on what terms—and how will you cover it?

HAWK (*L*) Cover it! Pshaw! Bring me the shares today, and I pay you tomorrow.   400

GROSSMARK Tomorrow!

HAWK (*aside*) Tomorrow the rise will have taken place.

GROSSMARK It is quite clear that in the situation in which you are, you are buying for Sparrow.

HAWK You think so?   405

GROSSMARK He must have given you the orders in the letter which announced his return.

HAWK Well, it is possible. Ah, Grossmark, you're a knowing dog! There is nothing escapes you. We shall yet have some excellent business together. Before the year's out, I shall have put ten   410 thousand pounds of commission into your pocket.

GROSSMARK (*overwhelmed*) Ten thousand pounds!

HAWK Bull the market with the Tobolsk Mines,° and get this letter inserted in the *Times*, and tomorrow we shall clear our twenty per cent. Swift! away.   415

GROSSMARK I fly! Good bye. (*Aside*) To think that I was about to send such a man to the Bench! (*Exit Grossmark, C and L*)

HAWK Ha, ha, ha! All the steam is on, and away we go! The moment Mahomet had three followers who believed in him, he had won his empire. I have moved the mountain.° Thanks to the pretended   420 arrival of Sparrow, I gain at least a week's delay—and a week always means a fortnight in a matter of payment. I buy shares to the tune of ten thousand pounds, in the Emeralds, before Prospectus can get at them—and, when Prospectus wants them, up they go! From today's affair, I see a clear profit of twenty thousand   425 pounds; with seventeen thousand pounds I pay my creditors, and am master of the place. (*Walks up and down stage*)

    Enter Thomas, C

THOMAS (*L*) Oh, sir!

HAWK (*R*) What is it, Thomas?

THOMAS Oh, sir, oh! 430

HAWK Well, what is it, I say? Speak.

THOMAS Old Earthworm offers me five pounds, if I will let him see Mr Sparrow.

HAWK Thomas, allow yourself to be bought.

THOMAS No objection at all, sir—but there's Mr Hardcore. He wants 435 to buy me—and all the others, they want to buy me. It's very pleasant, but a little puzzling.

HAWK Oh, sell yourself to all of them! You have my permission. It is the only way I can pay you your wages.

THOMAS Thank you, sir, I'll certainly do it. (*Going*) 440

HAWK Let them all see Sparrow. (*Aside*) Sir Harry will be sure to play his part well. (*Aloud*) When I say all—all except Grossmark. (*Aside*) He will recognize Mr Bradshaw.

THOMAS I understand, sir. Ah! here's Mr Noble. (*Exit Thomas, C*)
　　　Enter Noble, LD

NOBLE (*L*) My dear sir! 445

HAWK (*R*) Well, Noble, what brings you here?

NOBLE Despair!

HAWK Despair?

NOBLE Mr Sparrow has returned, and I hear that you have become a rich man again. 450

HAWK And is it that what alarms you?

NOBLE It is.

HAWK Upon my word, you are a strange fellow! I reveal to you my ruin, and you are enchanted! You learn my good fortune, and you are in despair! And yet you wish to be one of my family: why, you 455 are more like an enemy!

NOBLE It is my love which makes your fortune terrible to me. I fear lest now you should be no longer willing to give me your daughter's hand.

HAWK Frederick, we men of business do not all place our hearts in 460 our banker's book—our sentiments are not always reckoned up by double entry. You offered me the two thousand pounds which you had: it is not for me to reject you on account of a few thousands— (*aside*) which I have not.

NOBLE I breathe again! 465

HAWK So much the better, for I have a real affection for you. You are brave, generous, honest—you have touched me here, sir. (*Touching his heart*)
　　　Enter Grossmark and Prospectus, CD

HAWK (*to Grossmark, without seeing Prospectus*) Well?

GROSSMARK (*R, with confusion*) The business is terminated.   470

HAWK (*RC, gaily*) Bravo!

PROSPECTUS (*C, to Hawk*) Good day, old fellow!

HAWK (*aside*) Prospectus!

PROSPECTUS So, you have been buying before me, have you? I shall
be forced to pay dearer! Never mind! You have played your game   475
well. Let me pay my compliments to the Napoleon of Finance! Ha,
ha, ha!

HAWK (*troubled*) What does this mean?

GROSSMARK It seems Mr Prospectus does not quite believe in the
return of Mr Sparrow.   480

NOBLE (*L*) Oh, Mr Prospectus!

HAWK What! He doubts?

PROSPECTUS (*ironically*) Not at all—no longer! I fancied, indeed, at
first, that this return of Sparrow was the bold stroke that you told
me of yesterday.   485

HAWK (*aside*) Fool that I was!

PROSPECTUS And that, by means of the pretended return of this
Sparrow, you intended to buy for a rise tomorrow, though you had
not a penny today.

HAWK And you fancied that?   490

PROSPECTUS Yes! But when I saw that postchaise at the door—such
a perfect model of Indian carriages—I saw at once it was impossible to find its fellow in Long Acre, and all my doubts
disappeared. But Grossmark, why do you not hand Mr Hawk the
scrip?°   495

GROSSMARK The scrip? but—

HAWK (*aside*) Audacity alone can save me! (*Aloud*) Yes, the scrip—
come!

GROSSMARK Stay a moment. If Prospectus should be right—

HAWK (*haughtily*) Mr Grossmark!   500

NOBLE (*L*) But, gentlemen, Mr Sparrow is here! I have seen
him—spoken to him.

HAWK (*RC, to Grossmark*) Noble has seen him.

GROSSMARK (*R, to Prospectus*) I have seen him myself.

HAWK You?   505

GROSSMARK Yes, at the window.

PROSPECTUS Oh, I have not the slightest doubt of it! By the way, in
what vessel did Mr Sparrow come over?

HAWK What vessel? Why, the—why, the—oh! it was the *Triton*.

PROSPECTUS How inaccurate the newspapers are! They announced 510
it as the *Minnow*.

GROSSMARK Is it so?

HAWK No more of this, Mr Grossmark—the scrip!

GROSSMARK Allow me one moment. Unless this scrip be covered, I
should prefer seeing Mr Sparrow. 515

HAWK You shall not see him, sir! If I were to suffer you to see him
now, it would show that I allowed you to doubt my word.

PROSPECTUS Magnificent!

HAWK My dear Noble (*crosses to L*)—go and see Sparrow—tell him
that I have bought the scrip he ordered, and beg him to send me 520
(*with marked emphasis*)—two thousand pounds to cover it. (*Aside*)
At all events, you bring your own money!

NOBLE Certainly! (*Exit Noble, LD*)

HAWK (*with coldness*) Does that satisfy you, Mr Grossmark?

GROSSMARK Oh! Doubtless! doubtless! (*To Prospectus*) I say, he must 525
have come back.

PROSPECTUS Yes, when you have got your two thousand pounds.

HAWK Prospectus, I should be justified in calling you to account for
so insulting a doubt; but I am still your debtor.

PROSPECTUS Oh! don't mention it—for you must certainly have in 530
your spacious cash-box the means of paying it; and then your scrip
in the Indian Emeralds will bring you a fortune.

HAWK I understand your anger. (*To Grossmark*) You see where the
shoe pinches. (*Crosses to RC*)

PROSPECTUS (*LC*) The shoe will no longer pinch me, when I see 535
Sparrow's money.

Enter Earthworm and Hardcore, C

HARDCORE (*LC*) Oh, my dear friend!

EARTHWORM (*C*) Excellent Mr Hawk!

HARDCORE What an excellent man that Mr Sparrow is!

HAWK (*aside*) Good! 540

EARTHWORM What probity—what generosity.

HAWK (*aside*) Better and better!

HARDCORE What greatness of soul!

HAWK (*aside*) Go on!

PROSPECTUS Have you seen him? 545

EARTHWORM And spoken to him.

HARDCORE And been paid by him.

ALL Paid! (*Grossmark crosses to LC*)

HAWK Eh! What do you say? Paid?

HARDCORE Entirely, five hundred pounds in two bills.   550

HAWK (*R, aside*) Oh! I understand.

HARDCORE And eight hundred pounds in notes.

HAWK Notes?

HARDCORE Bank of England notes!

HAWK (*aside*) Now, I do not understand.° If they had been Bank of   555
Elegance,° it would have been clearer. Oh! I see. Noble must have
given it out of his money. Well! he'll bring so much less to
Grossmark, that's all.

EARTHWORM (*C*) And me too—me, who would willingly have
consented to a discount, a slight discount—I have received every   560
farthing!

HAWK In bills also?

EARTHWORM In excellent bills of fifteen hundred pounds!

HAWK (*aside*) What a magnificent fellow that Sir Harry is!

EARTHWORM And the other five hundred pounds—   565

PROSPECTUS Well, the other five hundred pounds?

EARTHWORM In ready money—here it is. (*Shows notes*)

HAWK (*aside*) The devil! Noble will only bring back seven hundred
pounds?

HARDCORE And, at the present moment, he is paying all the   570
creditors.

HAWK In the same way?

EARTHWORM Yes, by bills and ready money.

HAWK (*aside*) Ah! it's quite clear, Noble won't bring a penny to
Grossmark.   575

    Enter Noble, LD

NOBLE (*L*) I have executed your commission.

HAWK (*nervous*) Oh! you have—seen him—you have brought back
some money—

NOBLE Some money, indeed! Mr Sparrow would not hear of the two
thousand pounds covering.   580

HAWK (*aside*) I understand!

NOBLE He wrote a cheque for the whole amount.

HAWK (*rushing across to L*) Hey! what the devil's that! (*Earthworm,
Grossmark, and Hardcore cross to L*)

NOBLE A cheque for ten thousand pounds.   585

GROSSMARK (*R*) Ten thousand pounds!

PROSPECTUS It is true then. (*Runs off, CD and L*)

HAWK (*overcome*) A cheque for ten thousand pounds! I have it! I see
it! Ten thousand pounds! And where did you get that?

NOBLE Why, he gave it me.   590

HAWK He! Who?

NOBLE Why, Sparrow.

HAWK Sparrow! What Sparrow? Cock Sparrow?

HARDCORE (*R*) The Sparrow that's come back from India!

HAWK What India?   595

EARTHWORM (*R*) And who's paying all your debts.

HAWK Oh! I am going mad—I'm going mad! Am I, Hawk, to be the
victim of such Sparrows as that?
     Re-enter Prospectus, down C

PROSPECTUS There they are, and all paid! It was quite true!

HAWK All paid? Yes, paid—all paid! Damn it, they're all paid! I see   600
fire—the room spins round! This is fairy land—enchantment—
devilry!
     Enter Mrs Hawk and Julia, C; Sir Harry Lester, LD

MRS HAWK (*LC*) My dear, Mr Sparrow feels himself equal to seeing
you now.

HAWK (*RC*) Come here, my dear! You, Caroline—you, Julia—you,   605
Frederick. (*Noble crosses to LC*) All friends—you are not making
an ass out of me, are you?

JULIA (*LC*) Why, what's the matter with you, papa?

HAWK Tell me frankly—(*sees Lester, L*) Sir Harry, what is this?

LESTER (*L*) Lucky for me that I followed the counsels of your   610
wife—you would have had two Sparrows at a time, since good luck
brings you back the real one.

HAWK Has he, then, actually arrived? What! Sparrow—my dear
Sparrow?

PROSPECTUS (*LC*) What! You did not know it, then?   615

HAWK I? How the devil should I know it? Come back? Now I am a
man! Oh, I always said of him—'Sparrow has a heart—Sparrow
has the heart of an eagle! What integrity!—what probity!' (*Embracing Mrs Hawk and Julia*) Didn't we always bless his name? (*To Mrs
Hawk*) And you, Caroline—you, who bore all adversity so bravely!   620

MRS HAWK (*RC*) The delight overpowers me! To think of you,
rescued, rich!

HAWK (*C*) And honest. For my dear Caroline, and you, my children,
I will confess to you I was nearly succumbing. I was nearly beaten.
A giant of honesty might have fallen. But all that is over now. (*To*   625
Lester) Sir Harry Lester, I give you up your bills.

LESTER Oh, sir!

HAWK And I lend you one thousand pounds.

LESTER One thousand pounds! But I really do not know when—

HAWK No ceremony. Accept it! It's a fancy I have.   630

LESTER Then I do accept it.

HAWK Ah, what a sensation! How soothing, how noble! I am a
creditor! (*To creditors*) Look at me—I am one of you. I, too, am a
creditor! Magnificent development of human faculty!

MRS HAWK My dear, remember he is waiting for you.   635

HAWK That's true! Come, let us go! I have so often held up Sparrow
before the eyes of others, that it is high time I should behold him
myself. (*To creditors*) Gentlemen, we shall have no more business
together, but we remain good friends. If I have dealt too hardly
with you, forgive me. Remember, you yourselves first taught me   640
to handle the dangerous weapons with which I have kept you at
bay; and at parting, accept one word of advice from a man of the
world. When adversity comes, wait. Don't follow old Weller's
advice,° and run for a halter° at once; but bear up manfully and
cheerfully—go round with the world, and bide your time. I dare   645
not, I confess, attempt to justify the unwarrantable means I have
adopted to keep my head above water—though we all know that a
drowning man will catch at a straw. Still, this I do say—while
avoiding my errors, imitate the energy, perseverance, and good
humour, with which I formed a raft to float on till succour arrived; 650
and if you are honest fellows at heart, and really wish to pay, you
will get into smooth water at last, depend on it. Only play your
game boldly and steadily, till some good card turns up—then reap
the reward of your courage and your toil—burn the cards, and
eschew for ever—as I shall do—   655

THE GAME OF SPECULATION!

DISPOSITION OF THE CHARACTERS AT THE FALL OF THE CURTAIN

Mrs Hawk   Mr Hawk   Julia

Hardcore   Noble

Grossmark   Prospectus

Earthworm   Sir Harry Lester
R   L

THE LIGHTS O' LONDON

A New and Original Drama

In Five Acts

BY

GEORGE ROBERT SIMS

CAST

MR ARMYTAGE	Mr G. R. Peach
HAROLD ARMYTAGE	Mr Wilson Barrett
CLIFFORD ARMYTAGE	Mr E. S. Willard
MARKS	Mr J. Beauchamp
SETH PREENE	Mr Walter Speakman
MR SKEFFINGTON	Mr Wensleydale
SUPERINTENDENTS OF POLICE	Mr Layard, Mr Warren
CUTTS AND WATERS	Mr H. Evans, Mr Manning
CONSTABLES	Mr C. Cathcart, Mr B. Cullen
PHILOSOPHER JACK	Mr C. Coote
PERCY DE VERE, 'ESQ.'	Mr Neville Doone
TROTTERS	Mr W. Waite
PORTER AT CASUAL WARD	Mr J. B. Morton
JOEY	Master Worley
JARVIS	Mr Geo. Barrett
JIM	Mr J. W. Phipps
SHAKESPEARE JARVIS	Miss E. Edwards
MRS JARVIS	Mrs Stephens
BESS	Miss Eastlake
HETTY PREENE	Miss E. Ormsby
TOTTIE	Miss M. Clitherow
SAL	Miss Lizzie Adams
JANET	Miss A. Cooke
ANNIE	Miss G. Wright

First performed at the Princess's Theatre
10 September 1881

1.

The seat of Squire Armytage. Fine Park. Lodge-keeper's house L. Practicable.° Portion of Mansion R showing tree and seat beneath C. (Open lively°)

As curtain rises Squire Armytage discovered seated beneath tree C. He leans on stick. Marks the Lodge-keeper stands respectfully LC

SQUIRE (*RC on seat under tree*) Three years, three years today since he stood here as you stand now, Marks, and I bade him begone for he was no longer a son of mine.

MARKS (*LC sighing*) Ah! how well I remember it!

SQUIRE I was right, Marks. He was a good for nothing spendthrift, a disgrace to our name. 5

MARKS I sometimes think you might have given Master Harold another chance, Squire.

SQUIRE I bore with him until I could bear no longer, till the tales of his wild ways came down here and were village gossip, then I bade 10 him see my face no more, and he went!

MARKS Yes, he went out through your gates, a beggar.

SQUIRE And from that day, you have never seen your daughter.

MARKS No, she's written me now and again to say she was well in London, but from the day Master Harold went I have never seen 15 her, poor lass!

SQUIRE She went with him; he crowned his wickedness by enticing your child to share his vagabond life. Many a time when my old heart would have relented, I have thought of that—that he should have done this wrong to you—to you, the old Lodge-keeper, who 20 nursed him as a child on your knee, that he should have robbed you of the staff of your old age—bright, winsome Bess! The shame of it, I thought, would have killed me once. (*Rising*)

MARKS Poor Bess! Ah, Squire, I would walk a hundred miles, old and feeble as I am, to take her in my arms again and tell her I 25 forgive her, though she did break her poor old father's heart. (*Breaks down*)

SQUIRE (*consoling him*) My poor old friend!

MARKS It's him as won't let her come, poor wench! I'm sure of that. Come, Squire, in spite of all, wouldn't you be glad to see your 30 handsome son here in his old place again?

SQUIRE He is no son of mine. Not one foot of my land, not one
farthing of my money shall ever be his. Another stands in his place,
Clifford Armytage, my nephew; he will be Squire here after me. I
have no other son. (*Walks feebly towards house, exits R2E*)   35

MARKS (*alone*) Yes! Master Clifford will have all these fine estates,
he'll be Squire here. Master Clifford knows his book,° and fawns
upon the Squire like a hound as wants a bone, but he ain't fit to
black Master Harold's boots. (*Sits RC*) Well, let the Squire think
as he will about his boy, I'd give the world to see my bonny Bess   40
again. She went with him, never a doubt of that. They was little
sweethearts together, boy and girl. (*Music. Comes down R*) May be
he's married her, and he's too proud to let us know; she's been
true and loyal to him, which ever way it is. (*Bess enters RUE comes
slowly L at back*) It's only her poor father she's been cruel to! (*Sits*   45
R) Oh! Bess! Bess! my old heart aches to hear her sweet voice say
'Father' once again. (*Bess has crept cautiously to gate L pale and
ill-clad. Enters to Marks, whose back is turned to her. As he finishes,
she touches his arm. He turns and starts back as if he had seen a vision*)

BESS (*RC*) Father! (*Pause*) Father!   50

MARKS (*clasping her in his arms*) Bess, my darling!

BESS Father! (*Pause—business*°) Hush! Father, no one must know I
am here.

MARKS Has no one in the village recognized you?

BESS Look into my face, father, there are few who would recognize   55
in me Bess Marks of the old days. I've had so much trouble lately.

MARKS Trouble—and you never let me know!

BESS Listen, father, the last necessity has brought us here.

MARKS Us! Is Master Harold with you then?

BESS (*Goes up L to gate—Marks follows her—gets L. She points off*)   60
Yes, yonder, hiding like a thief on his own father's grounds,
waiting to see his father's servant, the old Lodge-keeper.

MARKS (*LC*) What does he want?

BESS He is weak and ill. We are penniless—starving—we have
tramped from London as far as this and can go no further. (*Sits*   65
L) Give us the shelter of the Lodge for an hour.

MARKS (*R of her*) And then—

BESS Harold must see his father. He must help us to leave the
country, it is our last chance.

MARKS My poor darling!   70

BESS You will, father, won't you? For my sake—for the sake of the
daughter you loved so fondly once.

MARKS And love so fondly still. (*Kisses her passionately*) I ask you nothing of the past, darling. I only thank God He has brought you back to my arms again. Ah, Bess, many a night I have looked up 75 at the stars and thought maybe up in the Great City° you were looking at them too, and I've said to myself—my Bess is an honest lass—she wouldn't bring her father to shame for the finest gentleman in the land.

BESS Father! (*Rises—embracing him lovingly*)   80

MARKS If I had not believed that, I don't think you would have found me here now. (*Bess turns her head away*) You are Master Harold's wife—ain't you my lass?

BESS Trust me, father. When the time comes, you shall know all. Let me look in your face, the dear old face as I see it now—perhaps 85 for the last time. Don't let it wear a frown.

MARKS It shan't, my lass. Tell me what you like. Whether you're Master Harold's wife or not, you're my daughter.

BESS And you'll let him come in?

MARKS Yes, I will. If the Squire turns me out, I will.   90

BESS (*going up to gate*) Then I'll call him in. (*Music. Waving her handkerchief off. Marks looks in same direction*)

MARKS Is that Master Harold—that man creeping along by the hedge?

BESS Yes, father!   95

MARKS Ah, my poor young master! (*Goes down L*)
        Enter Harold Armytage from RUE to gate LUE—is almost
        ragged. He smiles faintly and puts on a sham recklessness

BESS (*R*) Harold, father consents.

HAROLD (*C*) He's a brick.° Well, Marks, how are you? You see here I am come back like a long firm cheque.°

MARKS My poor boy! (*Hides face in hands*)   100

BESS I've told father what you want.

HAROLD Good lass! I don't know what I should do without you. Well, Marks, Bess has told you of the fix I'm in.

MARKS Yes.

HAROLD I must see my father alone tonight. No one but yourself 105 must know I'm here. I don't want my father's servants to pity me, and you see—(*laughing*) I'm not exactly dressed for company. Egad! They might almost think—(*Preene crosses from R to L stealthily*) I had changed clothes with a scarecrow coming along—and—

BESS (*R*) Don't joke, Harold! Every moment is of consequence. 110 (*Sits C*)

HAROLD (*C*) Yes, I know, Bess, but we must have some respect for appearances. I may be a scamp, but I'm none the less an Armytage, and want of pride was never a family failing of ours, and I think I have inherited my fair share of the article—and—(*breaking down— coming to Marks*) Hang it, Marks, I can't keep it up. The sight of the dear old home is too much for me. I'm utterly ruined and my only hope of salvation is in your hands. Get my father out here tonight, as soon as it's dark. I think he'll do what I want—if he doesn't—well—(*shrugging his shoulders. Noise heard off*)

BESS Hush, Harold—what was that? Let us go in. There may be someone about.

HAROLD Not now. I know this sleepy old place too well—besides, who'd recognize us? They'd take us for a couple of tramps begging of the Lodge-keeper, and so we are, aren't we, Marks? Ah, I never thought I should have to come back home like this!

BESS But now you have come—now you have conquered your pride, Harold, your father will help you.

HAROLD I'll ask him for your sake, Bess.

MARKS (*aside L*) She's his wife! It's his pride as won't let him tell me.

HAROLD It was not my fault we parted in anger. He was hot and hasty and said such things to me that no man could stand even from his own father. I determined to show him I was independent and could earn my own living. I went up to London and tried, and—and failed.

MARKS Failed?

HAROLD Yes, like many another fool who fancies when he sees the Lights o' London° he's found an Eldorado and only had to crawl back home again as I do now, a broken-down miserable man.

BESS It was for my sake you did this. But for me you could have struggled on.

HAROLD You! Why, I could never have lived through it but for you, Bess dear. Whatever our fate may be and tonight decides it, remember always this, that I would go through all my troubles again and again to have found such love as yours.

BESS (*rising*) I'm sure there's someone about. If your father knows you're here, he may refuse to see you. (*Marks goes up R*)

HAROLD (*LC*) Yes, he would help a stranger—not his own son.

BESS (*L*) Courage, Harold, don't meet him in anger.

HAROLD He shall say what he likes, and I will bear it for your sake.

MARKS Get into the Lodge—it's Master Clifford!

HAROLD The scoundrel who's robbed me of my inheritance. (*Crosses—business*)

MARKS Don't let him see you. I mistrust him. He's always about with   155
Seth Preene, a north country poaching chap. Mr Clifford is not the man to be Squire here.

HAROLD He's a smooth tongued sneaking hypocrite. It is he who has borne lie after lie about me to my father, and made him believe me a villain. Bess, darling, I'd almost give up my last chance   160
tonight to pay that fellow what I owe him.

BESS Harold, is this keeping your promise?

HAROLD No, it isn't. I can't afford to resent anything now.

MARKS (*L*) Get into the Lodge quick. (*Music*)

HAROLD (*to Bess—fiercely*) Bess, if my father had been like yours, it   165
is there I should have gone for shelter now. (*Pointing to Hall*)

BESS Courage, Harold, something tells me that the weariest part of our journey is done.

HAROLD (*down L with Bess. Sighs*) You don't know my father as well as I do, but we'll hope for the best.   170

They exit into Lodge

MARKS (*L outside*) Poor fellow! The Squire can't see him like that and not forgive him. It isn't in human nature to do it. It seems like a dream; she's under my roof. I almost expect the birds to wake up and sing again; they would if they knew she'd come. (*Exit into Lodge*)   175

Hetty enters R carrying novel, followed by Clifford. She sits under tree C. He crosses to LC looking about

HETTY It's too bad of you, Clifford, to treat me like this; you've plenty of time to speak with other people or to go out partridge shooting, but you can never spare five minutes with me.

CLIFFORD (*L of seat*) Don't be so unreasonable, Hetty. You know it isn't safe for us to be seen together. We are pretty safe here   180
though; the Squire's dozing and there's no one in the Lodge— what's the book?

HETTY 'The Village Beauty',° one Mrs Rouse lent me. I've read it before, but I was obliged to make some excuse for coming up here tonight.   185

CLIFFORD Don't care much about novels myself. How does it end?

HETTY She marries the Squire, and is a great lady, and has servants and diamonds, and oh! such lovely dresses.

CLIFFORD Quite your own story, Hetty. You're a village beauty, and some day will be a great lady.   190

HETTY You say that to tease me.

CLIFFORD Tease you, my pet; you know I'm too fond of you to do that.

HETTY Yes, you say you are, but if so why can't we go about together? Why am I always obliged to come up and read to old Mrs Rouse, the housekeeper? You said you'd drop into her room as usual, but you were too busy, I suppose.

CLIFFORD Well, you know how awkwardly placed I am. When we first knew each other I was simply the son of the Squire's poor brother, and it didn't matter what he thought of me. But now I'm his heir, I'm obliged to keep in his good books. I don't want to be kicked out as Harold was for running away with Bess Marks.

HETTY Ah! But Master Harold gambled, and led a wild life. Besides, he didn't marry Bess Marks, and you will marry me, won't you?

CLIFFORD (*sits L of Hetty*) Of course I will, but don't go chattering about it to your female acquaintances because if you do it will be all over the village and up at the Hall in no time and then—

HETTY Ah! do let me tell some of the girls, it would make them so savage.

CLIFFORD Look here, do you want to see me turned adrift? Would you like to marry me and have to scrub the floors and wear cotton gowns?

HETTY No.

CLIFFORD Then hold your tongue.

HETTY I hate poor people; sometimes I feel I could run away from our cottage, it is so mean and common and father is so unlike a gentleman.

CLIFFORD (*L of seat*) You were meant for better things, Hetty. What was that? (*Noise heard behind hedge*) Hush! I think I heard someone.

HETTY (*crosses to L*) Let me go! What will they say if they see me with you?

CLIFFORD Nothing!

HETTY Ah! you should hear the nice things they say in the village about Bess Marks. I hate village people; a girl can't dress better than they do but they chatter about her. Wait till I'm your wife.

CLIFFORD Only wait a little while and keep our engagement secret.

HETTY Yes, yes, I won't breathe a word about it to anyone—but father knows—you told him.

CLIFFORD He was prying about and watching us. He thought we were going to make a run-away of it, as if I didn't know my book

better than that. I told him what I tell you, that you shall be my
wife—hist! I'm sure there's someone behind that hedge. You'd
better run home at once. (*He strolls a little away*)

HETTY (*going towards gate LUE*) A lady! I shall be a lady and have   235
servants and diamonds! Oh! I think I should die if I had to be poor
all my life.

      *Exit through gate L and crosses R. Seth Preene comes from
      behind R hedge down to RC*

SETH Hist! Mr Clifford!

CLIFFORD (*starting*) Hulloa! Seth! You've been spying again. It was
you behind the hedge! (*Crosses and sits in chair R*)   240

SETH (*C*) Well, suppose I were. It's lucky as I do listen sometimes
for her sake and thine.

CLIFFORD What do you mean?

SETH Who do you think I've seen on this very spot? Why, Bess
Marks and Harold Armytage. Now then!   245

CLIFFORD What? (*Starts up*)

SETH And Master Harold's going to see the Squire and snivel and
get forgiven and it's a reg'lar plot agen your prospects, and my
lass's prospects, and old Marks is in it.

CLIFFORD Curse them! If they meet I'm done. Before the world, the   250
old fool's as stern as ever, but I've heard him muttering to himself
about his boy. (*To Seth*) Why, the other day I found him reading
Harold's schoolboy letters and he was crying over them.

SETH He ain't so hard agen Master Harold after all. I say, you
ain't—(*touching Clifford's arm*) Squire here yet, Mr Clifford.   255

CLIFFORD (*sits R*) He may alter his will at any moment. At present,
I know he's left everything to me. If Harold works the oracle°
tonight he will be forgiven, and your daughter will never be
mistress here.

SETH (*down by Clifford*) It 'ud break her heart, poor lass!   260

CLIFFORD (*thinking*) Harold has come down here secretly. How does
he look?

SETH Awful—ill—hard-up—shabby!

CLIFFORD He's on his last legs and desperate. (*Rising*) Seth, perhaps
he's come down here to rob his father, to force from him the   265
assistance he will not give.

SETH To rob my lass of what'll be thine some day.

CLIFFORD (*lights cigarette—Seth lights pipe*) Listen, Seth, everything
depends upon us now. Tonight decides whether we are to be rich,
or beggars.   270

SETH Your brain be quicker nor mine—tell me plain what it is you mean?

CLIFFORD If there were a robbery at the Hall tonight and a suspicious, shabby-looking fellow had been seen lurking about the premises, whom'ud you suspect?   275

SETH Why, shabby fellow, of course.

An ostler enters L, lights lamp over gate and exits

CLIFFORD In the library yonder, the Squire keeps his dead wife's jewels—this penniless outcast knows it. Seth, it's my idea he has come down to steal them.

SETH What's your idea's mine.   280

CLIFFORD At any rate, if the jewels were missing tonight it would be tolerably easy to fix suspicion on him, wouldn't it?

SETH Why o' course it would.

CLIFFORD I think I ought to give information to the police. There have been a good many robberies in this part of the country lately.   285

SETH You see your duty pretty clear, sir.

CLIFFORD Just walk as far as the police station with me! Hist! (*Marks comes from Lodge L and returns*) Old Marks is about! (*They separate*)

SETH Tell me quick, what do you want me to do?

CLIFFORD You go on first, I'll come round the other way; we'd   290
better not be seen together. I'll tell you as we go along.

SETH All right! (*Goes toward gate*) I'd do a good bit agen the man as 'ud rob my lass o' the best chance she's ever likely to get. (*Exit gate L*)

CLIFFORD (*alone—looking towards Lodge*) So, so, Mr Scapegrace, you   295
would come the prodigal son, would you, get your father to forgive you and kill the fatted calf. A pretty scheme, a very pretty scheme, but I think I can better it; it's my duty as the guardian of the family interests to see they're protected against this bad young man!   300

Music. Exits R2E behind House. Stage grows darker. Enter Marks and Harold from Lodge

MARKS (*R*) I may be wrong, Master Harold, but wouldn't it be better that you should go up to your father's house and see him there?

HAROLD (*C*) No, look at me. Why, the servants would refuse to admit me, and the dogs would mistake me for a tramp and fly at me. No, I don't want our people to see how low their young master   305
has fallen. Do as I ask or I shall think that you have turned from me now I am down on my luck!

MARKS Ah! Master Harold, I'd give my heart's blood to save you.

HAROLD Why, old friend, I believe it. (*Shakes Marks's hand—goes up to tree C*)   310

MARKS I feel like a traitor to him doing it but it's for his own flesh and blood that I'm false to him.

HAROLD Make haste, I can't bear to think that anyone should see me hanging about like this.

MARKS (*going towards R I E*) If it costs me my place here, where I was   315
born and bred, I can't help it.

HAROLD (*coming down to him*) Come, come, cheer up, cheer up, old man, it'll be all right!

MARKS (*coming back a little*) But it mayn't be all right, Master Harold.   320

HAROLD (*taking Marks's arm*) True, it may not. If it isn't, and I have to—(*hesitates*) leave her alone, (*placing hand on Marks's shoulder*) promise me, in the event of the worst, you will keep and shelter the only creature who cares a curse for me, my poor little Bess; that if they turn you out for this night's work, she goes with you,   325
and that whatever happens, you'll take care of her.

MARKS Master Harold—I am her father.

HAROLD Yes, and the owner of these broad acres is mine, but he has left me to starve. Promise that if he should refuse to help us, and I should have to leave my poor little girl, that you will shelter her   330
and keep her from want.

MARKS (*giving hand*) I promise!

HAROLD Now go—and good luck go with you.

    Music. Exit Marks nervously to house R

HAROLD (*alone*) He's promised, and he'll keep his word. Poor Bess, through all the weary years of want and trouble, she's been true   335
and loyal to me. Poor girl, it's rather hard upon her—but I dare not let them know she's my wife; as Bess Marks, my father would let her stay here in the Lodge, but he'd never forgive me for marrying his servant's daughter, and would turn her out and her father as he did me. But who knows, perhaps tonight he will let   340
me come home again, and in time I may soften his heart and tell him the truth about her, or at any rate he will give me the money to leave the country and in a new land we can lead a new life, and if he refuses—well, Bess is safe with her father at all events.

    Seth passes cautiously behind trees towards the house and conceals himself—Harold paces up and down

How slow old Marks is! Perhaps my father will refuse to come. If   345
he does, servants or no servants, I'll force my way into the Hall,

he shall see me! (*Looks anxiously towards house*) There he is! Can that be my father! Great Heavens! What a change. How ill and feeble he looks; have I been the cause of all this? I almost dread to meet him, after all. (*Draws back up L*) 350

Marks and Squire come on through library

MARKS If you will walk across to the Lodge, Squire, you can see the poor fellow yourself—he is in great distress.

SQUIRE (*following through window*) Genuine distress always has my sympathy. I'm glad you've fetched me.

MARKS (*closing window*) I knew you would be! 355

SQUIRE We should always do good when we get a chance. (*Starts*) Who's that?

HAROLD (*rushing forward*) Dad!

Marks crosses at back and exits L. Squire turns away

HAROLD Will you not speak to me? Father! Oh! don't turn away from me. (*Squire does not speak—after pause*) Heaven knows I have 360 suffered enough for all the wrong I ever did, but I haven't come down here to whine about that; all that I have suffered I no doubt richly deserved, but another has suffered with me and for her sake I have come to ask you to forgive the past and help me once more.

SQUIRE (*RC*) Harold Armytage, if I consent—if I break the oath I 365 have taken and help you again, how am I to know that this is not another piece of your villainy?

HAROLD Father, you've no right to say that to me. I am no villain. I have been mad—rash—a spendthrift if you will, but no man can call me villain, no man but my own father dare. 370

SQUIRE As you will! How am I to know that you are not masquerading in these rags to wring from me the price of a week's debauch?

HAROLD I am not the Harold Armytage I was! Father, you don't know what I have suffered! 375

SQUIRE (*aside*) My poor boy!

HAROLD I would rather have starved than come to you as I come now, but for another's sake.

SQUIRE The woman you have dragged from her happy home to share your shame. (*Agitated*) As my son I will do nothing for you. (*Going* 380 *R, returns*) As a stranger who comes to me with a tale of distress, true or false, I will help you.

HAROLD (*passionately*) I have never begged of a stranger yet. If I am a stranger to you—keep your money.

SQUIRE You refuse my help? 385

HAROLD I do. I have crept to your feet like a whipped cur; you, seeing me down, kick me. I will not give you the chance again. You will repent this to your dying day.

SQUIRE Scoundrel, do you threaten me?

HAROLD Yes, with a life-long remorse. You have already robbed me   390
of my birthright and given it to a stranger. What have I done to deserve it? Kicked over the traces now and then, and spent a little too much money, and three years ago when we parted, I said some hot angry words, which Heaven knows I've been sorry enough for ever since, but I have never given you the right to call me   395
scoundrel. I am still your son, although you seem to forget you are my father. And now when I come and tell you I am almost starving, and ask you to help me for the sake of the girl who clung to me when I hadn't a friend in the world, you not only refuse, but you insult me into the bargain.   400

SQUIRE Your rebellious spirit is still unbroken, Harold Armytage. You refuse my offer?

HAROLD I do!

SQUIRE I shall not stay here and listen to your threats. Shame on you to wreck the life of my old servant's daughter, and then use her   405
name as a means to extort money from me.

HAROLD It's a lie! An infamous lie!

SQUIRE Leave this place at once, sir! It wanted but your threats to prove how right I was in what I have done. I want to see your face no more. (*Exit R1E*)   410

HAROLD (*violently agitated—paces the stage*) Nor I yours! Refused and insulted! I might have expected it! Fool that I was to expect that there remained one spark of love in his hard old heart. I've done it this time. (*Sits under tree C*) Oh! what a hot-headed fool I am to be sure. If I had been a smooth-tongued hypocrite like that   415
sweet cousin of mine I should never have got into this fix, and now he'll live in my place, and I must wander forth an outcast. I don't care for myself, but—Bess, my poor little Bess! What will become of her now?

> *Music. Buries face in hands. The lights have been lit in the Hall and the Lodge by this time so that the triple action° can be seen by the audience. Footman draws curtains in C window of library*

BESS (*in Lodge with Marks*) Father, they are together now. Harold   420
does not return; how my heart beats.

MARKS Have no fear, my child. The Squire loves his son and will forgive him.

BESS Oh, father, brighter days may be in store for us, but the anxiety
makes my heart sick. I cannot stay here, I must go to him.   425

MARKS No, my darling, stay here with me. Harold will be back
directly and we'll have the good news from his own lips. (*Comforting her*)

HAROLD (*on seat under tree*) What am I to do? If I could have earned
money, I never would have come here to ask for it, but he's bred   430
me a gentleman with useless hands, and I must either beg or
starve, and she, my wife, what's to become of her! Can I drag her
back into the old life again—into worse—into Heaven knows what?
(*Rises*) No, she shall not sacrifice herself again for me. Bess, my
darling, I must leave you, but can I look into your sweet face and   435
say 'Good bye'? One look from those soft pleading eyes would
conquer me. No, I must go without one word. Bess, my darling,
forgive the pain I cannot spare you. (*Looks towards Lodge*) I will
go out into the world. (*Kneels by Lodge—plucks rose*) And fight the
battle of life alone. I will conquer and return to claim you, or I will   440
die and make no sign. My Bess, my only friend, my bonny
bright-eyed darling! Good bye, farewell! God knows when we shall
meet again. Good bye—good bye!

    Goes off through gate L terribly agitated

BESS (*in Lodge*) Father, let me go into the little room where I slept
as a child and pray for him.   445

MARKS Can you join your hands in prayer now as you did then?

BESS Yes, father, I have prayed for you every night since I left you.

MARKS God bless you! I want to know no more. If you can lift your
eyes to Heaven with his name upon your lips, you are his wife.

BESS Father! (*Puts her arm round his neck and her head sinks on his*   450
shoulder)

    Squire has entered library after footman has pulled curtains to,
    has taken deed box out of safe and is seated L of table—facing
    audience, opens window of library

SQUIRE Twice have I repented and revoked my will! (*Takes parch-*
ment out of box) This leaves everything to Harold, and cancels the
one I made when I disinherited him. (*Takes a packet of letters from*
box) Ruth's letters, faded and yellow. Poor Ruth! Poor mother!   455
Thank God! sweet wife, you never lived for the little Harold you
loved so well to break your heart as he has broken mine. (*Taking*
up a letter and reads) 'Baby Harold sends love to papa.' I was
abroad when she wrote that. Baby Harold! I can see him! A
curly-headed lad upon her knee. She worshipped him. Had she   460

lived he might have been a better man; so might I. Now he is an outcast and I am wifeless and childless. Poor Ruth! Baby Harold! No, my vengeance shall not survive me. (*Rises*) My dead hand shall not strike him. I cannot die and let Ruth's son be a beggar. Ruth, for your dear sake, I forgive him all. (*Music. Puts will and letter*   465
back into box)

> *Seth appears at back cautiously stealing through open window and steps behind curtain. Squire takes out jewel case and opens it*

Ruth's diamonds! They should have been Harold's wife's had he given me the daughter-in-law I wished him. (*Holds jewels up—diamonds sparkle in light*) How they glisten! And the bosom on which they heaved and fell is dust. (*Sighs*) This will in my son Harold's   470
favour shall remain. (*Has placed jewels in case and taken up will. Seth, who has come in at window behind him puts lamp out with right hand, seizes will with left. Squire turns on him, short struggle. Seth throws him through window, facing audience—down steps—seizes box and darts through window at back, crosses to L gate, is met by Clifford*)   475

CLIFFORD Well?

SETH Out o' the road! It's done!

> *Music. Rushes off through gate L*

SQUIRE Help! Thieves! Thieves! (*Rushes across stage, trips and falls heavily. Clifford crosses to R behind tree—pauses and comes down to Squire*)   480

CLIFFORD Great Heavens! What is the matter? You are hurt.

SQUIRE Yes, and robbed!

CLIFFORD Help! Help! Help!

> *Enter Marks from Lodge*

MARKS What's the matter? (*Helps Clifford to place Squire on seat C*)

CLIFFORD A robbery! The Squire is hurt!   485

> *Servants enter*

MARKS (*looking off through gate L*) Ah! they are bringing a man this way, they've caught him!

> *Harold is brought on by two constables followed by crowd of country people. Seth enters behind crowd*

HAROLD Why am I dragged back like this? What have I done? (*Sees Squire*) Father, you are hurt! (*Struggling*) What does this mean? Speak to me!   490

CLIFFORD Who has done this?

SETH (*coming down R of Clifford, with empty deed box in his hand*) That man! I saw him come out of that room with this box in his

hands. He ran up the road to the Six Acre field and gave two chaps
some papers and things out of it and flung it away.   495

HAROLD It is false!

CLIFFORD It is not false, Harold Armytage, you have robbed and
murdered your own father!

BESS (*pushing her way through crowd—down to L*) It's a lie! Who dares
say this thing of my husband?   500

ALL Her husband!

BESS Don't you know me, people? I am Bess Marks that was!

ALL Bess Marks!

HAROLD Bess! My poor Bess!

CLIFFORD You must answer to justice for what you have done. Take   505
him away! (*Movement. Bess rushes up and flings her arms round
Harold's neck*)

BESS No, no! You shall not take him from me! He is innocent, I tell
you! Harold! Harold! Say you are innocent!

HAROLD I am innocent, remember this, whatever happens!   510

BESS Thank God!

HAROLD (*shaking himself free*) Father, speak to me, tell them I am
innocent, tell them who has done this terrible thing!

SQUIRE It was my son! It was my son!

ALL His son! etc. etc.   515

> Bess swoons in Harold's arms as he rises

CLIFFORD Take him away!

HAROLD (*passing Bess to Marks*) Marks, she is my wife, remember
your promise! (*The two constables seize Harold. Curtain*)

2.1

Interior of the 'Armytage Arms', an old-fashioned room hung with sporting pictures. Large open fireplace R. Bar L. Snowy landscape through window. Three years are supposed to elapse between Acts 1 and 2. Lively to open.

Discover° Skeffington (a lawyer) and Seth Preene, before fire R. Mr and Mrs Jarvis eating at table LC. Jim sitting on drum L. Three rustics at bar drinking. At rise of curtain, one rustic exits door LC and crosses behind window to R

SKEFFINGTON (*sitting R by fire*) So you're doing very well here, Preene?

SETH (*standing before fire*) Yes, pretty well. But I didn't send for you to talk about myself. I want a little law business done and I want you to do it for me. You know how I came to get the money to take this place? 5

SKEFFINGTON I heard you had money left you.

SETH By an uncle in the West Indies, sir. Well, wi' this money there was papers. Now I often think as this house might be broke into, or I might die, and someone as had no right might come a rummagin' among them papers, so I want you to take charge of 'em and never give 'em up to nobody but me. 10

SKEFFINGTON Certainly not without your written authority.

SETH I thought you'd agree, so I had everything ready. Here's the packet, it's sealed because it's private. If I should die, why you can 15 open it. (*Gives him packet*)

SKEFFINGTON (*going towards door*) Very good. I understand! My clerk shall send you a proper receipt. (*Puts on hat. Seth helps him on with coat*)

SETH Allow me to help you on wi' your coat. 20

SKEFFINGTON If you would be so kind! Cold isn't it?

SETH Awful! About the sharpest winter we've had for many a year.° Good day. (*Skeffington exits door LC*) That's a load off my mind! (*Turning to Jarvis at table*) Well, guv'nor, so you're going to start this afternoon? (*At fire*) 25

JARVIS (*R of table*) Yes, we must be up in London as quick as we can. We open in Croydon this day week, with a h'extra company° and

new drama, written by my old woman there! Knocks Shakespeare
into a cocked hat, don't it Jim?

JIM (*L eating*) Um! Um! you're right, guv'nor, it do!   30

MRS JARVIS (*L of table*) Get along with you, Joe, but though I say it
as didn't ought, I ain't been a travelling about the country—fust
with father as had wild beasts and then with Joe here as has the
finest show on tour—for nothing.

SETH (*sits C*) Done pretty well here?   35

JARVIS Well! Pretty well, considering the weather. But we ain't took
enough to keep Jim in luxuries, have we, Jim?

JIM No, guv'nor, you ain't.

JARVIS No, but the boy's not here with us, that accounts for it.

MRS JARVIS (*sighing*) No! I often says to my good man, I says, 'Joe,   40
if anything was to happen to that boy of our'n, it would queer the
show.'

JIM (*eating*) Feenonynom!°

JARVIS Yes, he is a feenonymon and no mistake. There ain't nothing
that boy can't do. He helps the missus to write the dramas, don't   45
he?

MRS JARVIS Of course he do, and beautiful his h'ideas is, if they
could only be carried out.

JIM But they can't!

MRS JARVIS That the wust on it. You see it's a lovely h'idea to 'ave   50
a h'angel 'overing over the 'ero and savin' of 'im, and it ain't 'ard
to play a h'angel, only 'ow is 'e to 'over?

JARVIS That's exactly where it is, you see, and father, he says, if it's
to come on and h'off like a huming bein', father, he says, what's
the use of it bein' a h'angel? It's cheaper and more suitable to the   55
wardrobe to make it a huming bein' at once! That's the sort o' boy
Shakespeare is!

SETH Shakespeare! He is dead, isn't he?

JARVIS (*crossing to R*) Oh! yes, Shakespeare Senior is, been dead a
long time, mor'n forty year I should say, but we're talkin' o'   60
Shakespeare Junior. (*Going to fireplace and lighting pipe*) Shakespeare Jarvis, because he was born at Stratford-on-Avon!

Rustics go off door L and pass in front of window

MRS JARVIS And well I remember it, though it's sixteen years ago,
and me a playin' Medea° at the time, and much I feared, goin' on
that bloodthirsty, night after night, poor boy! through a six month'   65
tour, as perhaps he'd come to be hanged. (*Jarvis sits L of table*)
And all through no fault of his own.

SETH Why ain't the boy wi' you now?

JARVIS He's ill, poor chap! So we left him at our crib° in London
along of a good kind creature as lodges in our house and looks after   70
him, and takes care of him like a mother, don't she, Liza?

MRS JARVIS That she do. God bless her!

JARVIS And that's why we're a hurryin' on. The missus here wants
to see the boy again. She's a reg'lar soft-hearted 'un. You wouldn't
think so if you see her play Lady Macbeth; she plays it that   75
natural, the audience chucks things at her; and sometimes they
wants to go out and fetch the police.

MRS JARVIS Yes, and sometimes they don't come back again.

JARVIS But, come on Liza! We must be joggin' on. You finished,
missus?   80

MRS JARVIS Yes.

JARVIS You nearly finished, Jim?

JIM Not quite, guv'nor!

JARVIS No, you never would be finished while there was anything to
eat, Jim. Beat the drum and chuck the bills about;° we shall be   85
here next fair time may be. (*Exit Jim, LC door*)

SETH (*at window*) Well, a pleasant journey. You'll be well on your
road before night.

JARVIS I reckon we'll be a good twelve miles. (*Drains pot and buttons
up coat*)   90

MRS JARVIS (*crossing to fire*) I'll just have look at that fire and
remember it, it'll be a nice thing to think of, I daresay.

JARVIS (*at bar L paying bill, then turns to Seth*) I say, guv'nor, have
they found that convict as was seen on our road the day before
yesterday?   95

SETH (*C*) I haven't heard, poor devil! I should think he wishes he
was back in jail again in this weather. (*Mrs Jarvis has got to fire*)

JARVIS I should think so too. Why, it's cold enough to freeze a poster
to the wall without paste.

MRS JARVIS (*at fire*) A convict loose and on our road. Lor! Joe!   100
Perhaps he's a burglar! I hope we shan't be massacred in our beds.

JARVIS That 'ud be a tragedy for one night only, wouldn't it, missus?
As we couldn't announce till further notice.° Come along, Liza!
Good day, Mr Preene.

> *Music. Jim heard off, beating drum. Mr and Mrs Jarvis exit
> LC door*

SETH (*looking at watch*) Just got rid of them in time. Now Squire   105
Armytage, come as soon as you like, I'm ready for you. Janet!

JANET (*in bar*) Yes, sir!

SETH (*hands plates and things off table to her, then goes up to window*) He's generally pretty punctual. Here he comes down the hill drivin' like the devil and thrashin' his horse. He's a bully—but he's a coward. You can always tell a man by the way he drives his horse.   110

CLIFFORD (*shouting outside*) Hulloa, Preene, just send a boy to stand by this brute's head. (*Music*)

SETH (*opening door and calling off*) Jack, take the Squire's horse to the stable!   115

CLIFFORD Don't take him out;° I can't stay a minute. (*Enters at door LC*) Well, Preene, what do you want? (*Crosses to fire*)

SETH (*following*) I've been up to the Hall, half a dozen times, but you were out, so I left a message.   120

CLIFFORD (*at fire, back to Seth*) I'm in London most of my time.

SETH You find the Hall lonely maybe?

CLIFFORD Yes, it is dull.

SETH Why didn't you act fair and square by me and mine as you promised? Why ain't my Hetty up there now, mistress of it, and   125
making it a home for you as she would ha' done?

CLIFFORD It's not my fault if your daughter chooses to run away from home; you can't expect me to run about to find her with a parson in tow to marry us on the spot.

SETH It's a joke to you, perhaps, Clifford Armytage, but it's killin'   130
me, that's what it is. My Hetty, my lass, as I worked for and toiled for, as I *sinned* for—as she might be a lady—and then to go away without a word, never to write but once, just to say as she was in London. Sometimes I think she's dead, sometimes I think it 'ud be better if she was. (*Comes down a little*)   135

CLIFFORD Tut! tut! man. She's all right!

SETH (*looking at him*) Sometimes I fancy you know where she is, Squire; sometimes I think you've enticed her away, with your lies and false promises.

CLIFFORD Why should I?   140

SETH Why? Because I could ha' made you keep your promise and marry her!

CLIFFORD (*turns*) So I would, if she hadn't run away.

SETH I may be wrongin' you, I hope I am.

CLIFFORD (*crosses to L—sits on back of chair, R of L table*) I suppose   145
you didn't send for me to talk about Hetty?

SETH No, there was summat else.

CLIFFORD Money?

SETH You've guessed it first time.

CLIFFORD I've given you all you're likely to have. You have had this 150
place free and a tidy lump to start with. (*Leans on chair L*)

SETH I had a right to it!

CLIFFORD A pretty right!

SETH Quite as much as you had to the fortune you come into.

CLIFFORD My uncle's will left everything to me; no one can dispute 155
my title.

SETH Can't they? You've a short memory.

CLIFFORD Quite long enough to remember a good deal about you
before you had the Armytage Arms.

SETH There's a man in Chatham jail, if he knew as much as I do, 160
might say summat.

CLIFFORD Harold Armytage, the convict. He's doing his seven years
for robbing his father with such violence that ultimately led to the
old man's death.

SETH Harold Armytage did not rob his father—the blow which hurt 165
his brain and at last killed him, he received accidentally while
running after the real thief.

CLIFFORD (*goes up to Seth RC*) But you swore you saw Harold
Armytage commit the robbery. Don't forget that, my friend, that
you pursued him and saw him pass the jewellery and papers to 170
some accomplice who made off with them. He was convicted on
your evidence.

SETH And yours. But the stolen jewellery is in your possession now.

CLIFFORD And the papers, I suppose, are in yours?

SETH (*going R*) No, they were lost. I told you so before. 175

CLIFFORD (*following*) You don't know what they were?

SETH No! (*Pause. Clifford sits R of L table*) But I often wonder how
you would look if some day they turned up and that will in
Harold's favour which you suspected the old Squire of making was
among 'em. 180

CLIFFORD That would be awkward for you too—wouldn't it?

SETH Mayhap it might. (*Crosses to back of table*) But I don't care what
happens to me now my lass is gone, but for what I've done I want
my pay.

CLIFFORD You've had it. If I have any money to spare I know what 185
to do with it.

SETH (*comes down C*) Perhaps you allow Bess Marks so much a year?

CLIFFORD No, I don't!

SETH Well, then you ought. You let the old man die of a broken heart
and the lass go—Heaven knows where.   190

CLIFFORD I know where—she's in a situation or something of that
sort in London.

SETH Poor wench!

CLIFFORD I offered her money to leave the country, and she threw
it at me. Dirty pride!   195

SETH You've no dirty pride.

CLIFFORD (*rising*) Not a bit; I'd shake hands with you. (*Offers hand*)
Good bye!

SETH (*R*) Damn your hand, there's nought in it!

CLIFFORD (*going to door LC*) There isn't likely to be any more for   200
you.

SETH You refuse me the money?

CLIFFORD (*returning*) I do, and if you worry me any more, I'll turn
you out neck and crop, so now you know the man you're dealing
with.   205

SETH But you don't.

CLIFFORD Quite as much as I care about. Good bye! (*Going to
door—speaking off*) Bring the horse round to the door. Ta! ta!
    Music. Exit to LC door

SETH (*crosses to door, and slams it*) That's the sort of man you
are, Clifford Armytage. I can't blab without putting myself in   210
the hole, but I'll bring you to your knees some day, my fine
gentleman. It were for a mean hound like that I let a decent
gentleman go to gaol and broke Bess Marks' heart, and all for my
lass, my Hetty, and she's gone, gone wi' her bright eyes and pretty
face to what—I don't like to think. She were always a wilful   215
headstrong wench. (*Has taken pipe off mantelpiece and filled it—
pause*) By Heaven! if I thought as Clifford Armytage was at the
bottom of her going away I'd throttle him! (*Smashes pipe down on
hearth R, then walks L*) I'm glad I gave them papers to lawyer chap.
If the Squire thought as I'd got the will, there's nowt he wouldn't   220
do to get it.
    Janet enters L

JANET Master!

SETH What is it?

JANET (*giving cigar case to Seth as she speaks*) Squire dropped this
getting into his trap. (*Clears furniture*)   225

SETH (*taking cigar case*) His cigar case! (*Opens it*) He smokes good
weeds; I'll have one of them out of him at any rate. (*Lights cigar*)

Hullo! what's this? (*Takes paper out of case*) A receipt for a registered letter. (*Reads*) 'Mrs Armytage. The Hawthorns—Holly Grove, St John's Wood.' That's where Bess is! What's he up to   230 wi' her, a registered letter—that means money; then he's afeard on her and not of me. How's that! I must find that out. He's tryin' to square her and throw me over. Seth, my lad, you mun have a look in at this. I'll keep this, it may be useful some day.

  Music. Exit R1E. Scene changes

2.2

  A country road, heavy with snow. Bright moonlight night. The Jarvis caravan seen coming along the road° L to R. Jarvis walking by the side of the caravan singing

JARVIS   'Tis my delight
        On a starry night°
        In the wintry time o' the year.'

(*Draws caravan across stage. He is slapping his arms and keeping himself warm, as he crosses—he drops whip L; draws up R*) Hulloa!   5
I've dropped my whip! (*Picks up whip*) I shan't be sorry when it's Jim's turn to take the horse's head; the cold makes me feel as drowsy as them there syrups Iago advertises in the play.° (*Goes to caravan door*) Missus! Missus! She's asleep and Jim's a snorin' like a pig. 'Tain't likely as he'll wake up such a night as this. Well, I   10
suppose I must push on! (*Music. Sings again*)

      ''Tis my delight
       On a starry night . . .'

  Harold comes from RUE; he is in a convict dress

HAROLD Stop! stop! For the love of Heaven! Stop!

JARVIS (*L*) What is it mate—be you ill, or murdered—or—(*Stops   15
short*) Well, well, I'm blest! (*Moonlight shines on Harold's convict dress*)

HAROLD (*R*) Don't shrink from me; I don't want to harm you, I want your help. For two days, and nights, I've been hiding in ditches and behind thickets by day and crawling along under cover of the   20
night; all that time I haven't tasted bite nor sup. I'm perished with cold and my feet are cut to the bone. Give me a lift, for God's sake. Hide me in your 'van, help me and I'll pray for you all the days of my life.

JARVIS (*L*) You're a convict, mate, and you've escaped from jail. I'm   25
an honest man as pays his way and says his prayers for himself.
Why should I make myself as bad as you by helpin' you?

HAROLD I am an innocent man.

JARVIS Yes, most of you coves° generally are. Get out of my way and
let me pass! (*Going to van*)   30

HAROLD One moment: up in London there, my wife, that I would
give my heart's blood to save, lies dying. I swore in my cell when
she wrote that I might never see her again that I would. I
escaped—I got clear away and I've got here—here—where I can
almost see the Lights o' London. I can't move another step nearer   35
the Great City without detection.

JARVIS (*LC*) No, you'd look pretty conspicuous like that, I reckon.

HAROLD Think that my poor wife may be dying now, hungering
for a sight of me. I have risked so much to get so near. Without
your help I can get no farther, but must lie down here and die, die   40
in the snow, but you won't let me do that, you'll help me, won't
you?

JARVIS It's a felony you know, it's harbouring.

HAROLD Think of your own wife, if you should be parted from her,
for years, and then struggle to get within a few miles of her, and   45
be struck down and moan for help and no help came, for her sake,
for the sake of a wretched woman and a heartbroken man, have
pity! Have—oh, my head—my head! (*Reels—puts hands to head—
falls exhausted on face. Jarvis going R turns, goes to him and raises
him*)   50

JARVIS Dangit all, man, don't take on like that! Here, I'll help you.
Lord love you! Here, missus, missus! (*Goes to van, raps at door,
returns to Harold*)

> Mrs Jarvis puts her head out of door of van; she is wrapped in
> rug and things

MRS JARVIS Lor, Joe! What is it?

JARVIS Don't kick up a row; give us the brandy out.   55

MRS JARVIS Joe Jarvis, you don't mean to say you've woke me out
of my fust sleep just for a drink?

JARVIS Hush! there's a poor cove took ill here. (*Pouring brandy into
Harold's mouth*) Here, mate, have a pull at this!

MRS JARVIS Oh, lor a mussy!° (*comes down steps and crosses down to*   60
L) What a festive place to be took ill in. (*Looking at Harold*) A
convick! We shall all be murdered in our beds.

JARVIS Hush, missus, he's a poor devil as has escaped. He wants to
get to London to see his wife, don't you, mate?

HAROLD (*reviving, wandering*) Bess! Bess! Where am I? Ah! Who are   65
    you?

JARVIS You're all right, mate, you're with friends, ain't he, missus?

MRS JARVIS (*L*) I don't know that, Joe, it's compounding a felony.
    Here's a third act of a drama, and no mistake.

JARVIS Well, if you don't want to make it a tragedy, let's help him   70
    into the van.

HAROLD (*raising himself*) Oh, help me to get to London, to find my
    wife, who's dying! I am an innocent man!

MRS JARVIS All the convicks is as escapes. Leastways in all the
    dramas as I ever played in.   75

JARVIS (*R*) Well, if he's tellin' a lie, let it be on his own head; shall
    we take him or leave him?

HAROLD Don't leave me here to die. Let me only see my poor Bess
    again and then do with me what you will. (*Goes up*)

MRS JARVIS It's a rum start, you know, picking up convicks in the   80
    middle o' the night. I suppose we shall get into trouble with 'ard
    labour for harbouring—if it were to be found out.

JARVIS Yes, they'd put you in one prison and me in another. I don't
    like to talk about it. I couldn't live three months away from my
    wife.   85

HAROLD And I haven't seen my wife for three years. (*Breaks down*)
    Bess, my poor Bess!

MRS JARVIS Look here, young man, if you don't want to make me
    cry, drop it. I never did have a h'icicle in my h'eye, and I don't
    want one now.   90

JARVIS Cheer up, mate, the missus is coming round. She's allers a
    bit off colour when she's woke up out of her fust sleep.

HAROLD Then you'll take me with you?

JARVIS Come along, you can lie snug here. When you get to our
    home, you can find out where your missus is.   95

HAROLD I have her last letter in my breast.

MRS JARVIS Keep it there to warm your heart. Lor, how he shivers!
    You'll find plenty of things in there. There's a splendid ghost's
    costume complete in the corner, that'll keep you warm, only don't
    get a walkin' about or you'll frighten Jim.   100

JARVIS Jim 'ud be frightened if the ghost didn't walk.°

MRS JARVIS Joey, tell Jim as he's a leading tragedian as we met with
    accidental and he's on sharin' terms,° so he must be treated
    respectful. Good night—pleasant dreams. (*Crossing towards R*)

HAROLD (*kissing her hand*) May God bless you for all your goodness   105
    to me.

MRS JARVIS Poor fellow! There's something in his face as seems to
say, Liza Jarvis, you've done the right thing this time. Lord! Joe,
I'm in dishability° and never noticed it. (*Music. At door of van*)
Good night, Joey!   110
JARVIS Good night, Liza—there, old fellow, ain't she a brick?
HAROLD She is, and so are you. Bless you for all your goodness.
Bess, my darling, please God, I shall see you again soon.
    Gets up at back of caravan—it slowly moves as curtain falls

3.1

Outside a London police station. Open lively.

Policeman enters from L with little Child which he takes into station as lost. File of policemen come out of station and exit, R. Jack enters from L. Detective Cutts comes to door of station

JACK (*reading*) Murder—£100 reward. Desertion £5 reward. Escaped, a convict, £20 reward—a hundred and twenty five quid, staring a poor cove in the face!—I, what ain't got a blessed mag.°

CUTTS Why, Jack, the philosopher—what are you doing here?

JACK (*RC*) Enjoying a little light literature. I say, couldn't you prove as I committed that there murder, could you, and let me stand in the century° with you?

CUTTS (*C*) I'm afraid I should have to stand in the dock with you.

JACK Escaped, a convict—desertion of the wife and family. Well, I can understand a man running away from his wife and blooming kids, but he must be a discontented cove as would run away from a nice warm prison where he gets all his meals regular and plenty of nice light innocent amusement chucked in for nothing.

CUTTS You've never been in prison, Jack?

JACK No, I never had the luck to do nothing wus than be poor, and they don't punish a cove with board and lodging for that crime in this country.

CUTTS Down on your luck?

JACK Yes, I am, till I gets that ten pound reward for that bracelet as I found and was flat° enough to bring to a police station.

CUTTS You're a sharp fellow, Jack!

JACK No, I ain't, I'm a mug! Look here, guv'nor, would you like to learn a little bit of philosophy?

CUTTS I don't mind if I do.

JACK Well then, I'll tell you. Fools goes to the workhouse, rogues goes to prison. Why, cause every man as goes to the workhouse is a fool for not being a rogue. I say, when do you think the cove's a going to turn up with that reward. The gent said he'd call at the station and see if it was his. When I heard as it was advertised for I got hold of the address and I called there, and see a young lady and a gent; I told 'em I'd found it and took it to the station. Lor, it was a fine place and the young donah°—was a stunner!

CUTTS What did you say the name was?

JACK Mister Armytage. Rum ain't it, that's the name of this here
escaped convict. If he don't come quick about this here bracelet I   35
shall be on my beam ends.

CUTTS Armytage! Armytage! What do I remember about a jewel
robbery case in which that was the name?

JACK Hullo, here's the toff hisself!

Clifford enters L

CLIFFORD Is this the police station?   40

CUTTS Yes, are you the gentleman that's come about the lost
bracelet?

CLIFFORD Yes, is this the station to which it was brought?

CUTTS Yes, sir, and there's the man that found it.

JACK Yes, sir, I found it, sir. Picked it up outside the theatre, sir,   45
whilst I was calling a cab. I didn't wear it 'cos I thought it might
look conspicuous.

CUTTS It's all right, sir, but you won't be able to see it here.

CLIFFORD Why not?

CUTTS All lost property brought in goes to Scotland Yard; you must   50
go there to identify it.

CLIFFORD Of course! (*Crosses to R*)

JACK (*aside to Cutts*) I say, guv'nor, if he gets that bracelet, perhaps
he won't part with the spondulicks.°

CUTTS Yes, he will! They knew all about it at the Yard. They won't   55
give it up till he does part with the spondulicks.

JACK Oh, so long as my case is in the hands of the police I'm
perfectly satisfied! (*Exit L*)

CLIFFORD (*R, has been reading reward bills*) Escaped, a convict,
Harold Armytage! When was this?   60

CUTTS This week, sir!

CLIFFORD Is he—is he caught again?

CUTTS No, sir, got clean away.

CLIFFORD Supposing I have valuable information about him, to
whom do I give it?   65

CUTTS Well, as I'm on the job, you might as well give it to me.

CLIFFORD I know where the wife is; he's pretty sure to go straight
there. There's £20 reward.

CUTTS Yes, sir!

CLIFFORD And if you catch him—I'll give you another £20.   70

CUTTS Thank you—give me your name and address, please.

CLIFFORD Clifford Armytage, The Hawthorns, Holly Grove, St
John's Wood.

CUTTS (*has taken out notebook and written address in it*) By the bye, you'd better come with me; you'd recognize the wife going in and out. I shouldn't.   75

CLIFFORD I'll show you the house and I'll point the woman out to you, but I don't want to be seen in the matter.

CUTTS (*looking at name in book and then at reward bill*) Clifford Armytage! Harold Armytage! I understand, sir, family reasons. All right, sir, show me where the woman is and if the man's alive, ten to one we'll have him.   80

CLIFFORD May as well go down there at once. Have a cigar! (*Offering case to Cutts, who takes one*)

CUTTS Thanks, sir, don't mind if I do, sir.   85

CLIFFORD (*aside*) My interest in your movements, Bess Armytage, has not been thrown away after all. (*To Cutts*) Have you got a light about you?

CUTTS Light, sir? Oh, yes, sir! Don't you trouble about a light.
　　Music. Exit Clifford R1 E, followed by Cutts. Scene changes

3.2

Jarvis' house in Boston St., Boro'.° Doors R and L. Sofa R. Armchair L of fireplace. Clothes horse with theatrical dresses against wall L of fire. Window L in flat. Kitchen dresser with plates, knives, forks, etc. L. Table L. Chairs back of and at head of table. Theatrical properties. Swords, shields, bills, hanging against walls.

Discover Shakespeare Jarvis lying on sofa. Bess in armchair by fire, sewing, slop work°

SHAKESPEARE (*R*) Well, you are a oner,° Mrs Armytage, why, mother won't know this room when she comes back, and she won't know me—you've saved my life, that's what you've done.

BESS (*L of fire*) Nonsense, Shakespeare, I've only nursed you through a fever.   5

SHAKESPEARE Yes, and a pretty hot fever it was. Why, I ain't right on my pins° yet; I couldn't do a hornpipe, it 'ud be a breakdown.° I never thought I'd be in the show again, except as the living skeleton.°

BESS But you're getting better now.   10

SHAKESPEARE I ain't up to much yet. This is the first time the show's ever been without me.

BESS   But you haven't been idle—there's the new drama.

SHAKESPEARE   Ah! I think I've done it this time; there's a part for
   mother that'll suit her proper, and my part's a stunner. Shall I give   15
   you a bit of it now?

BESS   No, you must not exert yourself.

SHAKESPEARE   I know what I'll do. I'll get father to call a rehearsal
   before we start on tour and then you'll see it. I've called the
   virtuous heroine Bess, after you.   20

BESS   When do you expect them home?

SHAKESPEARE   Every day; they'll leave the caravan outside London
   with Jim and come on straight. Here's mother's last letter, (*taking
   out letter*) that the leading tragedian wrote for her. 'Dear Shakespeare, this comes hoping as you're better as thank God it leaves   25
   me and father at present. Business ain't good, we put two more
   murders in the last act of the "Idiot Witness"° but it don't draw
   like when you was the idiot.' Ah! Mrs Armytage, you ought to see
   me play the Village Idiot. 'Me and father sends best respects to the
   guardian angel as has nursed you, bless her, and I long for to take   30
   her in my arms and kiss her, no more at present from your
   affectionate mother, Liza Jarvis. P. S. We shall be home as soon as
   you get this letter.' There's something else.

BESS   What is it?

SHAKESPEARE   (*bashfully*) Kiss the guardian angel for me.   35

BESS   And you haven't.

SHAKESPEARE   I didn't know you'd let me.

BESS   (*crosses to him and kisses him*) Well then, I'll kiss you.

SHAKESPEARE   God bless you, Mrs Armytage; next to my mother,
   I think I love you best in the world, I've read this letter a   40
   dozen times. (*Puts letter away*) You're fond of reading letters, ain't
   you?

BESS   (*sighing*) Yes. (*Sits in armchair again*)

SHAKESPEARE   When I was ill and you thought I was asleep, I often
   used to see you take letters from your pocket and cry over them.   45
   They were from your husband, who's abroad.

BESS   Yes.

SHAKESPEARE   I'm sure he's a good fellow, or you wouldn't kiss his
   letters so. I hope I shall see him; when's he coming home? (*Crossing
   to Bess*)   50

BESS   I don't know. (*Breaks down*) Shakespeare, you're a good boy,
   and you'll never repeat what I tell you?

SHAKESPEARE   (*kneeling by Bess*) Never!

BESS (*putting her arms round his neck*) For years I have borne a sorrow
that has almost killed me, because I had no one to tell it to. Don't   55
mind me, it does me good to talk of my trouble and I haven't a
friend in the world.

SHAKESPEARE I'd go through fire and water for you.

BESS Yes, yes, let me speak or my heart will break. My husband,
whom I love so dearly, I haven't seen for three long years!   60

SHAKESPEARE Why doesn't he come home to you?

BESS He can't—he's in prison. (*Crying*)

SHAKESPEARE (*rising*) Don't take on like that—it half chokes me.

BESS Shakespeare, you will never breathe a word of this to anyone.
(*Rises*)   65

SHAKESPEARE Never!

BESS (*kissing him*) God bless you.

SHAKESPEARE No, don't, Mrs Armytage, I shall break down in a
minute, I know I shall, and then I'll cry like a baby. (*Goes up to
window and looks out*)   70

BESS (*to herself, seated at foot of table R*) I must bear my burden more
bravely than this; I must toil and struggle on and hope and pray.
Oh! the many, many weary years that must pass before he is free.

SHAKESPEARE (*excitedly—waving handkerchief at window*) Hullo!
There's a cab stopped at the door with four boxes on the roof;   75
why, it's father and mother and there's a new gent with 'em! Ain't
he popped into the house quick! Perhaps he's the new tragedian.
Father! Father!

JARVIS (*outside*) Hullo! Shakespeare, my boy!

BESS (*rising*) They mustn't see me like this. Shakespeare, I'm going   80
to my room. (*Aside*) I should break down if I saw them meet.
(*Music. Exit L door. Shakespeare comes down C*)
        Mrs Jarvis enters R with open arms

MRS JARVIS Shakespeare!

SHAKESPEARE Mother! (*Business. Embrace*)

MRS JARVIS Are you quite convalescent, my son and heir? I feel as   85
if I could eat you.

SHAKESPEARE Mother, you mustn't go without me again.
        *Jarvis enters R, stands at door with open arms—Mrs Jarvis is
        between him and Shakespeare*

JARVIS Perhaps, Liza, when you've quite finished with the boy,
you'll pass him on. I've got a part in this performance!

SHAKESPEARE (*going to him—they embrace*) Dear, dear, old Dad!   90

JARVIS My boy! My handsome boy!

MRS JARVIS Ain't he like his mother!

JARVIS (*sitting R of table with Shakespeare on knee*) It's as good as turning money away° to see you again!

SHAKESPEARE Is it, father?   95

JARVIS It ain't seemed like the old show without you!

SHAKESPEARE Ain't it, father? How did Jim play the Village Idiot?

JARVIS How did he play the Village Idiot! He's too much of a h'idiot to play anything. He was too natural, not like you. It weren't acting like yours and it didn't go. The people didn't take to paying a   100 tanner° for what they could see any day in the village for nothing.

MRS JARVIS (*L of table*) When he comes out of the tree and says to the dook, 'I seed you murder the girl, your grace' and begins to jabber,° the females used to get up and go out.

SHAKESPEARE I always used to make 'em laugh.   105

JARVIS Of course you did, and so you will again, I hope. (*Rises and goes towards door R*) But I must get those boxes stowed away in the next room or else somebody will be breaking their neck over them on the stairs. (*At door*) Liza, I'm blest if we ain't forgot all about the new tragedian.   110

MRS JARVIS The idea of leaving him out there. It was a meeting the dear boy as druv him out of my head. (*Embracing Shakespeare*)

JARVIS That's enough of it, Liza! (*Brings Shakespeare to RC*) Shakespeare, my boy, we are about to introduce a gent into this family circle, a mysterious gent as wants to keep dark whatever you sees   115 or hears. Mum,° and I'll tell you all about it.

SHAKESPEARE All right, father, I'm fly!° (*Jarvis exits R*) Is he our new tragedian, mother?

MRS JARVIS Yes, there ain't much of the low comedy merchant° about him. Bring him up, father; he is a bit shy, Shakey, and don't   120 like strangers. (*Music*)

JARVIS (*outside*) Come along, Mr—Mr Smith. There's only the family at home. (*Enter R followed nervously by Harold—he wears a long green cloak and slouch hat°*) There you are, sir! Make yourself at home, there's your manageress and there's our boy, Shake-   125 speare, as you've heard us both talk on so much. 'The Feenonymon.' (*Harold takes off his hat. Jarvis sits in armchair L of fire*)

SHAKESPEARE (*aside*) Oh my, ain't his hair short! (*Aloud*) Very pleased to see you, sir!

HAROLD You're very kind. (*Shakes hands with Shakespeare and goes*   130 *to R of fire. Mrs Jarvis L*)

MRS JARVIS Where's the guardian angel?

SHAKESPEARE She's gone to her room, mother.

MRS JARVIS Then I'll go up to her and give her a good motherly hug! 135

SHAKESPEARE Ah, she's been a good 'un to me! There'd have been no Shakespeare if she hadn't nursed me, bless her!

JARVIS (*At fire*) Liza, see if I can't come up?

MRS JARVIS Joe Jarvis!

JARVIS I always pays my way and I reckin I ain't out of debt till I've 140 thanked her for her kindness to our boy.

 Music. Bess enters L door, while they are talking

BESS I beg pardon, but I've left my work here!

HAROLD (*with a cry of joy*) Bess!

BESS Harold! (*They rush into one another's arms—Jarvis starts up*)

HAROLD Bess, my darling, my wife! (*Bess and Harold go to sofa.* 145 *Shakespeare down R. Jarvis up LC. Mrs Jarvis L*)

JARVIS His wife! (*Comes down C*) Blest if I thought I was leading up to this situation!

MRS JARVIS (*beckoning Jarvis and Shakespeare*) Joe! Shakespeare! We ain't on in this scene. 150

 Exeunt L door

HAROLD Bess, my darling, you are not ill, are you? (*Kneeling by sofa R*)

BESS (*on sofa*) No, Harold it's the joy, joy of seeing you again; can it be you? (*Puts hands over him*) My own dear husband! I dare not move, I fear to open my eyes suddenly and find I have but 155 dreamed you were holding me in your arms.

HAROLD It's no dream, darling! (*Kisses her*)

BESS (*starting up*) They have set you free?

HAROLD No, I have escaped! (*Showing convict's dress under his cloak*)

BESS Escaped! Oh, Harold! 160

HAROLD Do you think I could stop there week after week, without knowing if you were dead or alive? They stopped your letters, because I would not be a party to a piece of tyranny practised by one of the warders on a poor helpless lad, the scapegoat of the gang; they reported me for insubordination—for that they stopped 165 your letters. The last letter that was allowed to reach me told me that you had been ill and I pictured you in my cell ill, dying; the thought almost maddened me. I dreamed night and day of nothing but escape. At last the chance came; a fire broke out in the Governor's quarters; the men seized the opportunity to revolt. I 170 saw a desperate chance; three of us attempted to escape; two were

shot down, but I got free. (*Rises and comes down*) Free, with the
blessed country before me, free with the signpost pointing to
London where the only being I cared for in the whole world lay
as I thought dying.   175

BESS But I was better. I wrote to you and I wondered why they
returned the letters.

HAROLD It was cruel of them, Bess. I had to creep along the road by
night, but I saw your sweet face at the journey's end. It has been
a rough voyage but the haven is reached at last in your dear arms.   180
(*Sits by table—Bess kneels by him*)

BESS Oh, Harold, how I have longed for this moment! How I have
counted the weary months as they passed, hoping and praying that
God would spare me to see you again.

HAROLD My wife!   185

BESS (*starting*) You have escaped. They will hunt you down, Harold;
here in London are you safe?

HAROLD No, I must get away out of the country. (*Rising*)

BESS I will come with you.

HAROLD No, my darling, that cannot be; how I wish it could. I must   190
find some place where I can lie concealed till my innocence is
proved, then you shall come to me.

BESS Why may I not come now?

HAROLD You are ill and weak, Bess. You can't starve and tramp as
I may have to do.   195

BESS Oh, Harold! No, we must not part again. I would sooner die
now, now that your arms are around me and your dear eyes looking
into mine, than live here and not know whether you are alive or
dead. Had fortune been more merciful to us I should have shared
your happiness; you shall not suffer your misery alone. Where you   200
go, I'll go too. God has given you back to me and come what may,
my place is by your side.

HAROLD Come, Bess darling, don't let us talk of parting, just as we
have met after three long, weary years. (*Both rise*) These good
people are our friends and will help us. How strange that you   205
should be with them; the hand of Providence is on us. (*Sits L of
fire*)

BESS I have lodged here for two months.

HAROLD (*standing R of Bess*) With your father?

BESS No, alone; poor father never held up his head again after the   210
trial.

HAROLD Is he dead?

BESS Yes.

HAROLD My poor Bess, and you did not let me know this. (*Kneeling by her*)   215

BESS I knew it would only add to your trouble if you knew that I was alone in the world.

HAROLD My poor Bess! And I thought at least that you had your father to protect you. But how have you lived?

BESS By doing needlework for the city houses.   220

HAROLD (*looking at her fingers*) My poor girl! That is starvation! Oh, Bess, what have you done to be dragged down to this? How different things might have been but for those villains, Seth Preene and Clifford Armytage; on their false evidence I was convicted, through them my poor father died, believing me to be the cause   225
of his death. When I think of all the misery Clifford has brought upon us—the struggles, the poverty—and worst of all the long separation from you, I feel that if I were to meet that man, I should kill him.

BESS Harold, pray be calm. (*They rise*) Hush! they are coming back.   230
(*Knock at L door*) Come in!
    Mrs Jarvis enters L

MRS JARVIS I'm sorry to interrupt, but father's that hungry that if he don't have his dinner he'll get pitching into the property fowls.

BESS We'll go then.   235

MRS JARVIS No you won't! Here, father! (*Jarvis and Shakespeare enter L*) These young people want to run away already!

JARVIS Not yet, we're going to have a feed—a sort of family gathering to celebrate your return.

HAROLD But my clothes!   240

JARVIS It's all right, sir, I ain't forgot about the clothes. Here, Shakey!

SHAKESPEARE Yes, father!

JARVIS Here's five shillings. Go out and get—(*Mrs Jarvis laughs*)

SHAKESPEARE Look at mother laughing!   245

JARVIS What are you laughing at, Liza? I always was a bad hand at ordering a dinner. (*Goes up behind table*)

MRS JARVIS You ain't bad at eating 'em.

SHAKESPEARE (*R of table*) Let's have some spotted dog,° mother; I ain't had none since I was ill!   250

MRS JARVIS (*L of table*) Spotted bow-wow! What, fust?

SHAKESPEARE No, mother, after!

JARVIS (*Goes to Harold and Bess on sofa—shaking table cloth out*)
Never mind about the pastry. Here, Mrs Smith, what would you
like to have for dinner? (*Returns to table and lays cloth*)   255

MRS JARVIS Bless the man! As if she could think about dinner
under the circus°—I do believe, Joe, if I'd come back after you
hadn't seen me for five years, the fust thing you'd say, would be
'Liza—'

JARVIS (*interrupting*) Half pound o' beef, half pound of ham, half   260
quartern loaf° and threepence worth of duff.°

MRS JARVIS That's what you'd say to me, is it?

JARVIS No, that's what I'd say to Shakespeare, because my inside's
given the cue for dinner a long time ago.

SHAKESPEARE Am I to get that, mother?   265

JARVIS 'Am I to get that, mother?' There's a dutiful son for you.
Asks his mother if he's to obey his father's orders.

MRS JARVIS So he oughter. When his father ain't got no more idea
of ordering dinner than a blessed baby.

JARVIS Well, most babies as ever I knew had a pretty good idea of   270
h'orderin' their dinner, when they wanted it. When Shakespeare
was a h'infant he generally let you know when he was on the
premises.

MRS JARVIS Get along with you, Joe—though it's the honest truth,
many's the time I've had to cut out the last act of a drama when   275
he was a baby because he was that obstreperous.

SHAKESPEARE Am I to fetch what father says? Mother!

JARVIS Well, I'm sure—here's the company on strike now; once for
all, am I the boss of this show, or am I not? (*Business*)

SHAKESPEARE Yes. (*Crosses R*)   280

JARVIS That's all right. Now we can go on.

MRS JARVIS Get on, my boy, and be extraditious,° for your father's
a graspin' for his dinner.

SHAKESPEARE (*crossing to R*) All right, mother!

BESS (*rising*) Shall I go; the boy's not well.   285

SHAKESPEARE What! Why I ain't done anything for you yet, father
and mother, dash it all! Don't go and cut out the only bit of fat
I've got in my part. (*Bess returns to harold*)

MRS JARVIS Bless the boy, what a tongue he have got.

JARVIS Let him get a little ham with it. Look sharp and make   290
haste!

SHAKESPEARE (*goes towards R stopping for each item*) All right, father!
Half pound beef, half pound ham, half quartern loaf!

JARVIS Crusty—say it's for me.

SHAKESPEARE And three pennorth of duff!   295

MRS JARVIS And that's your notion of a dinner is it?

JARVIS And what's wrong with the notion?

MRS JARVIS And what about the beer? (*Shakespeare runs back*)

JARVIS I forgot all about the beer. I shall have to have a benefit° and
    retire, my faculties is a giving way. (*Mrs Jarvis gives beer can to*   300
    Shakespeare)

MRS JARVIS You never had much head, Joe!

JARVIS If he ain't quick with the beer, that won't have much head
    either. (*Shakespeare runs off R*) There, missus, let me help you.
    (*They lay table*)   305

HAROLD How good these people are to us.

BESS They have been so kind to me, Harold; many and many a time
    when I've had a bad week and I could not pay the rent, they have
    said what I did for them more than paid them.

HAROLD Hearts of gold, Bess! Hearts of gold!   310

MRS JARVIS There now! I feel hungry, I hope you do!

JARVIS (*anxiously*) Do you feel very hungry, Liza?

MRS JARVIS I do!

JARVIS Oh lor! Suppose they should cut it fat. There won't be
    enough; hadn't we better send for another couple of ounces?   315

MRS JARVIS Lor bless the man, one 'ud think I was a ostrich. Don't
    you mind him, Mrs Smith, he's full of his nonsense today!

        Shakespeare enters from R with things in bag—comes to table
        and puts them out

SHAKESPEARE Here you are, mother!

JARVIS Don't it look nice! Don't they take care of it! (*Shakespeare*
    is about to throw away paper that things are wrapped in) Here,   320
    don't waste the paper, that'll do to light the fire with. I say, Liza!
    Would it be very much out of place if I was to have a glass of beer
    just?

MRS JARVIS Lor! Joe, where's your manners?

JARVIS All right, Shakey, mother says I may, where's the beer?   325

SHAKESPEARE I forgot all about the beer. (*Seizes cans° and runs off*
    R. Jarvis gets hat off dresser—crosses to Harold and Bess, clears his
    throat)

JARVIS Ladies and gentlemen, in consequences of the non-arrival of
    the beer, this here performance cannot take place for several   330
    minutes, but the orchestra will play a selection of popular airs
    during the unavoidable interval. (*They all sit round table*)

MRS JARVIS Now, Mrs Smith, you sit here, and your husband there!
Lor! Joe, do sit still, you regular gives me the vertigo.

JARVIS I was only getting myself a chair; do you expect me to have   335
my dinner on my head. (*Business*) Oh, look what you have done!
You've given the lady the pastry first. They don't do that in
society; they always begins with the cheese. (*Business*)

HAROLD It's many a long day since you and I sat down to a meal
together, Bess.   340

BESS Yes, it seems like old times to have you by me.
Shakespeare runs on at door R. Shouts outside

SHAKESPEARE Father! Mother!

MRS JARVIS Bless the boy! How white he looks!

SHAKESPEARE There are two strange men at the door enquiring for
Harold Armytage—detectives!   345

HAROLD (*jumping up*) Detectives!

BESS (*flinging arms round him*) Harold, they shan't take you from me!

JARVIS (*at window*) Yes, they are watching the house! (*Shouts outside—business*)

HAROLD What can I do? I am caught like a rat in a trap! (*Looks   350
about—not knowing what to do*)

JARVIS Quick! They're coming to the door.

MRS JARVIS What can we do? Poor thing!

BESS (*falling on knees*) Save him! Save him!

HAROLD (*raising her*) Bess, my darling, courage! They shan't take me   355
alive.

SHAKESPEARE (*coming down*) Father! Mother! (*They go aside*) You
know the old play where there's a convict in it? Hadn't we better
rehearse it?

JARVIS Yes, that's it! The convict play. Come on, sir—come on, sir!   360

BESS Harold, they will drag you from me.

JARVIS This way, quick! We'll save you if we can. (*Drags Harold off
C door*)

BESS Harold! Harold! (*Falls into Mrs Jarvis' arms. She puts her in
chair R of table*)   365

MRS JARVIS Courage, my poor girl! Courage! They haven't got him
yet.

SHAKESPEARE (*at window*) Mother, there's a crowd half way across
the street—they're at the door, quick! (*Great noise outside*)

MRS JARVIS They're bursting the door open, they're coming up   370
stairs. (*Going to Bess*) Not a word if you value your husband's
safety; sit up and dry your eyes.

BESS Yes, I will, I won't let them see anything. (*Loud knocking at door R*)

MRS JARVIS Hoity toity! What's the matter? Are you the Gas, the 375
Queen's or the Water?°

WATERS (*outside*) Open in the name of the law!

MRS JARVIS Shakespeare Jarvis, open the door!

SHAKESPEARE (*opening door*) All right, mother!
    Two detectives, Waters and Cutts, enter R°

MRS JARVIS Well, I'm sure you might have sent a post card to say 380
you was coming and we'd a had our best clothes on.

WATERS (*RC*) All right, mum, I see you're fly.

MRS JARVIS Fly? I'll make you fly if you give me any of your
imperence.° This here's private property; as you ain't paid, I
suppose you've come in with a h'order,° where is it? 385

WATERS I'm in search of an escaped convict. There's my authority to search the house. (*Shows warrant and gives Cutts sign to
search*)

MRS JARVIS Convicks! Why lawks a mussy, man, what should we do
with convicks here? 390

WATERS I don't want to do anything unpleasant, my good woman,
so perhaps you'll stand aside and let me search the house!

BESS Ah! (*Moves towards door L*)

WATERS Who's this lady?

SHAKESPEARE One of our company; we're rehearsing. A drama. 395

MRS JARVIS Yes, we're rehearsing a drama for our next tour. It's
hard lines as poor folks as gets their living by performing should
be took up for what they're acting. (*L*)

SHAKESPEARE Look here, guv'nor, I play one of the Princes what's
murdered in the Tower,° why don't you hold an inquest on me? 400

MRS JARVIS And I play Lady Macbeth reg'lar. Have me up at the
Old Bailey for a murdering King Dunking!
    *During the above Cutts has been looking round the room and
    at last goes to door L, looks through and sees someone; turns
    and beckons to Waters who crosses quickly and enters room R.
    Bess rushes to door, Cutts seizes her—throws her to C and exits
    into room. Re-enter Waters and Cutts dragging Jarvis on
    between them. He is wearing Harold's convict dress. They cross
    to door R*

WATERS Oh, you're rehearsing, are you? Come along, my good man,
the game's up. Come along, Mr Harold Armytage. (*They exit R
door*) 405

Directly they are off, Harold enters from L room dressed as Jarvis

HAROLD Bess! Bess! My darling!

Bess turns with a shriek and falls into his arms. Picture. Curtain

4.1

*The Hawthorns, St John's Wood. Richly furnished. Doors R
and L. Opening C curtained. Open moderate.*°

Discover Hetty seated by fire L. Clifford by her

CLIFFORD (*L before fire*) What a discontented little puss you are,
Hetty. You've a beautiful house to live in, every luxury money can
buy; you're pretty, you're admired! What more can you possibly
want?

HETTY (*sitting L before fire—drumming her foot*) Oh! I'm tired of this   5
sort of life—it isn't real.

CLIFFORD It ought to be real—it costs me enough.

HETTY I hate to be mewed up here where no one who knew me in
the old days can come and see all the beautiful things I have.

CLIFFORD I bring lots of men here and they all admire you.   10

HETTY I don't want men to admire me, I want women to envy me.
(*Rising—going to him*) I want you to redeem your promise,
Clifford, I want to be your wife.

CLIFFORD (*in chair R of table*) I have told you there are reasons why
that cannot be yet. You have my name, you are called Mrs   15
Armytage, no one knows that you are not—(*writing a note*)

HETTY (*at back of him, with her arms round his neck*) I don't want to
be called Mrs Armytage—I want to be Mrs Armytage. I want to go
about openly and without fear. I want to drive about in my carriage
and pair in the place where I was poor. I want the mud of my   20
wheels to splash the people who used to chatter scandal about me.
Oh, Clifford, I'd rather have one year of that and die, than live
twenty years like this! (*Goes L and sits*)

CLIFFORD My dear girl, here you are Mrs Armytage, there you
would be Seth Preene's daughter. Your father keeps the Armytage   25
Arms. I don't want to wound your feelings, Hetty, but Seth
Preene's character is a little too well known for me to relish him
for a father-in-law.

HETTY (*crosses to R*) Father! Father! Always father; he has stood in
my path ever since I was born. As a child I used to blush when I   30
was pointed out as Seth Preene's daughter.

CLIFFORD But for your father you would have been my wife long
ago. (*Rises—goes to fire*) Get him to leave the country and I'll
marry you. (*Crosses to her*)

HETTY (*excitedly*) Really!   35

CLIFFORD (*both C*) Yes, you know yourself the life he has led; some
    day something may happen! How do you think I should like to see
    the father of my wife in the felon's dock?

HETTY Oh, Clifford! (*Sits R*)

CLIFFORD (*L*) If he really loves you, he will sacrifice himself for your   40
    sake.

HETTY He shall go. But you have not let him know where I am, you
    have not let me write to him. How shall I see him now, what shall
    I say? (*In chair R*)

CLIFFORD (*by her*) Say that ashamed of the name he bore in the   45
    village, you left him to earn your living in London, that I have
    found you out, renewed my promise to make you my wife on
    condition that he goes away.

HETTY If he has one spark of love for me, he will not stand between
    me and my future.   50

CLIFFORD Write to him to meet you somewhere in town. He'll come,
    never fear. He would give the world to see you again. The rest is
    in your hands. (*Crosses to L again and sits in chair by fire*)

HETTY Yes, it isn't much to ask of him; he's often said he'd go to
    the end of the world for me.   55

CLIFFORD (*aside*) If there is one weak spot where I can strike at
    Preene, it is there. She is not the girl to let anyone stand between
    her and her ambition! (*Aloud*) By the bye, Hetty, the bracelet is
    found; you'll have to go to Scotland Yard and identify it.

HETTY (*crosses and kneels by him*) Is it found? Oh, I am so glad!   60

CLIFFORD Yes, but you really must be more careful, diamond
    bracelets don't grow on trees, you know; besides, this is a family
    heirloom.

HETTY Clifford, when will you give me the diamond necklace?

CLIFFORD Give you, my dear? I haven't given you any of the   65
    jewellery. I'm afraid to do so, you're so careless.

HETTY Well, let me wear them; it only wants the necklace to complete
    the set. Oh, Clifford! It is so beautiful, let me have the necklace.

CLIFFORD You like diamonds?

HETTY I love them—I worship them.   70

CLIFFORD (*taking case containing diamond necklace out of pocket*) What
    would you say if I had brought it with me?

HETTY (*leaping up from her knees and clapping hands with delight*) Oh!
    let me see! (*Business with jewel case*)

CLIFFORD (*rises—Hetty crosses to R chair*) There! Only don't wear   75
    them in public, promise me that.

HETTY No! no! (*Kissing necklace*) Oh! you beautiful things! How you sparkle! How you gleam!

CLIFFORD What a child you are! Vain little puss! (*Looking at watch*) By Jove! Hetty, I must cut.° (*Crosses to her*) Don't forget to write 80 to your father! I've got to be at the club at six. (*Kisses her*) Now ta, ta! (*Aside—going C*) I've found the weapon to fight you with, Seth, at last! (*Exit C opening*)

HETTY I know what I'll do. I'll go and put these on in front of the glass and fall in love with myself. (*Goes off R looking at diamonds*) 85
          Enter Annie C

ANNIE Ma'am! (*Looks round*) Missus must have gone to her room. (*Knocks at DR*) Ma'am!

HETTY (*inside*) Yes!

ANNIE Here's a person wants to see you—he says Mr Armytage has given him a message for you. 90

HETTY The master has forgotten something, perhaps; show him in. Say I'll see him directly—then come in here to me. (*Music*)

ANNIE Yes, ma'am. (*Goes to C door and speaks off*) Will you step up please! Missus 'ull see you in a minute.
          Enter Seth C. Annie crosses to R and exits to Hetty

SETH (*looking round*) Missus! I thowt may be she were a servant here, 95 but I see how it is. I thowt that registered letter were queer; he's playing his own devil's game, and gotten her into his clutches as he got me. Poor Master Harold, him a felon, and his wife as he thowt so true to him, livin' in luxury and takin' money from the man who swore her husband's liberty away. Poor old Marks, it's 100 well for him as he's in his grave. Fathers don't count for much wi' their children now-a-days!
          Re-enter Annie

ANNIE (*crossing to L*) Missus will see you now. (*Exit C*)

SETH Missus! Poor Master Harold! If he come here and sees what I see he'll curse the hour he got free to find it out. (*Crosses up RC*) 105
          Enter Hetty R, jewels on her bosom

Hetty!

HETTY Father!

SETH Hetty! Mrs Armytage! Hetty Preene! What be you doin' i' this grand place? (*Seizes her*)

HETTY Don't, father! You hurt me! 110

SETH This be Clifford Armytage's house; what art thou to him, or he to thee? Mrs Armytage they call thee, be you his wife? (*She holds her head down; he releases her—gets RC*) My lass! My lass! This is why ye are breaking my heart, I who'd ha' made you a lady.

The cursed villain! He took you from me after all! Come home!   115
Come home! You shan't stay here with that man. (*Seizes her wrist*)

HETTY (*struggling*) Father, you hurt me! How dare you speak to me
like this? (*Breaks away from him*) Why do you come here to
disgrace me? (*Sits R*)

SETH Disgrace you? You're that man's light o' love, and you talk to   120
me of disgrace—I'd ha' made yer his wife if you had trusted to me,
instead of leaving me like you did. Shame on ye, girl, shame on
yer! (*L*)

HETTY (*half crying—sits R*) Don't! I won't be called names. I haven't
troubled you. Why do you come here to trouble me?   125

SETH Hetty, I'd ha' given every penny I had in the world and begun
life a beggar again, rather than ha' found you out like this; that ye
might hold up your head with the best in the land, I made myself
what I am. I sinned the blackest sin of my wicked life for you, and
for this.   130

HETTY Don't make a scene, father, I hate scenes. Why do you come
here and make me miserable, just when I was so happy. (*Half to
herself*) Just when I had the diamonds I longed for so. (*Rises*)

SETH Who gave you these?

HETTY Clifford!   135

SETH (*R*) Tak' 'em off! Tak' 'em off. (*Pulls necklace off her neck and
throws it down*) There's a curse in every stone.

HETTY Father! Don't—oh, don't! (*Picks necklace up in rage*) How
dare you do this?

SETH And it was I who put the cursed things into the villain's hands   140
to tempt my own child to shame! (*Down RC*)

HETTY You! They were Clifford's own! What had you to do with
them?

SETH I'd sooner ha' seen you lyin' dead in workhouse shroud than
like this.   145

HETTY (*shuddering*) Don't talk of such things. What have I done that
you should treat me like this?

SETH What ha' you done? You stand there the mistress o' Clifford
Armytage, and you ask me what you ha' done! D'ye think I
perilled my soul that ye should be that—to make my lass a—   150

HETTY (*stamping foot*) Father! You shall not speak to me like this! If
I am not Clifford Armytage's wife, why is it? Because of you,
because of the life you have led, because of your bad name. But
for you and the name you bear, Clifford would have made me his
wife long ago.   155

SETH (*in chair R*) Does he say this?

HETTY Yes. (*Goes to him, tries to take his hand. Kneeling by him RC*) Father, I may be his wife yet—it all rests with you.

SETH Wi' me—how wi' me?

HETTY (*coaxing him*) If you will go away—leave England, go somewhere, where there is no danger of—of anything you have ever done being brought against you, Clifford will make me his wife.

SETH An' it's you, you my own child that asks me to do this—you'd send me away—get rid of me and forget me.

HETTY I shall never be his wife, if you don't. While you live.

SETH Ah, say it! Say it! It only wants that, you'd like to see me dead that ye might be free o' me. Oh Heaven! My sin has found me out. He has told you to say this, he's struck at me like the coward he is from behind my own child.

HETTY You'll go away, father, won't you?

SETH No, I'll stay! (*Hetty rises R*) Stay and face the villain to make thee an honest lass. (*Crosses to L*) I won't ha' done his dirty work for nowt.

HETTY You'll ruin all—you've marred all my life and you would mar it still. It is you—you, father, who have dragged me down to what I am! (*Passionately*) You'll make me hate you. (*Rushes off to room R*)

SETH (*totters after her and sinks into chair L of table—buries face in hands*) My child! Hetty! Hetty! God forgive you! God forgive you! (*Rises angrily*) He has done this—he, with his foul tongue—it's a plot to get me away that he may be safe, but I'll baulk him yet. He shall marry Hetty, curse him! Or be the pauper again that he was! (*Looks towards R door*) I sinned! And I'll have the price of my sin!
    Music. Exit C door. Scene closes in°

4.2

Outside of workhouse—street seen as well. Practicable double doors with bell pull. Door R with step. Open lively.

Enter Mrs Jarvis and Shakespeare R; he is laughing

MRS JARVIS Don't laugh, Shakespeare, it isn't a laughing matter—to see your father, as he is honesty itself—a standing there in the felon's dock for all the world like William Corder in the last Act of 'Maria Marten'.° Your father would die rather than do a mean action. Once he took a fourpenny piece from a nussin' mother and gave her change for a threepenny, through the edge being worn, and found out his mistake; what did he do but give a penny back as they went out to every female with a h'infant in her h'arms, because he couldn't reconter the right one. That ain't the man as is to have his character sworn away in a police court.

SHAKESPEARE He'll be discharged, mother. The police said as nothing wasn't known against him, he's to meet us after it's all over. He'll prove he's a respectable; they won't do nothing to him. The bobby told me as they found out he was all right when I took father his suit of clothes this morning to appear respectable in.

MRS JARVIS Respectable! If he ain't I'd like to know anyone on the road as is. We're well known—nobody knowner; where we go once we can always go again.

SHAKESPEARE I hope father won't go again when he's out. (*Turns L*)
    Jarvis enters from L

MRS JARVIS Joe!

JARVIS Liza! (*Business*)

MRS JARVIS (*with emotion*) Don't mind me, Joe! I'm weak; it's bein' awake last night, a fancying perhaps they was a thumb-screwing you to get out what you know about the convict.

JARVIS I didn't like being locked up myself, but it's all right now. I'm remanded on my own recognizances for a week° and if nothing ain't found out against me I shan't hear no more about it. I did have a lark with 'em too!

SHAKESPEARE Did you, father?

MRS JARVIS I knew you'd give 'em as good as they give you.

JARVIS Well o' course I'd got real convick's clothes on, them as he escaped in, so it warn't no good pretendin' they were part of the wardrobe, so I says as I found 'em, and thought they'd been left by mistake and as I was goin' to play a convick in our new drama, I thought I'd try 'em on.

MRS JARVIS Did they believe you, Joe?

JARVIS No, they didn't, not much. Then they asked me why I didn't come to the station at once, why I didn't want to be took.

SHAKESPEARE They had you there, father.

JARVIS No, they didn't 'ave me there, father! 'Why I didn't want to be took,' I says, 'Well gents if you're agoin' to play a convick for your benefit,' I says, 'you don't want to be dragged through the streets, as you're made up.'

MRS JARVIS That was a good point, Joe!   45

JARVIS If the public can see you in the part for nothing, I says, it ain't
likely they'll pay. Mister Irving when he's a going to play Othello°
wouldn't like to walk down Bond Street with his face blacked.

MRS JARVIS Then they laughed, and let you go, I suppose!

JARVIS No, they didn't laugh and they didn't let me go; they wasn't   50
a good audience. They tried to make out as I'd got possession of
the government clothes. 'Them's the government clothes—are
they?' I says, pointing to the suit on the table! 'Yes, they are,' says
the magistrate. 'Then all I got to say,' I says, 'the sooner the
government changes its tailor the better,' but they let me go at last,   55
and here I am, Liza, hungry as a hunter and a thirstin' for—

SHAKESPEARE (dramatically) Revenge, father!

JARVIS No, my tea, my boy!

MRS JARVIS Come along home, father. You shall have the most
presumptious° tea you ever sat down to. Winks, whelks and   60
kippered attics,° a toad in the hole—

JARVIS I say, I suppose they got clean away—them two?

MRS JARVIS Lawks a mussy,° Joe—what d'ye think I've done?

JARVIS What?

MRS JARVIS Let them poor creatures go and forgot to give them any   65
money. And I don't believe as they'd got the price of a meal
between them!

JARVIS Dear, dear, where's your head?

MRS JARVIS It's been on my mind ever since, but I was that worried
about you.   70

JARVIS Well, let's go and have some tea, perhaps we may be able
to get at them yet. They're welcome to all as there is in the
treasury.

MRS JARVIS Lor! when I think what I've gone through with you only
away one night, it make my heart bleed for them, poor creatures.   75
(Affected)

JARVIS (sighing) Come on, Shakespeare! P'raps after tea we'll think
of something as we can put in the Telegraph, telling where we'd
meet 'em with some money.

SHAKESPEARE Yes, father, only if they ain't got any money how are   80
they to buy a Telegraph?

JARVIS (to Mrs Jarvis) Hain't he as sharp as a packet o' needles, Liza?
That boy will hand the name o' Jarvis down to prosperity. (Music.
Exeunt R)

> *Casuals° enter R and L, ring bell at door L. Admitted by*
> *workhouse Porter. Jack enters whistling—Trotters enters R*
> *calling wares*

TROTTERS Trotters!° Two a penny all fresh! Way ho, Jack, have a   85
trotter? (*Offering trotter*)

JACK No thanks, I don't dine today.

TROTTERS Out o' luck still, Jack?

JACK No, prospects is good. Picked up a bracelet worth a hundred
quid and got £10 reward for it.   90

TROTTERS Are you going in there? (*Points to workhouse*)

JACK Yes, unless I can h'indoose my banker to except a h'I. h'O. you,
till tomorrow.

> *Enter Percy de Vere Esq., very seedy*

PERCY Hallo, Jack dear boy! How d'ye do, dear fellow?

JACK Hallo! Percy de Vere Esq. He's got 'em all on,° ain't he? What   95
a fine subject for the waxworks. Visitors is requested not to breathe
on the image cause the wax might melt. Are we a stayin' at the
same 'otel, tonight?

PERCY Yes, cleaned out—stone broke!

JACK And when a cove's stone broke, he has to take to stone   100
breaking.° Your luck ain't been in lately; them estates of your'n
don't seem in a hurry to come.

PERCY No; by the bye, Jack, I heard you had a windfall.

JACK No, it was a bracelet fall—there's £10 reward.

PERCY I say, Jack dear boy, will you lend me a tanner?   105

JACK I've only two lending tanners, they're both out at present, but
you shall have the first that comes in.

PERCY Thanks awfully! Here's a pretty position for a gentleman—
my luck, my boy, I've had three fortunes and run through them
all. Damn it, sir, I kept my own racehorses once! Racehorses was   110
my ruin.

TROTTERS Will you have a trotter?

PERCY Ah, what ah!

TROTTERS No, not a what ah, but a trotter!

PERCY No thanks. Did you ever have anything to do with race   115
horses?

JACK No, the only horses he ever had anything to do with was
trotters and these trotters as don't go very fast, tonight.

TROTTERS You're right! Good night, Jack! (*Crosses R*)

JACK Good night—skip the gutter°. (*Exit Trotters R*) Pussy, touch   120
the 'otel bell. (*Percy rings bell—heavy bell—Porter opens door*)

PERCY I say, you fellar! Is my bed well aired?

PORTER Your what?

PERCY No, not your what, but is my bed well aired?

PORTER Thoroughly aired! You'll find it this way. (*Percy enters door*   125
    and is roughly pushed off R by Porter. Jack tries to follow—Porter
    stops him) Hallo! Jack, you here again?

JACK Yes, can't I have a shakedown?°

PORTER Ain't you got no work to do yet?

JACK No, I ain't!   130

PORTER Your philosophy don't seem to pay, then.

JACK No, rich men are never philosophers.

PORTER What does philosophy say is the use of such fellows as you
    in the world, Jack? Except to be a burden on the rates?

JACK (*standing half in door R*) Are you very anxious to hear what   135
    philosophy says on that subject? I'll tell you guv'nor; it says as it's
    coves like me as keeps coves like you. Now you can send me up a
    cup of coffee and two doorsteps° in the morning. (*Music*)

PORTER (*pushes him in R*) Go on with your imperence! (*Exit—shuts*
    door behind him—a pause)   140
        Harold and Bess enter L

BESS (*RC*) I can't go another step—let me sit down, I shall be better
    directly. (*She slips down on step and Harold sits beside her*)

HAROLD For God's sake, my darling, don't break down here. Come,
    come, cheer up, you don't feel ill, Bess, do you?

BESS No, I'm only tired, I want to sit down here a little, I feel so   145
    sleepy. (*Her head falls a little forward. Harold lets her rest it on*
    him—looks into her face)

HAROLD But you cannot sleep here, my darling! Bess! Bess! here in
    the streets we are not safe a moment. (*Music*)

BESS (*still dreaming—puts out her hand and takes his mechanically*) We   150
    will go to the country together; we shall be happy there—London
    is so cold and cruel.

HAROLD (*soothing her*) Yes, we will go away into the country
    again.

BESS (*holding out hand*) We've had many troubles, but they'll soon   155
    be over; we're on the road to home, aren't we?

HAROLD (*aside*) Her mind is wandering. (*To her*) Yes, yes my darling,
    on the road to home.

BESS My dear old home, I seem to know every hedge row—every
    wild flower. How sweet the honeysuckle smells—and listen to   160
    the birds—look Harold! Yonder's the Lodge and there's father

standing at the gate waiting for us. Father! (*Tries to rise—staggers— falls back into Harold's arms*)

HAROLD Bess, don't, my darling, we can't stop here.

BESS No, Harold, it is so pleasant, here in the old park, beneath the   165
dear old tree. Harold, I'm so hungry.

HAROLD (*aside*) Hungry! She hasn't tasted food all day. Hungry, and
I am penniless and homeless in this Great City. (*To her*) You want
food, you shall have it. (*Aside*) If I steal it.

　　　　*Enter two old gentlemen in evening dress with overcoats R. They
　　　　cross to L*

FIRST GENTLEMAN (*as they enter*) You'll come out well if you do as   170
you say. £200 is a very pretty subscription.

SECOND GENTLEMAN Well, the mission° is a most deserving one;
these savage tribes are most interesting.

HAROLD (*has risen—comes to them*) I beg your pardon but—

FIRST GENTLEMAN I never give to beggars in the street.   175

HAROLD I am not a beggar. I'm a poor devil with a sick wife and no
money; she's ill, and I want to get food and shelter for her. I can't
beg; will you lend it to me?

SECOND GENTLEMAN Lend! What will be the next dodge, I wonder!

FIRST GENTLEMAN Come along, this may be a snare.   180

HAROLD There's my wife yonder on the doorstep. Look at her; you
wouldn't let her starve for a few shillings, would you?

FIRST GENTLEMAN If your distress is genuine, you can get relief. Go
tomorrow to the Charity Organization Society; the office is closed
tonight. They will enquire into your case, refer to your employers,   185
and the places where you have previously lodged, and then
doubtless give you a letter of recommendation to some Charitable
Society.

HAROLD Tomorrow, man—but tonight she may die. Do you think I
would beg if it were not a case of life and death?   190

FIRST GENTLEMAN What an impudent fellow. (*Policeman enters L*)
Here, policeman, this man is annoying us. (*They move off L still
talking*)

SECOND GENTLEMAN By Jove, old fellow, how well that £200 for
the heathen will look in tomorrow's papers. (*They exit L*)   195

POLICEMAN Now then, what are you annoying people for, eh?

HAROLD I was a fool, I heard them talking of their charity, and I
asked their help.

POLICEMAN What do you want help for?

HAROLD What for? Look here!   200

POLICEMAN Here missus, you mustn't sit there! Does she belong to
you?

HAROLD She's my wife!

POLICEMAN Poor wench! She does look queer too. Well, mate, take
her away, there's a good chap.   205

HAROLD Where am I to take her to?

POLICEMAN That ain't my business.

HAROLD Whose business is it, I should like to know, in this cursed
city?

POLICEMAN Ain't you got no home?   210

HAROLD No.

POLICEMAN Well, you'd better take her in yonder, they'll see to her
there.

HAROLD Where's that?

POLICEMAN The workhouse! (*Aside*) Poor devils. They look as if   215
they'd seen better days. (*Goes to Harold—looks around—takes
brandy flask out of pocket*) Here, your missus wants to pull herself
together a bit; give her a sup of that when nobody's looking—it's
brandy.

> *Harold takes brandy and gives Bess some. Policeman goes off L,*
> *meets Inspector, salutes him. Inspector crosses, look at Harold*
> *and Bess and exits R*

HAROLD What am I to do? Tonight every casual ward in London   220
will be searched and a printed description of me posted at every
police station—it's certain capture to go in there, but better that
than she should die in the streets. I'll do it.

(*Goes to door—rings—then goes to Bess and raises her*)

Come, darling, I've found shelter for tonight.   225

PORTER (*at door*) Well, what d'ye want?

HAROLD Shelter for the night.

PORTER Come on, then, the wind's enough to blow one's head off.

BESS Harold—what place is this?

PORTER The workhouse—did you think it was the Grand Hotel?   230

BESS No, no, Harold, we must not go there!

PORTER Now then, are you coming in?

BESS (*dragging Harold back*) No, no, no!

PORTER What d'ye want to come annoying people for then? (*Goes in,
slams door*)   235

HAROLD Come then, we are in God's hands now, may he be more
merciful than man. (*Music. Bess staggers*) Don't give way now.

BESS I'm better now!

HAROLD That's my brave Bess. Keep up, my brave girl, don't give
way now, we shall be home soon.   240

   Harold supports her as they exit R. Scene changes°

4.3

The Slips,° Regents Park.

*Discover Man and Sal on tree L. Boy asleep by steps R.
Policeman with lantern on steps R*

POLICEMAN (*comes down steps and crosses L*) The slapin' beauties! (*To
Man and Sal on tree L*) Now then, wake up! You know it ain't
allowed.

MAN All right, guv'nor, you might ha' let us had another forty winks;
I was dreaming.   5

POLICEMAN Dreaming as you dwelt in marble halls,° perhaps?

MAN Well, this here doss° is cold enough to make a fellow dream
that. (*Pushing Sal*) Sarah! Sarah! Sal! d'ye hear, get up; the copper
says we're to move on.

SAL Shan't!   10

MAN There you are guv'nor, I ask you as a man, what's a cove to do
when his old woman says she shan't.

SAL We ain't doin' no 'arm.

POLICEMAN No, of course ye ain't, you're the h'innercentest young
couple as ever was seen. Out of work, I suppose, ain't ye?   15

SAL Yes, we is.

POLICEMAN Well, it's a good job! I don't like to hear of your bein'
too busy. Come, off you go! Get up! Get up! Get out of that, my
ould cauliflower.

MAN I suppose you think we ain't respectable.   20

POLICEMAN Stop that! I know ye.

MAN Sal, he knows us. Come and stand us a drink.

POLICEMAN Come, clear off, all the watches is gone home° long ago.

SAL We ain't thieves!

POLICEMAN No, of course not. Sling your hook.°   25

MAN Wait till I've buttoned up my ulster.°

SAL Oh, you nasty, disagreeable old Scotchman!

MAN Get away with ye, he ain't a Scotchman, he's a h'Italian!

POLICEMAN I'll give you Italian!

MAN Come on, Sal! 30

SAL Wait a minute, Adolphus! (*Arranges shawl*) I shall soon want a new Mother Hubbard.°

MAN Hi! Can I get a hansom° near here?

> *Business—Man and Sal exit L grumbling, Policeman crosses R, flashes lantern on Boy under steps*

POLICEMAN Hello, boy, what, have you took to dossin' then?

BOY (*getting up*) Please, sir, I didn't know I was doin' no 'arm, sir! 35

POLICEMAN No harm; why, you're laying up enough rheumatics to last you your natural life. Why don't you go home?

BOY Ain't got no home, sir.

POLICEMAN Ain't got no home. Where's your father?

BOY Father's a doin' three months for smashin' mother's nose with 40 a quart pot.

POLICEMAN Well, where's your mother?

BOY She's doing six months for stealin', sir.

POLICEMAN A nice family—what did she steal for?

BOY To get the money for a lawyer, sir, to speak up for father. 45

POLICEMAN (*aside*) What fools the women are! (*To Boy*) Well, my boy, you can't stop here!

BOY No, sir? Where shall I go?

POLICEMAN How the deuce should I know—poor little devil! Look here! I suppose if I was to find you a night's lodging, you wouldn't 50 be grateful?

BOY Oh! I should, sir! I'm that cold and stiff I feel as if I hadn't got no 'ands or feet, or no stummick, sir. (*Coughing*)

POLICEMAN Well, what would you say if I was to run you in?

BOY Will you, sir? Oh, thank you, sir! I should be able to have some 55 victuals regular and be comfortable of a night. (*Delighted*)

POLICEMAN Yes, and the doctor 'ull put that there cough of yours all right. Now don't go and hurt yourself with joy, and I'll promise you three months.

BOY Thank you, sir! What shall ye say I've done? Shall I prig° yer 60 handkerchief, sir?

POLICEMAN No, you're wanderin' without visible means of subsistence,° that's enough.

BOY Please tell the beak° tomorrow I'm a regular thief, will you?

POLICEMAN Why? 65

BOY Because if you don't he'll send me to a reformitory and I'd sooner go to quod,° sir.

POLICEMAN All right, young 'un. I'll see you put away luxurious for the rest of the winter. Come on, the station's just round the corner. I'd do more for you if I could. (*Music. Exit both L2E*)   70
    Harold and Bess come across bridge—down steps to tree L

HAROLD We can rest a little while, Bess.

BESS If I could only rest a little I should be better then. (*They sit*)

HAROLD That's my own brave Bess! Now we won't be miserable any more. Courage, my darling, we will start again directly you have rested. By tomorrow night we may be at St Albans with the   75 Jarvises and then our pilgrimage will be over. No one will think of looking for the escaped convict in a travelling show.

BESS Harold, I'm so sleepy.

HAROLD Lay your head on my shoulder and sleep then. We are safe for a little while here; there is no one about but homeless   80 wanderers like ourselves.

BESS (*dreamily*) Harold, dear, you've never been sorry you married the little country girl, whose father was your father's servant?

HAROLD Sorry! Bess, my darling, God knows there has been little enough of romance in our married life, but I'd sooner sit here   85 tonight an outcast in this desolate park with you by my side than be my father's heir, with the finest lady in the land for my wife.

BESS God bless you, Harold!

HAROLD Now try and sleep. Wrap your shawl tightly round you and don't be afraid of anything or anybody. (*Kisses her—business*)   90 Nobody shall disturb you here. Heaven bless her! But for her, I should have broken down long before this. Poor girl! She has set her heart on it, that we shall get to St Albans and be with the Jarvises, but there's many a mile between this and that and I dread the worst; I dread the worst! (*Arranges himself in an easy attitude—*   95 *gradually his head goes down a little*)
    Clifford enters R on to bridge, smoking cigarette. Seth follows,
    but keeps in shadow

CLIFFORD (*stops in C of bridge*) What a beautiful night! I'm glad I walked instead of letting Hetty call with the carriage for me. This is the night to brace a man up after having gone the pace°, to sharpen his faculties and set his nerves. (*Sees Seth*) Hallo, fellow!   100 What do you want? (*Raises stick. Seth has touched Clifford on shoulder*)

SETH Clifford Armytage!

CLIFFORD Damn it, Seth! What do you want to startle a fellow like that for? I thought you were after my watch and chain.   105

SETH I saw you at the theatre tonight with my lass, my Hetty.

CLIFFORD Yes, she told me you'd been, and made yourself objectionable. Why can't you let the girl alone? She's happy enough.

SETH You have taken from me the only thing I loved in this world, Clifford Armytage. You taught my girl to hate me, to deceive me, 110 and to leave me; now I want reparation.

CLIFFORD Come to my place tomorrow and we'll have a talk, I'm in a hurry now.

SETH No, I followed you from the theatre to your club. I could have stopped you as you came out and said what I had to say, but for 115 her sake, I didn't. I don't want her name bandied about in the street. I followed you from your club here. Here I can say what I have to say. Clifford Armytage, you must make my lass your wife and at once.

CLIFFORD I've promised her to if you leave the country. 120

SETH You'll do it wi' me *in* the country. I'm her only friend. Shut o' me° you'd snap your fingers at both o' us.

CLIFFORD Very well, if you stay you stand in your own daughter's light. I'm not going to run the risk of having my father-in-law in Newgate° some fine day. 125

SETH The blackest sin of all my wicked life I sinned as she might be your wife. You tempted me to do it wi' your lies and your false promises. Now let me tell you what I'll do. Unless Hetty shows me her marriage lines° within a fortnight, I'll tell all as I knows of the robbery at Armytage Hall. 130

CLIFFORD Bah! they wouldn't believe you. The case was tried and proved, when Harold Armytage was convicted.

SETH Ah! for stealin' the jewels that I saw on Hetty's neck this afternoon. The jewels I stole and you received. There was a reward offered for them, and a description published by you. It was all 135 done to make the robbery look genuine. Take care it does not bring the robbery home to you.

CLIFFORD Thanks, Preene, forewarned is forearmed. Now I know your amiable intentions, I'll take care the jewels are put out of sight altogether. 140

SETH It's too late, man, every servant in the place has seen them. Now I gie ye fair choice; make an honest woman of my lass as ye swore you would do—or—

CLIFFORD I'm not to be bullied into anything of the sort. (*Tries to walk away. Seth stops him*) 145

SETH You refuse?

CLIFFORD I do; do your worst!

SETH I will do my worst—Clifford Armytage, ye're no Squire, ye're the penniless beggar you were before I perjured myself. You've no right to one penny o' the old Squire's money. It all belongs to the   150 man we sent to Chatham gaol—the man they're hunting down now—Harold Armytage!

CLIFFORD (*furiously*) It's a lie!

SETH A lie is it? In the box I stole, there were jewels and papers—the jewels you had, the papers I kept. One on 'em was a will, Squire's   155 last will, mind ye, and it left all the estates to his own son, Harold Armytage!

CLIFFORD I don't believe it.

SETH Ye'll believe it tomorrow—the will was made, I ha' got it.

CLIFFORD (*turns suddenly—seizes him by the throat*) You damned   160 traitor! (*Music*)

SETH Leave go o' me, or it will be the worse for you. (*Struggles*)

CLIFFORD I'll shake the life out of you, if you don't tell me where those papers are!

SETH Leave go—or I'll—(*Clifford pushes him over side of bridge—Seth*   165 *hangs for a moment or two*) Help! Help! (*Clifford strikes his hand and makes him let go. Seth drops into water.° Clifford dashes off RUE*)

BESS (*starting up alarmed*) Harold! Harold!

HAROLD They shan't take me alive! What is it?

SETH (*coming up*) Help! Help! Help! (*Sinks again*)   170

BESS There, over there, there's a man struggling in the water! (*Harold rushes up on to bridge, flinging his coat off. Bess follows him*) Harold, what are you going to do?

HAROLD Save a life! (*Jumps off bridge into water. Bess stands on the bridge—gazing half-frantic after Harold*)   175

BESS Harold! Harold! (*Harold comes up with Seth clinging to him. He seizes bank and holds on*)

SETH (*recognizing him*) Harold Armytage!

HAROLD Seth Preene! (*Business. Curtain*)

5.1

The Boro', Saturday night.° Open lively.

FIRST COSTER° (*with fish on barrow LC*) Here ye are, fine cod fish! Fourpence a pound! Fine plaice! Sprats a penny a pound! I'm blowed if I can do any trade tonight, one 'ud think the people couldn't see the fish!

JACK (*with can*) Never mind, mate—they can smell 'em. 5

FIRST COSTER What cheer, Jack old man! Come into a forchin'?

JACK No, been honest and got a reward, picked up a diamond bracelet worth a hundred quid and got a tenner.

FIRST COSTER What's that there? (*Pointing to Jack's barrow*)

JACK That's the tenner invested. 10

FIRST COSTER Last time I see you, you was talking of going into a light business.

JACK Yes, selling matches, that's a light business, but this is better.

FIRST COSTER What is it?

JACK Well, it's a bit of philosophy; the weather's variable, so I 15
thought I'd be independent of it. Look here, penny ices on one side and baked taters° on the other, specially adapted to the English climate. Hullo! blest if it ain't turned cold again. Here, paternize° Philosopher Jack, and warm your hands with a hot tater.
(*Shouts from costers*) 20

FIRST COSTER (*to a woman looking over fish*) Here you are, mum, fine fresh soles!

WOMAN (*smelling fish*) Fresh! Why, they're quite strong.

FIRST COSTER Strong, are they? Well, you should have bought them last Saturday when I offered 'em to you. 25

> *Business—shouts. During shouts, Clifford and Detective Waters
> enter from R down to C*

CLIFFORD They were with these people and they must know something about him.

WATERS Well, if they're friendly with them, sir, they ain't likely to tell me. The bird was flown right enough, when my mate searched the place. 30

CLIFFORD Why didn't your mate come with you?

WATERS He's on a jewel robbery job, I believe.

CLIFFORD I believe this fellow and his wife are still secreted there; they've no money and they couldn't get far.

WATERS Well, if you believe that, we'll try the place again, but we   35
shan't find 'em.

CLIFFORD Not if you go knocking at the door and asking for them.
Get in quietly when no one sees you, and I've an idea you will find
your man. You're scouring the country when he's right under your
nose.   40

WATERS How are we to get in?

CLIFFORD I'll manage that. These Jarvises don't know me. I'll pump
them and if I can get into the house any way I'll soon see if the
bird's there.

WATERS You ought to have been in the Force yourself, sir.   45

CLIFFORD Well, the Force does want a few good heads, but my
ambition does not lie that way. I'll get in somehow. Watch me;
have a couple of men handy and I'll let you in.

WATERS How can you let us in?

CLIFFORD Leave that to me. Look out, there's somebody coming   50
out! If I'm seen with you they'll be suspicious. Keep about and
watch me.

> *They separate and move off among crowd. Shouts. Coster and
> whelk barrow man moves off. Cutts has entered L and comes
> down C to Jack*

CUTTS Come here, Jack, I want to speak to you. There goes the gent
who lost the bracelet.

JACK Yes, I've had my eye on him for the last five minutes.   55

CUTTS Well, how's business, Jack?

JACK Dreadful bad!

CUTTS How's that?

JACK Why, it's all owin' to foreign competition.°

CUTTS I say, Jack, tell me again what the gent said to you when you   60
went to the house about the bracelet?

JACK What he said to the donah? He said 'Look here, my girl, you'll
have to be more careful, if you'd lost that bracelet you'd have spoilt
the set.'

CUTTS Oh, then he's got the set. Jack, are you prepared to swear to   65
what you say?

JACK I never said nothing in my life as I would not swear to. (*Goes
up C*)

CUTTS (*taking out reward bill*) £100 reward—jewels stolen from
Armytage Hall! That bracelet is among the lot; that young   70
woman's got the jewels, her name's Mrs Armytage. Armytage!
Armytage! That's the name of the young fellow who was put away

for stealing the jewels. I've read that bill a dozen times and things
begin to look queer. If that young lady's maid only does her duty
tonight, I'll compare this lost bracelet with the jewels in about half   75
an hour. It's so late, I'd better be off, or I'll be too late. Good
night, Jack!

JACK Good night! Have a bit of hokey-pokey°—before you go?

> *Exit Cutts R. Business—shouts. Coster off R. Enter Mr and Mrs*
> *Jarvis and Shakespeare from house with market basket. Jarvis*
> *is looking suspiciously about; they come down C*

MRS JARVIS Come on, Joe, I ain't got Sunday's dinner yet.

JARVIS (*LC*) All right, my dear, only don't go in for no luxuries,   80
cause it won't run to it.

SHAKESPEARE Shall I carry the basket, mother?

MRS JARVIS Not if I know it! You'd be stoppin' to study character
and somebody'd be helping theirselves to our Sunday dinner.
(*Jarvis looks about suspiciously*) Lor! Joe, what are you looking   85
about for?

JARVIS I don't know, but I never comes out now without expecting
to be took up or followed. I'm only out on my own recognizances,
you know, and them bein' there—

MRS JARVIS Hush, father, why don't you go and tell everybody at   90
once as they're in the house?

JARVIS I ain't comfortable, Liza! He says as it's all right, as his
innocence is a going to be proved, but they've been there three
days and nothing ain't come of it. It's harbouring, you see, and this
time I'd be put away for it.   95

SHAKESPEARE Who's to know they're there, father?

JARVIS Why, the police, my boy, I never sees one now without a
goin' red from the roots of my feet to the soles of my hair.

MRS JARVIS Nonsense, Joe! We're a doin' our duty to our neighbour;
you wouldn't have us give 'em up, would you? I know as it'll be   100
all right; they told me all about it when they came back that night,
nearly froze to death, and in my house they stops if I has to be a
convick myself for it.

> *Clifford calls Waters' attention to Jarvis*

JARVIS 'Taint you as 'ud catch it, it's me. The law supposes a wife
to be under the influence of her husband.   105

MRS JARVIS Then the law knows nothin' about women; it's no good
talkin', Joe!

JARVIS You want to get rid o' me, that's what it is, you've got
somebody else in your eye.

MRS JARVIS No, I ain't, Joe.   110

    Clifford has gone to Jarvis' door and knocked

SHAKESPEARE Hullo! what's that cove want at our door? (*Runs up to him*)

JARVIS At our door! Liza, it's a warrant; good-bye, write to me in prison sometimes, there'll be a vacancy in Jarvis' Temple o' the Legitimate° this tour. You'd better advertise in the *Era*° for   115 another partner.

SHAKESPEARE (*comes down*) It's somebody wants to see Mr Jarvis.

MRS JARVIS Go and see who it is, Joe.

JARVIS Not me, it's a trap! Shakespeare, if it's all right, give me the tip° in yonder. (*Bolts into public house. Waters follows him*)   120

MRS JARVIS I never did see such a man as your father's got.° He's afraid of his own shadow now. (*Goes up to Clifford who is at door knocking*) What might you please to be a doing with that knocker, sir!

CLIFFORD (*comes down RC to her*) I want to see Mr Jarvis.   125

MRS JARVIS He ain't at home. I'm Mrs Jarvis; if you've anything to say to him, you can say it to me.

CLIFFORD Certainly, you had a poor woman staying here some time since, a—a Mrs Armytage?

MRS JARVIS Well, supposin' we did?   130

CLIFFORD I am a friend of hers. I know her story, and if I could find her I'd give her and her husband enough money to leave the country.

MRS JARVIS Very kind of you, I'm sure; I travel about the country in this line. (*Showing him a large poster*) If I should happen to see   135 'em among the audience, I'll let you know. (*Aside, looking at his feet*) He ain't got the police boots on!

SHAKESPEARE (*coming to Mrs Jarvis*) There's the teck° hanging about, mother, as took father.

MRS JARVIS Is there? Then this is one of 'em in private boots.   140

    Jarvis comes out from the public house looking very uncomfortable. Sees Clifford talking to Mrs Jarvis, tries to attract Shakespeare's attention—then exits quickly L1E followed by Detective

CLIFFORD Then you couldn't give her this money for me?

MRS JARVIS Oh, yes, I could if I was to see her.

CLIFFORD Come, isn't she in your house still? I know that her husband came there and escaped and your husband was taken by mistake. We are both friends to these poor creatures.   145

MRS JARVIS I've told you she went away and I know nothing more.
  Lawks a mercy man, do you think as we've got nothing else to do
  but harbour convicts? How's the show going to get on if my master
  gets six months; no thank you, once bit twice shy. Good evening,
  sir. Come along, Shakespeare. (*They move L. Clifford goes R*)   150

SHAKESPEARE I must go and tell father it's somebody after the
  convict. (*Runs up and goes into Blue Pigeon,*° *then comes to Mrs
  Jarvis directly*) Mother! Mother! Ah! there you are! Father ain't
  there.

MRS JARVIS Not there, Shakespeare! You don't think as they've gone   155
  and took him away sudden in a cab or—

SHAKESPEARE No, mother—he's up the street somewhere; let's go
  and look for him. (*They go up among crowd, and off LUE*)
         Jarvis comes on quickly from L1E

JARVIS Phew! I've got away from him; it's the first time as ever I
  broke the laws o' my country and it'll be the last; I'll get indoors.   160
  (*Has been mopping his forehead with handkerchief, goes up to door and
  in crossing drops handkerchief. Puts key in door—opens door half way*)
         *In the meantime Waters has entered L1E. Clifford crosses from
         R to L, picks up handkerchief with stick and throws it to Waters
         who goes to Jarvis and brings him down R*

WATERS Hi, you've dropped your handkerchief!

JARVIS (*leaving key in door*) Thank ye, sir.

WATERS Busy neighbourhood this?   165

JARVIS (*business*) Is it?

WATERS Don't you live here?

JARVIS (*business*) Me, oh lor no! I'm a foreigner! (*Gets further away
  from Waters as he speaks*)

WATERS I thought you lived here! Beg your pardon.   170

JARVIS Don't mention it, it's only a case of mistaken idemnity,°
  that's all. (*Exits R quickly. Clifford during this scene has got into
  house—now returns to Waters and give him key of door*)

CLIFFORD (*at door*) Wait about with your men. If they're here, I'll
  give you the signal, then come in at once.   175

WATERS There are some queer characters here; hadn't I better come
  with you?

CLIFFORD No, I have my revolver with me. If I don't return in ten
  minutes, break into the room over the shop. (*Goes in, closes door.
  Waters crosses and exits R*)   180
         *Church clock strikes 12. Man turned out of public house, comes
         down C. Police file in from R1E. Man runs off L. The last*

policeman remains near door of public house, till the stage is clear. Potman brings him beer. Business and exit. Stage clear. Ready with rise during this business. The rise goes up discovering Scene 2.° Music.

5.2

The interior of the Jarvises. Planned scene°—staircase etc. etc.

Discover Harold seated L of table. Bess at window—she comes and puts penny on table

HAROLD (*starting*) What's that for, Bess?

BESS Your thoughts!

HAROLD (*cheerily*) They were worth it. I was thinking what a pleasant life it will be roaming from place to place with the Jarvises, free and without fear.   5

BESS Won't it be beautiful, and we shall be together. Look, Harold, how far away the lights seem to stretch tonight; beyond them lies the country that I long to see again.

HAROLD (*taking her hand*) Do you remember, Bess, the night we first saw those lights together, when you came at a word from me to be   10
the good angel of my life?

BESS Oh! how beautiful I thought them then; I couldn't believe they could shine and gleam upon the misery such as I know now there lies within them.

HAROLD We were going to make our fortunes, weren't we,   15
dear?

BESS Oh, what dreams we had in those dear old days, Harold!

HAROLD Last night while you slept, I sat and watched at the window till the black night lifted, and the lights went out and another dawn broke over the Great City; then I seemed to see the far off hills   20
loom through the mist. It was an omen, Bess.

BESS A good omen?

HAROLD Yes, it seemed to tell me that another dawn was about to break for us, and that we should see the peaceful country again, that lies where our yearning eyes have turned so often. (*Pointing*)   25
Beyond the London lights. It has been a weary pilgrimage, but there will be rest for our tired feet at last.

BESS Soon, Harold, soon, if Preene keeps his word. But when do you think he will come?

HAROLD I have expected him every hour. Tonight was the night he 30
promised we should know all.

BESS Sometimes, Harold, I grow nervous and wonder if he will keep
his promise.

HAROLD He seemed in earnest; besides I risked my life for him—I—

BESS Why did he tell us to come here? 35

HAROLD Because it would be impossible for him to find us, if we
were roaming about the country. 'Tell me where I can find you in
three days' time,' he said, and this is the only place I could think
of—he swore that he would undo the mischief he had caused and
prove my innocence. 40

BESS But, Harold, why should he do it? What is the gratitude of such
a man worth?

HAROLD Nothing, but there is a stronger sentiment than that
working for us in Seth Preene's heart.

BESS What is that? 45

HAROLD Revenge. Clifford Armytage has wronged him as well as
myself; he knows who really stole the jewels and he can prove it if
he likes. It's all coming right, sweetheart!

BESS And then we shall go away!

HAROLD Yes, and be happier than ever. Why, I've almost forgotten 50
I'm a rich man's son; if I could only clear my name of the prison
taint, let Clifford keep the estates and let me keep my little Bess.
I know who'd have the best of the bargain.

BESS It must be past twelve. Preene won't come tonight.

HAROLD No, I'm afraid not. 55

BESS Oh, Harold, if he should have got us here to have you taken
again!

HAROLD Don't think of anything half so terrible as that, Bess. Hush!
What was that? (*Clifford ascends stairs*)

BESS (*rising and going to door*) It's Preene! (*Opens door, then slams it* 60
to very suddenly) It's Clifford Armytage! (*Bolts door and stands with*
back to it)

HAROLD (*starting up*) I am caught!

BESS Harold! Harold! What will you do?

HAROLD Let them in, quick! Pretend I've escaped—throw him off the 65
scent, it's our only chance! (*Hides behind curtains—Bess opens door*)
Clifford enters—looks around

BESS Clifford Armytage!

CLIFFORD (*crosses to door L*) Yes, you didn't expect friends tonight
evidently or you wouldn't have bolted the door.

BESS (*at door R holding it open*) You are no friend of mine. What do   70
you want here?

CLIFFORD (*looking about*) I heard you were in trouble. I've found you
out and come to help you.

BESS You help me! D'ye think if I were starving and a crust could
save me, I'd take it from your hands—I'd rather die.   75

CLIFFORD What harm have I done you?

BESS (*passionately*) Such harm, that were I a man, you wouldn't ask
that question twice!

CLIFFORD I'm sorry for you; you've thrown yourself away on a
worthless blackguard.   80

BESS Coward! You have blighted and ruined his life, you have put
a stain upon his name, you have made him a hunted outcast,
but I am free and I do not fear you. This is my room and I order
you to leave it; you shall not insult my husband—and in my
presence.   85

CLIFFORD A pretty husband! A scamp who marries you and drags
you down to poverty, a felon who robs his own father, and leaves
his wife to starve.

HAROLD (*coming from behind curtains*) But not to be insulted by a
cowardly blackguard like you.   90

CLIFFORD Ah! I thought I'd have you out. (*Goes to move to door R*)

BESS (*fiercely*) Stop him, Harold! (*Harold stops him*) He has robbed
you of your inheritance—he's plotted your liberty away—he has
hunted you down and now when even a fiend might pity us, he
would betray us. All our misery we owe to him; he is in your power   95
now, thrash him within an inch of his life! (*Music*)

HAROLD Now, Clifford Armytage, it's man to man! (*Business of fight*)
*Waters has entered from R with two policemen to street
door—goes inside and shuts door*

BESS It's your life against his, Harold—if he cries out again—kill
him! (*Harold and Clifford have seized one another; Harold throws
Clifford against door L which bursts open; they both get into room.°*   100
*Clifford draws revolver, Harold snatches it from him and forces him on
his knees against door which is shut and presents revolver at his head.
Waters has rushed up the stairs to door R*)

WATERS (*shouting*) Open the door!

HAROLD If you speak one word, you're a dead man.   105

BESS (*during fight between Clifford and Harold keeps scene going,° calling
to Harold*) Hold him down, don't let him speak—they are breaking the door in! (*Bess closes door L*)

As the police break down door R, Bess crosses to door L and stands with back to it, panting. Waters bursts door R open and enters

WATERS Now then, missus! Where is he?

BESS Who?   110

WATERS Your husband.

BESS He has escaped.

WATERS Then where's the gentleman who came up here just now?

BESS (*defiantly*) I don't know!   115

WATERS What are you standing there for? Come away! (*Tries to pull her away*)

BESS (*struggling, hysterically*) I won't! You may kill me, but you shan't pass!

> *Clifford makes a plunge at revolver which goes off; Harold throws him off, opens window and jumps out. Waters throws Bess off—she shrieks*

BESS Harold, save yourself!   120

> *Clifford throws door open° and shows Waters Harold jumping out of window. Waters jumps out after him; as Harold goes to rush across to R he is met by Inspector and policeman, both of whom he knocks down. Waters then pinions him from behind. Business. Simultaneously with pistol shot, crowd outside start murmurs which gradually increase in volume. Crowd enters from all directions shouting. Policemen come on from all directions and keep crowd back. Clifford and Bess during this have entered from house, crossing room and down staircase. Clifford rushes at and seizes Harold. Bess comes to Harold, but is thrown down by Clifford. Free fight. Scene closes in.° Shouts kept up till opening of next scene*

DISPOSITION OF CHARACTERS

Crowd Police				
	Inspector Waters			
	Police Harold		Police	
	Clifford		Police	
	Bess (on ground)			
Police			Police	
Police			Police	
Police			Police	
R			L	

5.3

Interior of Police Station. Policeman wheels on desk from R for Inspector who enters RIE. Cutts enters RIE, opens dock—crosses to L. Harold and Bess dragged on through door L. Harold placed in dock. Policemen keep crowd back. Rest of police in places as marked.

DISPOSITION OF CHARACTERS

```
                               Police
     Police                              Police
          Harold
Police              Bess        Police        Police
     Inspector      Waters    Clifford      Police
                                       Cutts
   Policemen
 Crowd
 R                                           L
```

INSPECTOR (*at desk*) Keep the crowd back! Keep them back!

HAROLD (*in dock RC, Bess by him*) Courage, Bess, Seth Preene hasn't forgotten us; it is Clifford Armytage who is at the bottom of this.

BESS (*kneels to Clifford C*) Spare my husband, say you were mistaken.

HAROLD Don't kneel to him, he's a liar and a coward. Look at your   5
work, you pitiful hound. (*Furiously*)

CLIFFORD (*LC. Coolly to Inspector*) This man is violent; he should be handcuffed. (*Harold makes a movement as if to get at him—police restrain him. Row at door—Jarvis' voice heard*)

JARVIS I will come in. Here, Liza, give me into custody will you?   10
   Jarvis breaks through crowd—enters at door LC followed by Mrs Jarvis and Shakespeare

INSPECTOR Who are these people?

WATERS They're the people where this man had been hiding, sir.

INSPECTOR Let them remain; they may be important witnesses.

SHAKESPEARE I'm the best 'Witness' on the road,° ain't I, mother?

INSPECTOR Silence! Who is this man?   15

WATERS Harold Armytage—the escaped convict; he's given me a rare hunt, but I've got him this time!

INSPECTOR Who identifies him?

CLIFFORD I do.

INSPECTOR Your name?   20

CLIFFORD Clifford Armytage. I identify him as the man who committed the jewel robbery at Armytage Hall and was sentenced to seven years' penal servitude.

HAROLD It's a lie! It was a vile plot to rob me of my inheritance!

INSPECTOR Does anyone else identify him? 25

    Seth Preene enters quickly through crowd at door followed by Skeffington

SETH Yes, I do!

CLIFFORD (*alarmed*) Seth Preene!

HAROLD Seth Preene at last! (*Eagerly*) Tell them what you know, man! (*Pointing to Clifford*) Look, look at that villain's face, how white it goes! 30

SETH (*slowly*) I identify this man as Harold Armytage who was convicted of the jewel robbery and sentenced to seven years' penal servitude, but the man who committed the robbery was I—Seth Preene!

CLIFFORD (*hissing through his teeth*) You fool! 35

HAROLD Thank God! At last! At last!

BESS (*wildly to all*) You hear, my husband is innocent! You'll let him go, won't you?

SETH I held my tongue long enow. (*To Harold*) You saved my life and I swore I would save you. I stole the jewels and that man received 'em. (*Pointing to Clifford*) Now I give myself up. 40

CLIFFORD It is a lie! These men are accomplices!

INSPECTOR It is no lie, sir! You gave your name as Clifford Armytage; the stolen jewels for which a reward was offered three years ago have been found. 45

CLIFFORD Found?

CUTTS Yes, by me, at your house!

CLIFFORD (*aside*) Hetty has betrayed me! Curse her!

HAROLD Now, Clifford Armytage!

CLIFFORD (*fiercely*) Damn you! You're an escaped convict still; it's a plot between two thieves! 50

INSPECTOR It's no plot! Here are the jewels! (*Producing jewels*) They tally with the reward bill.

SETH My lass! My lass!

HAROLD It is you who were a thief's accomplice! 55

CLIFFORD (*fiercely*) It's a lie!

HAROLD (*quietly*) Hadn't the man better be handcuffed—he's violent.

CLIFFORD These jewels are mine, I have a right to them; they form part of the estate, left me by my uncle!

SETH No, they don't! The estates belong to him! (*Points to Harold*) 60

SKEFFINGTON I have the late Squire's will in my possession—it revokes the one in Clifford Armytage's favour.

SETH That was stolen with the jewels and I kept it till it was wanted.

CLIFFORD Traitor! (*Tries to get at Seth—a policeman stops him and after a short struggle he stands pale and sullen*)   65

HAROLD (*coming C*) Bess, the clouds have burst and the bright days will come at last! (*Bess comes C with him*)

BESS At last, Harold! At last!

INSPECTOR You are not free yet. You will be charged with being a convict at large.   70

SKEFFINGTON But the facts have been laid before the Home Office, and I can tell you this, that should your innocence be proved as it will be, by Preene's confession and the discovery of the jewels, you will at once be granted a free pardon.

JARVIS A free pardon for what he never done? There's poetical   75
justice° for you!

HAROLD Bess, my darling, our trials are over; in a little while I shall be free and rich—

BESS And happy! Then we'll go back to the dear old home!

HAROLD All the happier perhaps, for the trials we have passed   80
through. May our brighter days knit only closer together the love that has never wavered! (*Tableau. Curtain*)

THE MIDDLEMAN

A Play

In Four Acts

BY

HENRY ARTHUR JONES

CAST

CYRUS BLENKARN	Mr Willard
JOSEPH CHANDLER, of the Tatlow Porcelain Works	Mr Mackintosh
CAPTAIN JULIAN CHANDLER, his son	Mr Henry V. Esmond
BATTY TODD, Chandler's managing man	Mr H. Crane
JESSE PEGG	Mr E. W. Garden
SIR SETON UMFRAVILLE	Mr Ivan Watson
DANEPER, Reporter	Mr W. E. Blatchley
VACHELL	Mr Royston Keith
EPIPHANY DANKS, of Gawcott-in-the-Moors	Mr Cecil Crofton
POSTMAN	Mr T. Sydney
DUTTON	Mr Rimbault
SERVANT	Mr Hugh Harting
MARY } NANCY } Blenkarn's Daughters	{ Miss Maud Millett { Miss Annie Hughes
MRS CHANDLER	Mrs E. H. Brooke
MAUDE CHANDLER	Miss Agnes Verity
LADY UMFRAVILLE	Miss Josephine St Ange
FELICIA UMFRAVILLE	Miss Eva Moore

First performed at the Shaftesbury Theatre
27 August 1889

1.

Drawing-room at Tatlow Hall. Discover Chandler at open window left addressing crowd without. Daneper, at chair R of LC table, taking notes of speech. Sir Seton Umfraville yawning left. Lady Umfraville and Mrs Chandler on settee C. Maude and Felicia RC. Batty Todd, above table L, applauding and shouting 'Bravo' in a very enthusiastic manner. As curtain rises, great cheers are heard without L. When the cheers subside, Chandler, a smug, fat, prosperous-looking man of fifty, with the manners of an upper class commercial man, continues his speech

CHANDLER (*continuing speech with considerable hesitation*) Yes—gentlemen—as your worthy mayor has called me—a King of Commerce—ah—ra—I'm proud of the title—(*Shouts outside* 'Hear! Hear!' *Cheers continued. Todd always cheering and clapping his hands*) I'm proud of representing that great commercial spirit of the age which—ah—ra—has made England what she is today—(*Cheers outside,* 'Hear! Hear! Bravo!') Which—ah—ra—has covered her through the length and breadth of the land with—ah—ra—railways and factories and mines—and chimneys and steam-engines—and—so—on—I—ah—ra—(*gets stuck, stops*) 10

TODD (*after a short embarrassing pause*) Hear! Hear!

CHANDLER (*floundering*) I repeat—ah—ra—which—(*Looks helplessly round at Todd*)

TODD (*prompting in an undertone*) Energy—lofty business spirit.

CHANDLER (*primed*) That energy—that lofty business spirit, that 15 faculty of organization which provides labour for thousands and which—ah—ra—(*slight cheers outside and a single 'Bravo'*) whatever may be the result of next year's election, you—ah—ra—you will find plenty of light refreshments in the marquee. (*Tremendous cheering outside. Todd again very demonstrative. Chandler, looking* 20 *very much relieved comes away from window to Lady Umfraville, wipes his forehead*)

TODD (*L, comes down, prompting him*) Fireworks!

CHANDLER Yes, I forgot. (*Goes back to window—Todd returns to former position—is received with cheers, commands silence by a gesture*) 25 There will be a grand display of fireworks on the lawn this evening. (*Great cheers, repeated three times. Goes to C. Todd drops down LC.*

*Chandler comes down to Todd and Sir Seton. Chandler, very
anxiously to Todd*) Well, Todd?

TODD (*LC*) Wonderful! Eh, Sir Seton? Wonderful!   30

CHANDLER (*anxiously*) Candidly, Todd?

TODD On my honour! You know I never flatter. (*Aside to Chandler*)
I've fished up old Danks! I'll bring the old blackguard in while he's
tolerably sober. (*Exit through window L*)

> *Captain Julian Chandler enters R into conservatory, sits down
> moodily in chair next to table. Dutton follows him with brandy,
> soda and cigarettes. Chandler C talking to Lady Umfraville*

MRS CHANDLER (*seated on settee C*) Maude, darling, where is Miss   35
Blenkarn? (*Julian listens attentively*)

MAUDE (*seated up RC*) In her room, mamma.

MRS CHANDLER Couldn't she be helping the servants in the tent?

JULIAN (*listening, mutters to himself*) No, Mother, I'm hanged if she
shall. (*To Dutton*) More brandy! (*Takes spirit decanter, pours   40
himself*) You can go! (*Sit and smokes moodily. Dutton goes off R*)

> *Re-enter Todd L at window, speaks off*

TODD Come in, Mr Danks! (*Goes to Daneper*) Now Daneper, my boy!
Here's a pretty little picturesque incident going to happen! Dodge
it up° for your paper. (*Goes back to window*) Come in, Mr Danks!

> *Enter at window L Mr Epiphany Danks, a very aged rustic,
> slightly tipsy and rather deaf, Todd conducting him to Chandler*

TODD Mr Chandler, this is Mr Epiphany Danks of Gawcott-in-the-   45
Moors, the oldest man in the county. He will shortly exercise, for
the first time in his life, that franchise which the wisdom of our
legislature has conferred upon him.° (*To Daneper*) Have you got
that down? (*Daneper nods, goes on writing. Todd continues*) Such is
the fervour of his political convictions and his admiration of your   50
glorious public spirit that for the mere pleasure of shaking you by
the hand he has performed the astounding feat of walking every
step of the fifteen miles from his residence at Gawcott-in-the-
Moors. (*Todd nods direction to Daneper, who replies by nod. Todd gets
up L to Daneper. Danks crosses to Chandler*)   55

DANKS (*shaking hands with Chandler with one hand, affectionately
pawing him with the other*) Druv over in Sam Rawlins's van—me
and old Bet Turney—stopped at every blessed public° as us come
along—la! What a morning we had, to be sure! (*Beams benignantly
on Chandler*)   60

CHANDLER (*embarrassed by Danks's affection*) Very proud, Mr Danks,
to grasp your honest hand! Very proud!

TODD (*L of table, dictating to Daneper*) Mr Chandler's warm and
    tender nature was moved to tears by this touching proof of political
    devotion on the part of the patriarch of Gawcott!   65

DANKS (*still retaining Chandler's hand*) Yaller, bain't you?

CHANDLER Yes, yellow is our colour, Mr Danks.

DANKS I be yaller! (*Shouts feebly*) Yaller for ever! Damn they there
    blues, I say! (*Waving his hand in the air*) No more and no less!
    Damn 'em!   70

TODD (*dictating to Daneper*) Mr Danks, in a few terse, well-
    considered phrases, expressed the sternest condemnation of his
    political opponents.

CHANDLER (*C, to Todd*) Get him away, Todd.

TODD (*LC coming up to Danks on his L*) After your exertions you   75
    must be in need of refreshments, Mr Danks!

DANKS (*suddenly drops Chandler's hand*) Grub? Where? (*Between
    Chandler and Todd*)

TODD (*leading him to window L*) This way.

DANKS (*again insists on shaking hands with Chandler*) Well, good-bye!   80
    (*Wrings Chandler's hand*) Don't you be afraid of them 'nation
    gallows blues!° (*Reassuringly to Chandler*) *I* shall vote for 'ee. I be
    the oldest man in this here county! Born Epiphany Sunday,° annie
    domino! (*Todd gets Danks up to window L. As Danks passes Sir Seton
    he stops and wants to shake hands with him, holds out hand. Sir*   85
    Seton doesn't respond. Danks cannot understand it) Yaller, bain't you?

SIR SETON Yellow, Mr Danks, but inexpansive.

        *Chandler watches Sir Seton, shows annoyance that Sir Seton
        won't indulge Danks. Danks still holds out hand. Sir Seton
        shakes his head, but points to Todd who immediately holds out
        hands to Danks*

DANKS (*effusively to Todd*) I like you! There ain't no nasty pride
    about you! You be yaller! So be I. (*Glares viciously at Sir Seton,
    shouts feebly*) Yaller for ever! Hurray! Well done our side!   90

        *Todd gets him off at window L and returns, dictating to Daneper
        who is writing throughout*

TODD (*L of table*) The rustic Nestor,° after a truly remarkable display
    of political sagacity, then took his departure.

FELICIA (*seated up RC*) What a charming circle of friends a par-
    liamentary candidate gathers round him, Mr Chandler!

CHANDLER My dear Miss Umfraville, for the good of my country,   95
    there is no sacrifice too great for me! (*Going up to Felicia RC. Mrs
    Chandler and Lady Umfraville rise, go down to Sir Seton L*)

Music. Waltz. Enter Mary into conservatory, gets behind Julian's chair, speaks to him in a low tone. She is on his L

MARY You must go?

JULIAN (*without looking up, same tone, speaks in front of him*) Yes, by the night mail.

MARY (*showing great disappointment, steadies herself, speaks in a low, earnest tone*) I *must* see you before you leave. (*Julian looks up*) Hush! (*Passes on into drawing-room, gets to RC of settee*)

MRS CHANDLER Miss Blenkarn, I'm surprised you haven't employed yourself in the marquee! (*Julian rises angrily and comes to drawing-room door*) The servants have so much to do on a day like this—

JULIAN (*R in doorway of conservatory*) How does what the servants have to do concern Miss Blenkarn?

Maude and the Umfravilles all show embarrassment

MRS CHANDLER I think it very inconsiderate, Julian, of a young person in Miss Blenkarn's position—

JULIAN (*interrupting*) Miss Blenkarn's position in this house is companion to my sister, and considering the obligations we are under to her father—

CHANDLER (*C very much upset, interrupts*) Obligations! What obligations? (*Comes down to back of settee*)

JULIAN Why, you know, father, it was his invention that made your fortune.

CHANDLER (*terribly upset*) What! What on earth will get into your head next? (*Julian is about to speak*) Hold your tongue, sir! (*Goes up stage. Chandler goes up stage to R of C opening and crosses to Daneper and Todd L*)

JULIAN Sir!

MARY Captain Chandler, please say no more! I will go and help. (*Going up C*)

JULIAN (*R*) No. (*Mary stops*) Not unless the others go too, Maude!

MAUDE (*very pleasantly, rises*) Very well, Julian, I'm ready to do anything. Pour out anybody's tea, kiss anybody's baby, anything to advance the political education of the nation! Let's all go! It will be rather jolly. Come along! Now, Mary! (*Takes Mary's arm. Mary throws a grateful look at Julian and exit with Maude at back C to L. Felicia rises, comes to back of settee. Chandler is with Todd*)

MRS CHANDLER (*crosses to C*) Really, Julian, if you hadn't been leaving us today for ever so long, I should be very angry with you!

(*Exeunt Mrs Chandler and Lady Umfraville at back C to L. Chandler*   135
is meantime conferring with Daneper and Todd. Sir Seton is occupied
with paper)

FELICIA Won't you come with us, Julian? (*Going up and looking back*)

JULIAN (*indifferently*) Yes—if you like. (*Going to her*)

FELICIA You're not a very amiable lover, considering I'm going to   140
lose you for months, perhaps years, and that you may get lost or
killed in Africa! (*Exeunt Julian and Felicia at back C to L. Exeunt*
Todd and Daneper to R conferring about proofs)

CHANDLER (*comes down to Sir Seton*) Sir Seton—(*Sir Seton puts down*
paper) it would be of immense advantage to my candidature if you   145
were to—to—a—to—a mix a little with my guests.

SIR SETON (*seated L*) Should be delighted, Chandler, but leap-frog
and skittles are rather out of my way.

CHANDLER A little cordiality, a little friendly intercourse—with such
persons as Danks, for instance, goes a great way.   150

SIR SETON (*rises*) It does with me. (*Crosses to C and up*)

CHANDLER (*following a little*) And now Julian and Miss Umfraville
are engaged—and you promised—

SIR SETON (*C, a little angry; controls himself. Turns to Chandler*) My
dear Chandler, let us understand one another. You're rich—I'm   155
poor! I've had to turn out of Tatlow Hall. You've turned into it.
I've only one child and I want to spare her the continual struggle
with genteel poverty that her mother and I have gone through.
And naturally I want the old place to be hers. You agree to settle
so much upon her the day your son marries her, and I shall use   160
my influence amongst my county friends to get you into Parliament. There our agreement ends, (*going C*) and as for playing
skittles with Mr Danks—excuse my plain speaking—I'll see your
election damned first!

CHANDLER (*cordially*) Oh, quite so! Quite so!   165

Exit Sir Seton, at back C to L

CHANDLER (*aside*) If I could only get into Parliament without him!
(*Music stops. Chandler goes L of settee C*)

Enter Todd from conservatory R

TODD Oh, by the way, sir! Have you looked through the proofs of
the interview for Saturday's *County Herald*?

CHANDLER (*in front of settee; pulls proof from pocket*) Yes, here they   170
are. Not up to your usual form, Todd. (*Sits C*)

TODD What's wrong?

CHANDLER I think you might make a great deal more of my philanthropy. You've said nothing about my building the new congregational chapel at Little Hoggesdon.   175

TODD (*R*) Yes, but now you've joined the Church—

CHANDLER I take a very broad view of these matters. You might mention that!

TODD (*taking notes*) Very well. Profoundly sincere religious convictions, but no narrow bigotry.   180

CHANDLER That's it. By the way, about that subscription to the Wesleyan Sunday Schools—I should think a ten pound note, eh?

TODD You gave twenty to the Baptists. All the fat will be in the fire if you don't treat 'em both alike.

CHANDLER Very well, twenty then. I wish there weren't quite so   185
many sects. It gives one a very poor opinion of religion.

TODD When you've got to subscribe to them all, it does. But you can't get into Parliament without it.

CHANDLER (*running over proofs*) 'Great business energy.' That's all right! 'Paternal care of work people, not a man, woman or child in   190
the Tatlow Porcelain works who wouldn't gladly lay down his life for Joseph Chandler.' That's very good indeed, Todd—'Most affectionate husband and father—sacred shrine of domestic happiness—'

TODD That always goes down with the British public.   195

CHANDLER Just so. (*Reads*) 'Under his fostering care, the Tatlow Porcelain works have grown from a mere hovel to cover two acres of ground and to afford employment for five hundred hands. The discovery some twenty years ago of a peculiar process of glazing by an ingenious workman named Cyrus Blenkarn—' (*Stops, an-*   200
noyed) What's the object in mentioning Blenkarn's name?

TODD Well, as the fact of his invention is so well known—

CHANDLER Well known! Of course, it's well known, so what's the good of mentioning it? Where would his invention have been if it hadn't been for my capital and business energy in working it?   205
Besides, I paid him for it, two hundred pounds. And look how good I've been to him ever since—always advanced him money on his wages to fool away on his crack-brained inventions that never came to anything. No! It's not necessary to mention Blenkarn. (*Rises*) He shares in the glory of belonging to the works.   210
That ought to be enough for him. (*Crosses to L and sits at writing table*)

Julian enters from back, comes LC

TODD Very well, I'll alter that paragraph. (*To Daneper, who enters from conservatory R and comes into drawing-room R of Todd*) All right, Daneper! (*R*) I'll bring round the proofs tonight. (*Daneper is going towards LC table*) By the way, Daneper, (*seeing Julian*) I could give you a few notes about Captain Chandler. They might be of use to your editor. (*To Chandler*) Eh, sir?   215

CHANDLER Certainly. (*Goes L to chair and sits*)

> Daneper comes to Todd, corner of settee, takes note-book and pencil. Julian listens with growing anger

TODD (*dictating*) Our local hero, Captain Chandler, having covered himself with glory in the last Egyptian campaign,° is again about to visit Africa. He has nobly volunteered to accompany the relief expedition in search of the renowned African traveller, Sir George Hinchinbrook. The deadly perils of the Central African desert—   220

JULIAN (*comes down C to Daneper and Todd*) Stop that confounded flummery, Todd. I'll give you the particulars myself. (*Daneper turns to Julian, who dictates*) Captain Julian Chandler, having got himself into a devil of a mess at College and in the Service and being dunned by all the Jews in Christendom,° (*Todd goes up R to LC at back*) has been obliged to accept his father's offer to pay off his debts on condition of his settling down and becoming respectable—   230

CHANDLER (*L, interrupting*) Julian! This is scandalous!

JULIAN (*taking no notice of Chandler*) But not wishing to tie himself up at present, he was jolly glad to get the chance to cut away to Africa.   235

CHANDLER (*fuming*) Julian! (*Rising*)

JULIAN The Tatlow brass band accompanied Captain Chandler to the railway station, and played a selection of the liveliest airs, to testify their delight at the prospect of there being one blackguard the less in the county. Put that down, Daneper, and let them know the truth about me! (*Crosses in front of settee and exit R and through conservatory*)   240

CHANDLER (*upset, fuming*) Really, this is monstrous! I never heard— (*Crosses to R following Julian. Daneper crosses to table L*)   245

TODD (*comes down LC*) Never mind, sir. I'll put that all right. (*To Daneper*) That's all right, Daneper. Tell Mr Snoad I'll call at the office by-and-bye and bring him all particulars myself.

DANEPER (*L*) Very well, sir, good-day. Good-day, Mr Chandler. (*Takes up notes from table, puts them in pocket and exit at window*)   250

TODD (*C, soothing Chandler*) Don't trouble, sir. I'll see the *Herald* has it corrected. (*Chandler anxiously sits C*)

CHANDLER Thank you, Todd. You think my speech made a good impression? (*Todd LC*)   255

TODD Excellent! Magnificent! Wonderful!

CHANDLER (*seated, seizes Todd's hand; wrings it effusively*) I never met a man with a stronger natural judgement than yours, Todd! You never mind telling me the truth candidly and fearlessly!

TODD Why not? What object is there in telling lies? By the way, sir,   260 when you get into Parliament, you will allow me to help you in your parliamentary duties?

CHANDLER Naturally, Todd, naturally. Statistics always bother me, Todd. Now you're very good at statistics.

TODD Don't you trouble about statistics. You let me know what you   265 want to prove, and I'll guarantee the statistics shall be all right.

CHANDLER Thank you, Todd.

TODD And I suppose I shall continue the management of the Tatlow works as well.

CHANDLER Of course, Todd. (*Rises*) Of course. (*Going up C*)   270

TODD And perhaps at some future time you will admit me to a partnership. (*Following*)

CHANDLER (*C, turns on Todd. Aghast*) Partnership, Todd? (*Very much upset*) Really, you surprise me—just as I had taken you into my confidence in everything. It's too bad, Todd. It's encroaching   275 on my good nature! You have the honour of belonging to the works. You share in the glory that attaches to the name of Joseph Chandler. I think that ought to be sufficient.

TODD (*humbly*) Very well, sir. I'll say no more.

CHANDLER No, don't, there's a good fellow. Go and see that   280 everybody's attended to. I shall be out amongst them soon. (*Exit C and L*)

TODD Ah, that's gratitude, that is! Where would Joseph Chandler have been if Batty Todd hadn't worked him? (*Exit at window L. Music.*)   285

    Re-enter Chandler, Maude and Felicia at back C and L from garden

CHANDLER (*brisk, oily, polite, to Felicia, coming down C*) Well, how are all our friends enjoying themselves?

MAUDE (*at back of settee*) All the old people have gravitated to tea, and all the young to kiss-in-the-ring!° (*Goes to door of conservatory*)

CHANDLER Well, so long as they are satisfied. (*Coming down LC*)   290

FELICIA Don't you think kiss-in-the-ring is somewhat too satisfying? I speak from observation, not from experience. (*Sitting C*)

CHANDLER (*C*) Oh, quite so! Quite so!

   Enter Lady Umfraville and Mrs Chandler, at back C and L from garden

LADY UMFRAVILLE (*coming down L*) Well, I'm disappointed! It seems this wonderful man is not here!   295

CHANDLER (*LC. Mrs Chandler joins Felicia C and sits R on settee*) What wonderful man?

LADY UMFRAVILLE (*L of Chandler*) This workman of yours who made that lovely dinner service you gave us!

CHANDLER (*contemptuously*) Oh, Blenkarn!   300

LADY UMFRAVILLE (*sits L*) Yes, I must see him! I'm sure he's quite a genius! I adore genius!

CHANDLER (*LC, nettled*) Genius! I don't call a mere inventor a genius, Lady Umfraville!

LADY UMFRAVILLE No? What's your idea of a genius then, Mr   305 Chandler?

CHANDLER My idea of a genius is—a—ah—a—practical man, a man who doesn't invent anything himself, but has the insight, and courage, and shrewdness to see the value of another man's invention, and the energy to secure it and work it: a man who, by sheer   310 force of business enterprise, raises himself to the position of a great public benefactor and provides labour for thousands of his fellow creatures. (*Getting eloquent*) That's the type of genius that I admire, and that's the type of genius that suits our modern civilization!

LADY UMFRAVILLE And the only type of genius that seems to   315 flourish in it! (*Felicia and Mrs Chandler rise and join Maude R*)

FELICIA What's your idea of a genius, Maude?

MAUDE (*at doorway R*) I never saw one! I shouldn't know one if I did.

   Enter Cyrus Blenkarn, at back C from R, in shirt sleeves, with no coat; hair long and untidy: a keen, pale, thin man, with bent form, sharp features, restless, absent, distracted manner. He stands a moment or two at doorway, looking for someone. Seeing Chandler, he comes eagerly down to him

CYRUS Mr Chandler, could you give me an order° for the iron fittings for my new kiln? (*C*)   320

CHANDLER Really, Blenkarn, this is very unceremonious! (*LC*) How do you expect people to trust you when you are always throwing your money away in useless experiments? How much will the fittings come to?

CYRUS I'm afraid they'll come to nearly twenty pounds, sir.   325

CHANDLER Can't you manage with ten?

CYRUS I'll try to make it do, if you'll leave the order open.

CHANDLER No, no. Todd will give you an order for fifteen tomorrow. (*Turning to Lady Umfraville*)

CYRUS But I want to start today. I can't afford to waste any more   330
time. I've wasted so many years already. Can't I have it today?

CHANDLER My dear good man, you can surely wait till tomorrow
before you begin to squander my money. (*Turns up stage to window.
Cyrus is going up C*)

LADY UMFRAVILLE (*seated L*) Ah, Mr Blenkarn! That lovely dinner   335
service Mr Chandler gave us was your workmanship, wasn't it?
(*Cyrus assents*) I'm glad you put your own mark on it!

CHANDLER (*L, shows annoyance*) Ah—ra—Blenkarn—ah—ra (*comes
down to Cyrus, LC*) I think that's rather an absurd practice of
yours, putting your own private mark on your best pieces. It's not   340
necessary—not necessary—I wouldn't do it again if I were you.

CYRUS Very well, sir. (*His face falls; he shows intense disappointment.
Turns up C. Music stops.*)
        Todd enters at window L

TODD The balloon's going up! (*Todd and Chandler get up L. Cyrus
up C*)   345

MAUDE Oh, we must see the balloon. Come along everybody. (*Crosses
up C. To Felicia*) Where has Julian got to? (*Maude and Felicia get
C. Mrs Chandler at back of settee*)

FELICIA I don't know. (*Joins Maude*) He can't expect me to be
always running after him.   350

MAUDE When I have a lover, I shall expect him to be always
running after *me*, and he may think himself lucky if he catches me!
(*Exeunt Maude and Felicia at window L. Mrs Chandler joins Lady
Umfraville at window L. Todd and Chandler have been talking at
window L.*)   355

CYRUS (*C, catching sight of Todd*) Mr Todd, could you please let me
have an order for some iron fittings?

CHANDLER (*interrupting, taking Cyrus away to R. Mrs Chandler and
Lady Umfraville at window to see balloon*) Can't you see Mr Todd
is busy upon my parliamentary business today? (*Softening*) Come,   360
go and fetch your coat and enjoy yourself for once. There's a
balloon and fireworks, and I daresay I may make another speech.
Enjoy yourself, my good man! Enjoy yourself! (*Exit at window L,
followed by Todd*)

Cyrus R, stands absorbed, disappointed. Nancy appears at back C from R

NANCY May I come in please, Mrs Chandler?   365

MRS CHANDLER Certainly, (*advancing a little to C*) but you really ought to teach your father to take care of himself. (*Lady Umfraville gets to window with Mrs Chandler*) Make him a little more presentable, if he's going to stay. (*Aside to Lady Umfraville*) Mr Chandler allows these Blenkarns to take the strangest liberties.   370 (*Exeunt Mrs Chandler and Lady Umfraville at window L*)

Nancy comes down R to Cyrus, who has stood baffled, listless, disappointed, hearing nothing of above conversation. As he is crossing to window L she takes him by the shoulders, and shakes him vigorously

CYRUS (*C, turning*) Eh? Oh, Nancy!

NANCY Where's your hat? Where's your coat? (*Cyrus rouses himself from his abstraction by an effort*)

CYRUS Coat?   375

NANCY Where did you take it off? Think!

CYRUS (*thinks. After a pause*) I don't think I put it on, Nancy.

NANCY Where did you wear it last?

CYRUS (*after a pause*) I wore it to church last Sunday. Didn't I?

NANCY (*with a gesture of despair*) How could you come to Mr   380 Chandler's in such a state?

CYRUS (*innocently*) What state?

NANCY Look at yourself. (*Pointing to his clothes*)

CYRUS (*looks himself up and down*) Yes, it does look rather shabby, but—it isn't Sunday today, you know.   385

NANCY You told me you weren't coming to the garden party.

CYRUS I haven't come to the garden party. I came to get an order on Mr Woolaston. (*Suddenly starting off*) I wonder if Mr Woolaston— (*going L*)

NANCY Listen! (*Catches him by the arm and pulls him back*) Now you   390 are here, you're going to stay and enjoy yourself with me and Mary. (*At mention of Mary's name, Cyrus' face lights up with great animation and joy*)

CYRUS Mary! Where is she? Why don't you bring her to me?

NANCY You shall see her directly if you behave yourself. (*Looks all   395 round*) There's nobody about! Sit down. (*Pushes him into seat C*) Let me make you tidy! (*She goes round to back of settee, takes out small brush and comb from pocket and begins to comb his hair*) Did you have your dinner?

CYRUS Dinner?   400

NANCY Yes, I left it in the oven!

CYRUS Did you? Then why didn't you tell me so?

NANCY I told you so four times and showed it to you baking.

CYRUS Did you? Then I suppose I must have had it! Yes, I
remember now. I did have it. It was delicious. I'm very fond of   405
Irish stew.

NANCY Irish stew! Why, it was veal pie. (*Gives a pull at his hair which
makes him jump*)

CYRUS Was it? I thought it was Irish stew!

> *Jesse Pegg enters at window L, a young workman dressed in his
> Sunday best, with hair carefully pomatumed° into a triangle
> three inches high in front. Knowing he is intruding, he stands at
> window a moment or two before he ventures to whisper*

JESSE Miss Nancy! Miss Nancy!   410

NANCY (*curtly*) Well?

JESSE (*comes in, treading very gingerly on carpet*) The balloon's just
going up! I've saved you such a splendid place, close to me. (*LC*)

NANCY How horrid of you!

JESSE (*with desperate earnestness*) Do come along.   415

NANCY I can't. If you're not busy you might—

JESSE (*eagerly*) Anything! Anything! If it's for *you*.

NANCY It isn't for me, it's for him. Run home and look all over the
house and all over the works till you find his hat and coat and
necktie, and bring them all here. You'll find me somewhere about   420
when you come back. See how quick you can be.

JESSE All right, I'm off. (*Going up C*)

NANCY Oh, Mr Pegg! (*Jesse stops C*) You'll find a veal pie in the
oven. I wish you'd take it out.

JESSE For *you*! If it's for you.   425

NANCY Certainly. It's for my supper tonight, if it isn't burnt to a
cinder.

JESSE Thank you! Thank you! I'm so proud to be allowed to run on
your errands. (*Runs off at back C to R*)

NANCY (*aside*) To think that little me should make such a fool of   430
such a sensible fellow as Jesse Pegg. (*Cyrus is leaning forward
absorbed in thought. Nancy takes him by the shoulders, pulls him back
in his seat and begins combing his hair*)

CYRUS If they could make tht china a hundred and twenty years ago,
why can't it be made today, Nancy?   435

NANCY Hold your head still!

CYRUS (*getting excited*) You believe it's to be done, don't you?

NANCY Yes, if you only keep quiet.

CYRUS I'm sure of it! (*Getting excited, wagging his head to and fro*) All the old receipts° are wrong—I've tried them all. I tell you this, Nancy—(*starts up violently. Nancy has hold of his hair*) 440

NANCY Will you sit down? (*Puts him into settee again*)

CYRUS (*sits down submissively*) Shall you be long, Nancy?

NANCY Two minutes if you keep still. Half an hour if you don't.

CYRUS (*schooling himself, sits very quiet for two or three seconds, then plaintively*) It's very kind of you, Nancy, but you comb my hair too much. You do nothing all day long but comb and make me tidy! 445

NANCY (*at R corner of settee*) That's the reason you're such a dandy!

    Enter Mary at window L

MARY (*comes down very gently*) Father! (*Going to him, L of settee*)

CYRUS (*his manner changes to intense delight*) Mary, my dear! I haven't seen you for nearly a fortnight. You're quite well, my dear? (*Kisses, still seated*) 450

MARY Yes, quite well.

CYRUS (*looking anxiously at her*) You're looking pale and worried—eh, Nancy? 455

MARY No, no, it's nothing! I'm quite well! Let's talk about yourself. Tell me how you're getting on with your work. How have the new vases turned out?

CYRUS Spoilt! They wouldn't stand the firing!

MARY Never mind. Every failure brings you nearer to success. 460

CYRUS (*very much touched, gently takes her hand and covers it with kisses*) God bless my Mary! You're always kind to me! There's nobody in the world understands me but you, dear! (*Kissing her hand. Mary withdraws it with a pained expression*)

    Jesse Pegg enters at back C from R with Cyrus' coat, hat, necktie. He is panting, breathless, exhausted, sits in chair L, holds out coat, etc., helplessly to Nancy, panting

NANCY What's the matter? (*Crossing behind settee to him, LC*) 465

JESSE (*hand on heart, breathless*) I've brought—hat—coat—all—(*drops the things helplessly into her hands. She takes them*)

NANCY What made you run so fast?

JESSE (*with a look of reproach*) You commanded me—to make haste.

NANCY (*Mary fastens Cyrus' wristband*) I didn't tell you to bring on an apoplectic fit! Here, Mary! (*Giving clothes to Mary, who takes them*) Make haste! (*Looking out of window*) They're all watching the balloon—you'll have time to finish him before they come back. 470

Mary takes things, gets round to R of Cyrus, puts them on settee, helps Cyrus to rise, ties his necktie, makes him generally comfortable and tidy. Jesse has sat panting, slowly recovering

NANCY (*returns to him*) Oh you stupid!

JESSE I did it for you, and you reproach me! (*Rising*) I wish I was 475 dead.

NANCY Well, don't run yourself to death on my errands. Make it a case of felo-de-se.° (*Goes to window L*)

JESSE (*looks at her ferociously for a moment, then goes determinedly to Cyrus LC, holds out his hand*) Good-bye Mr Blenkarn! 480

CYRUS (*surprised*) Good-bye, Jesse?

JESSE I can't endure it any longer. Her scorn drives me mad. Good-bye.

CYRUS But I can't spare you, Jesse. You're the best workman I ever had. Where are you going? (*Nancy leans over back of chair L*) 485

JESSE I don't know whether I shall commit suicide or go to Australia. (*Affected*) You'll think of me sometimes, Mr Blenkarn—and there's that bit of Brussels carpet° I bought for her—you can keep that—and if anything does happen to me—let her look at that carpet, and remember that Jesse Pegg would have used his heart's 490 best blood to dye its crimson pattern if she had only asked him! Good-bye. (*Going up C*)

NANCY (*L, calling him*) Mr Pegg! (*Jesse stops*) If it wouldn't trouble you, I should like to see the sack race. (*Goes up a little to corner of table*) 495

JESSE Trouble! Trouble! (*Coming down to her*) I'll get you a place. Where would you like to sit? (*Snatching at her hand*)

NANCY In some place where you can't possibly get a chance of squeezing my hand. (*Drags her hand away and runs off at window L. Jesse follows. Cyrus sits on settee C. Mary kneels on his R*) 500

MARY (*RC, having finished toilet operations, fondling him*) Father, wouldn't you like me to come back home and live with you always?

CYRUS Of course I should, for my own sake—but we must think of your future!

MARY My future! (*With a look of shame and pain which Cyrus does not 505 see*)

CYRUS Yes, dear! (*Arm round her neck*) You see I'm a careless, thoughtless old fellow, and all the money I get goes somewhere. I don't know where it goes, but it does go somewhere, doesn't it?

MARY (*caressing him*) Dear father, I'm glad you don't like money. 510

CYRUS Oh, but I do like it! I'm very fond of it! I should like to be very rich; then I could carry on all my experiments: but I'm afraid I shall always be poor.

MARY Never mind. God can't think much of money. Look at the people he gives a lot to!   515

CYRUS (*musing*) It doesn't matter for myself and Nancy—we shall always be able to shift for ourselves, but—you're not like us. Ah, you don't know how proud I am of you, dear! And you're in your right place here amongst great people! I want you to stay here always. I want to think when I'm at home, 'Mary's safe—whatever   520 happens to me, she's provided for. She's a lady, and some day perhaps some great man will see her and fall in love with her.'

MARY No, no, father! There's no fear of that!

CYRUS Eh?

MARY I mean—you're a very foolish old fellow to put such fancies   525 into my head! You mustn't be proud of me any more—never any more (*rises and gets to R*)—you'll break my heart.

CYRUS Why, Mary my dear, what's this?

MARY I mean you'll make me vain. Don't talk any more about me. Tell me about your work. (*Comes to him*) How are you getting on   530 with your new kiln? (*Sits on settee on his R*)

>   *Julian enters C from R*

CYRUS (*Music. Schottische*°) Stopped! I wanted to work at it today, but Mr Todd was too busy to let me have the order for the fittings, and I've got no money to buy them!

JULIAN (*coming down LC*) How much do you want, Mr Blenkarn?   535

CYRUS Oh, Captain Chandler, sir. How do you do, sir? (*Rises, takes hat from settee as he does so. Mary rises. She has shown slight confusion and alarm at Julian's voice*)

JULIAN How much do you want?

CYRUS For the fittings, sir? I'm afraid they'll come to nearly twenty   540 pounds. (*Julian takes out note-case*)

MARY (*R*) No—Captain Chandler—please not—it wouldn't be right for my father to take money from you!

JULIAN Why not? All our money came from your father's invention. We owe him more than we shall ever pay him! Here, Mr Blenkarn.   545 (*Giving notes*)

CYRUS (*takes them; shows them to Mary*) Thank you! Thank you!

JULIAN Don't thank me! I wish I could make it more, but I'm not very flush myself—(*goes a little to L*)

CYRUS Then I ought not to take this—(*offering it back to Julian*)   550

JULIAN Yes—yes—take it. You ought to be at the head of the firm, instead of working for us. Besides, I shall get plenty out of the governor before I start.

CYRUS Oh, well, then you'll excuse me (*thrusts notes in side pocket of coat*)—I'm so much obliged, so much obliged. (*Is going off C*)   555

MARY (*RC*) Father, where are you going?

CYRUS To Mr Woolaston's to buy the fittings. Good-bye, dear. (*Going*)

MARY But Mr Woolaston is here at the garden party. He has shut up his shop for today. (*Going up to him*)   560

CYRUS Has he? Then he must open it again. I can't have my kiln stopped for a garden party. (*Crosses to L, taking money from pocket again*) Thank you, Captain Chandler—it's so kind of you, so kind. You'll excuse me. I must go—I want to get these fittings. Thank you! Thank you! So kind! (*Shakes hands with Julian, going off at*   565 *window L with great animation*)

MARY You shouldn't have given him that money!

JULIAN Why not?

MARY Can't you see—it seems like—(*stops ashamed*) Julian, how can I ask you? You must marry Miss Umfraville!   570

JULIAN Marry her? No! I mean to get out of it some way or the other! (*crosses to R then back to C and sits C*) I hope to heaven I shall get my quietus° out in Africa, and there'll be an end of me!

MARY (*on his L*) Hush! You mustn't talk like this.

JULIAN How should I talk? I've acted like a blackguard and a   575 scoundrel. And you've been such a brick to me, Mary, as staunch as steel, as true as gold! What must you think of me?

MARY I forgive you, Julian!

JULIAN Don't forgive me! Hate me and despise me! I hate and despise myself!   580

MARY No—no—Julian, you love me still. (*Embrace*)

JULIAN Love you! You know I do! You know I'd marry you tomorrow if I dared.

MARY If you dared.

JULIAN How can I? With nothing but beggary to offer you. And   585 to take you out to that cursed climate to die with me. No! I've brought enough misery on you—I won't wrong you any more.

MARY Oh, Julian, (*goes L*) what can I do? What can I do?

JULIAN Stay here, Mary. If I live and come back to England, (*enter   590 Chandler at back C from L*) you shall be my wife. If I die, as I hope

I may—well! I shall know you are safe and happy. Maude's fond
of you, and you will always have a home here. If there's one thing
I'm thankful for, it is that your secret will never be known.

MARY (*LC*) Julian, (*looks at him*) it must be known. (*Drops her eyes*)   595

JULIAN (*shows surprise and fear, then bursts out—rises*) Oh, what a
scoundrel I've been! What a coward and a fool I was to let my
father gull me into this marriage. (*With great tenderness, going to
her, puts his arms round her*) Mary!

> Chandler comes forward C to back of couch. They both show
> surprise and consternation, and fall apart. Mary shows intense
> shame

CHANDLER (*C, looks from one to the other*) Miss Blenkarn, Mrs   600
Chandler is asking for you. (*Mary stands speechless and overwhelmed*) Do you hear, madam? Mrs Chandler is waiting. (*Mary
slowly exits C to L. Chandler turns to Julian, sternly*) What's the
meaning of this?

JULIAN (*R, summoning courage*) It means I've been a blackguard!   605

CHANDLER (*RC*) What! You don't mean to say there's any chance of
a public scandal?

JULIAN No, there shall be no public scandal if I can stop it!

CHANDLER Stop it! You must stop it! You know what these Tatlow
people are. If this affair gets wind, it will lose me hundreds of   610
votes. (*Music stops*) Come now, what do you mean to do?

JULIAN (*calmly*) I mean to marry Miss Blenkarn.

CHANDLER What!

JULIAN Look here, sir, I've been a fool. Don't force me to be a
coward as well!   615

CHANDLER I shall force you to keep your word to Miss Umfraville.

JULIAN You will?

CHANDLER I shall. Sir Seton's influence is necessary to me. If you
break off your engagement with his daughter, he will withdraw his
support.   620

JULIAN But, father—

CHANDLER I shall not argue the point with you, Julian. Come, the
time's short. What do you say?

JULIAN (*R, firmly*) I shall marry Miss Blenkarn.

CHANDLER (*C*) Very well, sir. Then I shall not pay a farthing of your   625
debts; I shall publicly disown you for my son and when you leave
this house today, you'll never return. Do you hear, sir? So pack
up, and be gone. (*Rings bell up L above window*)

JULIAN Very well.

CHANDLER And when you and your precious madam are starving   630
together, (*going to him R*) you'll think what a fool you were not to
accept my offer of a comfortable provision for her! (*Cyrus enters
out of breath, L*)

JULIAN (*seeing Cyrus*) Hush!

CYRUS I can't find Mr Woolaston anywhere. Have you seen him, sir?   635

CHANDLER No, Blenkarn, no.

CYRUS They told me he had gone into the house too. (*Cyrus goes up
LC and leans on chair for a moment, then up C opening looking for
Woolaston*)

CHANDLER (*to Julian*) You'd better think it over, young man.   640
(*Softening, drawing Julian down stage*) Come, Julian, I don't want
to be hard on you for this bit of boyish folly. But be reasonable.
You must see that if you split with the Umfravilles just now, it
will ruin all my hopes, destroy my honourable ambition.

JULIAN (*indicating Cyrus*) But his hopes—*his* ambition for Mary—her   645
life, poor girl! (*Exit Cyrus C and R as if he had seen some one*)

CHANDLER I'll take every care of her, I promise you. Don't break
your engagement now, Julian. I wouldn't mind it in a year's time,
when once I'm safe in Parliament. Come, you'll let things stay as
they are.   650

JULIAN (*excited and raising voice*) I can't—it's cowardly—it's black-
guardly!

    Cyrus re-enters

CHANDLER Hush! (*Looks round*) Then you'll marry her and bring
her to beggary. Mind, I'm determined.

JULIAN (*after a pause*) If I do nothing to break with the Umfravilles   655
for a year, will you pay off my debts and give me the two thousand
you promised?

CHANDLER Certainly, I will. I—

CYRUS (*comes down C*) Mr Chandler, would you let one of the men—

CHANDLER (*RC, irritated*) What is it, Blenkarn, what is it? (*Takes*   660
him to window L)

CYRUS Why, it's Woolaston—

CHANDLER (*impatiently*) Yes, yes, anything you please! Send one of
the men—

CYRUS Thank you, sir. (*Going off*) Here, Tom, Mr Chandler says—   665
(*Voice dies away as he exits at L window*)

CHANDLER (*to Julian*) Well? Yes or no?

    Servant enters C from R

JULIAN (*R*) We'll let things stay as they are.

CHANDLER A very sensible decision. (*Shakes hands*)
> *Enter Todd, window L, Mary appears at back C from L*

SERVANT (*down C*) You rang, sir?   670

CHANDLER (*RC*) Yes, let Mrs Chandler and the family know that Captain Chandler has received an urgent telegram from London. He will leave by the five o'clock up express, instead of the night mail.

JULIAN What?   675

CHANDLER (*to Servant*) Tell Williams to have everything ready. (*Exit Servant through window L*)

JULIAN There is no need for me to leave before the mail.

CHANDLER (*after a look at Mary, determinedly*) I think there is.

TODD What's this? Captain Chandler going at once? I must wake up   680
the brass band and get some men to take your horses out of the carriage and draw you to the station, eh, sir?

CHANDLER By all means! By all means! (*Going back to settee. Todd exits hurriedly at window L*)
> *Enter Maude, Mrs Chandler, Felicia, Lady Umfraville and Sir Seton*

MAUDE (*to Julian*) Julian, is this true? Are you obliged to go this   685
afternoon?

MRS CHANDLER (*to Julian*) Must you go, Julian?

CHANDLER (*comes down between Lady Umfraville and Felicia*) Yes, he is urgently required in London tonight. Miss Umfraville, there is only just time to bid him good-bye.   690

JULIAN Our adieux have already been said. Have they not? (*Crosses to Felicia*)

FELICIA Yes, I suppose so. (*Takes off a flower she has been wearing*) There's a keepsake for you.

JULIAN Good-bye. I'm not good enough for you, Felicia.   695
> *Re-enter Todd at window L. Sir Seton drops down L. Julian embraces Mrs Chandler and then Maude*

TODD (*at window, to crowd outside*) Now then! Three cheers for Captain Chandler! Hip! Hip! Hurrah!
> *Crowd cheer, band strikes up march in distance, getting nearer and nearer till curtain. Dutton enters with Julian's hat, coat, gloves, etc. Cyrus enters L, crosses behind to R. Talks to Todd for a moment, then goes toward C opening, trying as he does so to attract Mary's attention*

JULIAN Now, Dutton, look sharp! (*Dutton hands him hat, etc.*)

MARY (*aside*) Will he go without a word?

Julian is saying good-bye all round, embraces his mother, sister

JULIAN Good-bye Maude! Mother! Felicia! (*Crosses to Sir Seton. All*   700
follow) Good-bye, Sir Seton. I leave Felicia in your care. If
anything happens to me—

CHANDLER (*LC, looking out of window*) The carriage is ready, Julian.
You haven't a moment to waste. (*Dutton exits at conservatory R*)

JULIAN (*to Mary*) Good-bye, Miss Blenkarn. (*Looks round to see if he*   705
*is unobserved. Cyrus comes down RC. Then Julian turns to her and
says furtively*) Mary, I—(*sees Cyrus, stops*)

MARY (*nerves herself with great fortitude*) Good-bye, Captain Chandler! I hope you will—I—I—I—(*breaks down, almost fainting, her
father catches her in his arms*)   710

CYRUS (*RC*) Mary, what is it? Mary—

JULIAN Miss Blenkarn!

CHANDLER (*comes from window to C, touches him on the shoulder*)
Come, sir, come! Time presses!

JULIAN But Miss Blenkarn is ill—   715

CYRUS Yes, she's—

MARY (*with desperate effort recovers herself*) No—no—I'm quite well.
(*In a firm, determined, cheerful voice*) I hope you will have a pleasant
journey, Captain Chandler. Good-bye. (*Stands calm and motionless
throughout, betrays no emotion*)   720

JULIAN Good-bye. Good-bye, Mr Blenkarn. (*Offers hand to Cyrus*)

CYRUS Good-bye, Captain Chandler! (*Grasping his hand*) Good-bye.
Thank you! Thank you! I shall get to work tonight. Your kind
present. God bless you! God bless you. (*He wrings Julian's hand.
Julian hastily withdraws it and rushes off. Band very loud*)   725

CURTAIN

*Picture.° Julian gone. All looking off at window. Ladies waving
handkerchiefs, with the exception of Mary who is standing in
conservatory door, weeping. Curtain*

2.

Cyrus Blenkarn's house, the next day. A plain sparely furnished room, with cheap wainscoting and whitewashed walls. A fireplace down stage right: a door up stage right. At back, corded to the wall, are a pair of steps which can be let down from Cyrus' workshop so as to furnish access to its door, which is some six or seven feet from the stage° in the back wall. To the right of these steps on the wall at back are shelves with various specimens of china and earthenware. To the left of the steps a cupboard. Across the corner at left is hung on rod a chintz curtain, which being drawn aside discloses a bench with materials for painting china and a chair in front of the bench. A window over the bench: a pair of high steps just below the chintz curtain, LC, a door down stage left. In front of the fireplace a long table with materials for painting china. Vase on table. Behind the table a chair in the centre of a strip of new, gaudy, crimson-flowered, Brussels carpet. Discovers Nancy on top of steps, LC, arranging the curtain over Jesse's bench. Jesse is looking on. Nancy has just fixed the curtain in such a way as to hide Jesse's bench

NANCY (*on steps*) There! Now when that's drawn you can't possibly see me! (*Coming down steps. Jesse offers to assist her*) Go away, Jesse, go away!

> *She comes down steps folding them up R, Nancy crosses to table R. Jesse puts steps against wall, R, then goes to Nancy's table, R*

NANCY Come! Get to your work! (*Jesse hesitates*) Get to your work! (*Jesse goes L. Nancy follows him*) Fix all your attention on it, and don't so much as remember that I am in the room!   5

> *He goes reluctantly behind the curtain up L and sits at his table. Nancy draws curtain. She goes to her table R, seats herself at work, takes up vase and begins to paint it. Jesse gradually moves the curtain and peeps round it. She takes no notice but goes on painting, holding out the vase at full length to get the effect*

JESSE Miss Nancy! Miss Nancy!

> *Nancy, sublimely unconscious, is studying the effect of vase*

JESSE (*shouts*) Words are cheap enough, aren't they?

NANCY It disturbs your peace of mind when I speak to you.

JESSE (*drawing curtain back and looking round*) It disturbs my peace   10
of mind a great deal more when you don't speak to me.

NANCY Then why do you stay here? Why don't you go into the
works?

JESSE And leave your father? You know he must have a workman
always handy to help him. I will never leave your father. (*Rises.*   15
*Nancy takes no notice. Jesse comes determinedly down to her, stands a
moment, then shouts fiercely at her*) I will never leave your father!
(*Thumping on the table*)
> Nancy quietly puts down her vase, takes him by the arm,
> marches him up to his bench, seats him at it, then in a cold,
> magisterial voice

NANCY If I see or hear anything more of you for the rest of the
morning, I won't speak to you for a week. (*Goes back to table R,*   20
sits)

JESSE (*meekly*) Thank you. You shan't! I'll be as quiet as a mouse.
Thank you so much! Thank you! (*He gets quietly to work, painting
vase on table*)
> Enter Chandler L and Mrs Chandler, followed by Maude,
> Felicia, Sir Seton and Lady Umfraville

CHANDLER Good morning, Nancy. (*Comes to C*) I want to see your   25
father.

NANCY (*glancing at ladder*) I'm very sorry, sir. His ladder's up.

CHANDLER Oh nonsense! Nonsense! Blenkarn! Blenkarn! (*Goes up C.
The others cross to Nancy's table*)

JESSE (*L*) Shy something heavy at his door, sir, and if that don't fetch   30
him, I'll go round to the back and break a window. That's almost
safe to bring him.
> Chandler goes to Cyrus' ladder, and bangs at it three times with
> increasing vigour with his walking stick. Cyrus opens door an
> inch

CYRUS (*through chink of door*) Run away! Run away! Go and do some
errands! Go and take a long walk! Don't come back again! (*Slams
door*)   35

CHANDLER (*loudly*) Blenkarn! Blenkarn! I say—

CYRUS (*opening door and looking out*) Eh? Oh! (*Lets down ladder, stands
at top if it very much embarrassed*)

CHANDLER (*LC*) Come down, Blenkarn, I want to speak to you!

CYRUS (*coming down ladder*) I'm very sorry, sir—I didn't know it was   40
you, or I shouldn't have told you to go and do some errands!
(*Comes down to Sir Seton and Lady Umfraville*)

CHANDLER (*aside, as he goes down L*) His girl hasn't told him yet.

CYRUS (*apologetically to Sir Seton and Lady Umfraville, R*) I beg your
   pardon. I'm obliged to have that ladder, because as soon as I set   45
   to work, a lot of people will come bothering me, and I can't get
   rid of them. (*Nancy frowns and makes signs*) I don't like to tell them
   they're a nuisance. And they always come just as I'm doing
   something important, don't they, Nancy?

NANCY (*flatly*) No! (*Glaring at him*)   50

CYRUS (*C*) Yes, they do. You know they do.

CHANDLER (*LC*) Blenkarn, I want you to show Sir Seton and Lady
   Umfraville over the works. You can explain the processes so much
   better than anybody else. (*Cyrus' face falls*)

CYRUS Not this morning, Mr Chandler. I'm very busy this morning.   55

CHANDLER (*contemptuously*) Busy! My good man! You've been busy
   these last twenty years, and what have you done?

CYRUS (*pause*) Well, I invented the glaze. The works were bankrupt
   when—

CHANDLER When I bought your patent, and brought my energy and   60
   capital to bear on it. Come, Sir Seton and Lady Umfraville are
   waiting. You've got a lot of odds and ends here. You might begin
   by showing them your bits of old Tatlow!

CYRUS Delighted, I'm sure—(*showing great reluctance, languidly takes
   a teapot from cupboard, without interest*) Teapot—date 1750—made   65
   by Aaron Shelton—(*C, with sudden flash of enthusiasm*) Look at it!
   The new Tatlow would melt like wax in it. I've baked it for weeks
   and there isn't a crack in it. If I could only make a piece like that
   before I die! And I will! I will!

CHANDLER (*LC*) Not you, Blenkarn! You'll never do it!   70

CYRUS Oh, yes I will!

CHANDLER By the way, you're always wanting money. You might
   sell me your collection.

CYRUS No, I won't sell that, Mr Chandler. (*Turns up stage. Restores
   teapot to place, takes out dish*) Dessert service—1762—made by—   75
   by—(*gets bewildered, looks round helplessly*) I can't remember
   anything this morning—

SIR SETON (*RC*) Chandler, we'll look round the works at some other
   time when Mr Blenkarn is at liberty—(*Cyrus grasps Sir Seton's
   hand*)   80

CYRUS (*very warmly*) Thank you! Thank you! (*Chandler goes up stage,
   LC*) I'm just at work on the model for my new kiln, and it's very
   complicated—the fact is there are nineteen different ways of doing

it, and I don't know which is right—and if you'll excuse me—
(*going towards cupboard C to put down dish, sees Jesse at work*) Oh,   85
there's Jesse Pegg! He knows the works a great deal better than I
do, don't you, Jesse?

JESSE (*seated L*) Yes, Mr Blenkarn, I'm ready. (*Rising*)

SIR SETON Come along then, Mr Pegg. (*Crosses to LC*) We'll say good
morning, Mr Blenkarn! I can see you'll be glad to get rid of us!   90

CYRUS Yes, I shall. And if you'll come some other day when I'm not
busy—in about six months' time—or a year—I'll show you round
myself. Jesse, mind you show them everything, and—and—(*bolting
hastily up ladder*) Good morning. Good morning. So proud I've
seen you, so proud. Good morning! Good morning! (*Draws up*   95
ladder and exit into room, closing door)

JESSE If you'll come this way, please—(*going to door L and stopping*)
        Enter Todd L. He remains up stage L and signs to Chandler

MRS CHANDLER Nancy, you will come with us. My daughter and
Miss Umfraville are going through the works; they will require
your assistance.   100

NANCY Very well, Mrs Chandler. (*Ladies cross to door L. Exeunt*
Maude, Felicia, Mrs Chandler, Lady Umfraville, Sir Seton, Nancy
and Jesse)

CHANDLER (*RC*) What is it, Todd?

TODD (*LC*) Needham has brought the contract for the new works.   105
He wants it signed at once.

CHANDLER I'm a little doubtful, Todd, about these extensive alter-
ations. (*Puts hat and stick on table R*) It mortgages all my capital
for years. Suppose business was to go wrong—

TODD You ain't losing faith in yourself?   110

CHANDLER I shall never lose faith in myself, Todd. But suppose this
old fool (*indicating Blenkarn's room*) was to find out the secret of
the old Tatlow—

TODD Well?

CHANDLER It would knock all our present ware out of the market.   115

TODD He'll never find it out.

CHANDLER No, and if he does, I could buy his patent of him for a
five pound note. (*Going to corner of table R*)

TODD Yes, to be sure. (*Aside, going LC*) Unless I bought it for ten.

CHANDLER Very well, Todd. Then we'll sign the contract and start   120
the works at once.

TODD (*going to Chandler RC*) Right. And if business gets a little shaky,
you can turn the whole concern into a limited company, and clear out.

CHANDLER Oh, quite so, quite so. (*A knock at door*)
    Enter Postman L with letter. Chandler RC, Todd C

POSTMAN Good morning, Mr Chandler. 125

CHANDLER Good morning, Carter.

POSTMAN (*crosses to table R*) Letter for Mr Blenkarn. As usual at this house, if there's only the old man at home, you might knock the blessed walls down and none would hear you. (*Puts letter on table R near Chandler, and exits*) 130
    Chandler turns for hat and stick, sees letter. Todd watching. Chandler turns suddenly, nearly catching Todd, who looks the other way. Chandler aside, glances at letter, shows alarm and surprise, puts his hand over letter

CHANDLER Todd, step across to Needham and tell him I'll be there to sign the contract in five minutes.

TODD Yes, sir. (*Watching him, aside*) What's up, I wonder? There's something in that letter. (*Going off slowly L*)

CHANDLER (*peremptorily*) Did you hear? 135

TODD Yes, sir. (*Exit quickly. Chandler watches him off, then turns quickly to letter*)

CHANDLER (*after a look around*) From Julian! London postmark! What can he have to write to Blenkarn about? Unless it's—(*looking at letter, and looking round*) I suppose it would be considered 140 dishonourable to open a letter—as a rule—and yet in a case of this kind it may be my duty—(*looks round at Blenkarn's door, opens letter, takes out a slip of paper and an enclosed envelope reads slip of paper*) 'If you love your daughter Mary, be sure she has this privately at once.' (*Reads address on enclosed envelope*) 'Miss 145 Mary Blenkarn.' (*Hesitates*) My public career is at stake. (*Opens letter*) 'Mary, come to me at Paris at once at the above address, and I will make you my wife before I leave for Africa. We are hurrying on, so don't delay. If I am obliged to leave Paris before you arrive, I shall leave all instructions for you to follow me. Make the best 150 excuse you can at home. Don't let them suspect you are coming to me. I enclose notes for your journey. (*Business of pocketing banknotes*) Oh, my dearest, can you ever forgive me? Ever your Julian.' (*Looks round, goes to fire, hesitates for some moments, finally puts letter on fire*) There, you young fool! I've saved you 155 from the fruits of your folly, and you'll thank me some day! (*Before the letter has burned, enter Maude and Felicia L. They are coughing. Chandler, standing at fire, watches the letter burn*) What's the matter, Maude?

MAUDE (*To Chandler*) We've been nearly choked in that horrid   160
tile-room! Oh, Papa! (*Felicia sits down LC*) Is it necessary for the
women and girls to do that terrible work?

CHANDLER Necessary? Of course it's necessary. What would become
of England's commercial prosperity if they didn't do it?

FELICIA (*LC*) It's a wonder they're not all suffocated.   165

CHANDLER (*L of table R*) Oh, they get used to it. In fact, after a time
I believe they really get to like it. They must like it, or they
wouldn't love and respect me as they do.

MAUDE I suppose, papa, there's no doubt they do love and respect
you?   170

CHANDLER Doubt! You heard the Mayor's speech yesterday? I never
heard a more glowing eulogium upon any man's private and public
virtues than he pronounced on mine.

MAUDE Yes, but, papa, you get all your wines and spirits from him.

CHANDLER (*very much upset*) Wines and spirits! Good heavens! That a   175
child of mine should take such an incredibly low view of human
nature as to suppose that a respectable wine and spirit merchant
should be influenced in his political views by paltry considerations of
trade! Get rid of such cynicism, my dear, get rid of it! It's degrading!

MAUDE But you are a splendid customer to him! (*Goes to R of Felicia,*   180
LC)

CHANDLER (*getting to C*) I encourage all local enterprise. You must
surely see, Maude, that I am a great public benefactor to the town
of Tatlow. Look at the entertainments yesterday—the fireworks
alone—had the man down from the Crystal Palace° on purpose.   185
Really, it does seem cruel that I should be obliged to point out my
benevolence to my own daughter. But I suppose I must bear to be
misunderstood, Miss Umfraville, like those other noble philan-
thropists who have preceded me.

FELICIA (*seated LC*) Yes, which?   190

CHANDLER Well—ah—ra—several. It would be invidious to mention
any *one* in particular.

MAUDE (*taking out watch*) Quarter past twelve. (*To Felicia*) Shall we
have a gallop before lunch?

FELICIA (*rising and going to door L*) Yes, and get the dust of that   195
tile-room out of our throats.

MAUDE I shall never go there again. (*Going towards door L*) Oh, papa,
I wish for those poor girls' sakes that England could do with a little
less commercial prosperity.

   Exeunt Maude and Felicia

CHANDLER (*RC*) It's strange how little the members of my own 200
family seem to appreciate me. (*Goes to fireplace, stirs ashes with poker*) Yes, it's quite burnt. Now, if I can persuade the girl to hold her tongue and leave the neighbourhood without saying anything to her father—(*comes to C*)

    Enter Todd, L

TODD (*crosses LC*) Needham's waiting for you to sign the contract. 205

CHANDLER I'll go to him. (*Crosses to door L. Todd about to follow*) By the way, Todd, you might just draw old Blenkarn, pump him a bit.

TODD (*LC*) I will. Rely on me.

CHANDLER We must take care to be on the safe side, Toddy. (*Winks* 210 *very slowly at Todd, who winks very slowly back at him. Chandler laughs. Todd laughs. Chandler exits L. As soon as Chandler has gone off, Todd relaxes his wink, lays his finger to the side of his nose*)

TODD Yes, we must take care to keep on the safe side, guv'nor. What luck some men have! What a position I could have made for myself 215 if I had only happened to get hold of a greenhorn like old Blenkarn! (*Crossing to R*) Ah well, the old boy's just as green as ever! (*Cyrus opens his door and appears at top of ladder. The ladder descends*) Here is the old moonraker!°

    Cyrus comes down ladder steps, muttering to himself, without noticing Todd

CYRUS It won't come right—all my time wasted— 220

TODD (*R, very cordially*) Ah, good morning, Blenkarn! Good morning!

CYRUS (*C, waking up*) Good morning, Mr Todd. My perforated bricks won't fit—they're all wrong, I must get some more baked. (*Comes to L of table R*)

TODD Of course. Tell Cousins to take your order. 225

CYRUS (*gratefully*) Thank you. (*Going L*)

TODD How are you getting on with your new experiments?

CYRUS Splendidly.

TODD (*going up ladder*) I should like to have a look at what you're doing. 230

CYRUS (*turning and coming C, back to audience*) You can't. I never let anybody go into that room, except my daughter Mary. She's the only one that knows my secrets.

TODD (*going up further, hand on door*) Oh, but I might be able to give you some advice, to help you. 235

CYRUS Nobody can help me. (*Fiercely*) Come down! You shan't go there. Do you hear? Come down, I say!

TODD Oh, very well. (*Comes quickly down, stands RC up stage by ladder. Cyrus goes up ladder, locks door and puts key in pocket. Re-enter Jesse and Nancy, L. Jesse takes off coat. Nancy crosses R and seats herself at table R. Jesse sits L to work*) You know, Blenkarn, I take an enormous interest in you.

CYRUS (*on steps*) Oh, do you?

TODD You don't know what a good friend I've been to you!

CYRUS (*mechanically*) No—yes—no—I forget. (*Comes down steps. Going L*)

TODD And I mean to stick to you, I do! (*Takes Cyrus by the arm. They come down RC together*) Now, if you make any discovery that means money, why not bring it to me?

CYRUS Eh?

TODD You can't work it yourself—you've got no capital—well, we work it together and make a fortune out of it. See? Well, that's agreed between us. That's settled. (*Seizing and shaking Cyrus' hand*)

CYRUS No, I don't think so, Mr Todd. (*Withdrawing his hand*)

TODD No?

CYRUS Mr Chandler has been a good master to me. He has always advanced me money on my wages to carry on my experiments, and I think I ought to give him the first chance.

TODD (*glibly*) Of course! Of course! I was speaking entirely in Mr Chandler's interest. Naturally, I should take it to Chandler—great, noble-hearted man, Chandler! Oh, I love him quite as much as you do. (*Aside*) Damn him, he'll get your invention if I don't look smart. (*Crosses to door L. Aloud*) Well then, you bring it to me, and I'll take it to Chandler. (*Exit*)

CYRUS (*after pause, during which he looks blankly round about him*) Now what was I going to do? Oh, I know. (*Going L*)

JESSE (*has been listening from his seat up stage. Rises and comes down LC*) Mr Blenkarn! (*Peremptorily stopping Blenkarn*)

CYRUS Yes, Jesse?

JESSE I'm going to talk to you for once in a plain, straightforward way!

CYRUS No, don't, Jesse! (*Trying to pass him*) I'm going to get some bricks perforated.

JESSE (*stopping him bluntly*) You'll stay and get your common sense perforated first.

CYRUS Well, what is it, Jesse? (*Pause*) Make haste. (*Takes off spectacles and puts them in his pocket*)

JESSE Years ago you invented the glaze which put the Tatlow
porcelain works, figuratively speaking, on their legs, put the town
of Tatlow, figuratively speaking, on its legs, and put Joseph
Chandler Esquire, figuratively speaking, on his legs, and made
him, as the Mayor said yesterday, an ornament, a glory and a
bulwark to the British nation.

NANCY (*at her bench, shows great interest*) Hear! Hear! Hear!

CYRUS (*turns and looks at Nancy surprised, then fidgets to get away*)
Yes, I know, Jesse—but you're wasting my time.

JESSE (*fixing him relentlessly*) And what are you today? Are *you* a
glory, an ornament and a bulwark to the British nation? No! Are
you putting up for Parliament? No! Are *you* owner of Tatlow Hall?
No! Are *you* President of the Young Men's and Young Women's
Mutual Improvement Association? No! Have you got a banking
account?

CYRUS (*laughingly*) A banking account!

JESSE No! Have you got a high hat? No! Or a brass knocker? Or a
decent coat to your back, or a decent pair of shoes to your feet, or
a sixpence to bless yourself with? No! No!! No!!! No!!!!

NANCY (*enthusiastically*) Hear! Hear! Hear! Hear!

CYRUS (*after another look at Nancy*) I can't help it, Jesse.

JESSE You must help it! You shall help it! And it is in the firm
belief that you will help it, when you make your next invention, (*waxing more eloquent with Nancy's encouragement*) that I grasp
this opportunity of telling you, Mr Blenkarn, what a fool you've
been.

CYRUS Thank you, Jesse, I know I've been a fool! I know I ought to
have cared more for money! (*Turning away to R*) But there are
thousands of men who can make money—it isn't a very clever trick
after all. (*Seeing vase on Nancy's table*) There isn't a man in the
world today who could make that vase! What would it matter to
me if I had all the money in the country so long as I couldn't turn
out a bit of work like that! You don't understand me, my lad.
(*Patting Jesse on the shoulder, crosses L*) Nancy doesn't understand
me. My Mary understands me! (*Exit, L door*)

JESSE There, Miss Nancy, you told me to speak to the point. Now
did I?

NANCY You were quite eloquent, Mr Pegg.

JESSE Was I? (*Approaching her fondly*) If I was eloquent on that
subject, what should I be on the subject of love?

NANCY (*seated at table R*) Dreadfully tiresome, so please don't begin.

JESSE (*L of table R*) I must. I'm going once and for all to lay bare all   320
the anguish of my heart.

NANCY (*unconcerned*) Oh, please don't! Ugh!

JESSE Aye—laugh at me, jeer at me, trample on me! (*Going to C*)

NANCY I don't want to trample on you! I've got your nice Brussels
carpet to trample on.   325

JESSE You trample on my gifts!

NANCY What did you buy the carpet for?

JESSE That its crimson flowers might whisper of my love to you and
be a symbol of its blooming for you—when every shred of that
Brussels carpet has melted into oblivion!   330

NANCY Oh, I thought you bought it to keep my feet warm. (*Rises,
takes her chair off the strip of carpet, moves the carpet away
from bench, throws it away from her to centre of stage*) Take your
carpet! (*Puts her chair back, and sits and goes on with her work at
table R*)   335

JESSE (*has watched with growing indignation*) You refuse my gift?

NANCY I can't take it now I know what the pattern means. (*Jesse, C,
stands savagely looking at her for a few moments, then deliberately sets
to work, rolls up the carpet very resolutely*)

JESSE I was not unprepared for this crisis, madam. (*Puts carpet on   340
barrel L. Goes up to his bench, drags from under it a very large,
well-worn, bulgy carpet bag, with a bit of stocking and a coat arm
hanging out of the side*) When you flouted me last night, I packed
my poor belongings. (*Drops bag on stage C*) Cold, heartless serpent!
You've withered every spark of good in my nature! Now it matters   345
not what becomes of Jesse Pegg! (*Putting on hat and coat*)

NANCY (*unconcerned*) Where are you going, Mr Pegg?

JESSE To ruin, to madness, to despair!

NANCY You'll just catch the 1.15 if you make haste.

JESSE (*takes up roll of carpet and bag, shoulders the carpet, carries the   350
bag*) I shall. Some day, basilisk, you may be sorry you didn't
accept my Brussels carpet in the spirit in which it was offered.
(*Pausing at door L*) I am going.

NANCY (*unconcerned, painting her vase—in a very pleasant tone*) Well,
good-bye, if you must go.   355

JESSE I mean it this time. Farewell! I warn you, inhuman, heartless
monster, that you have wrecked me body and soul. When anybody
asks you 'who murdered Jesse Pegg?' say, 'I did.' (*With a shriek
and a groan rushes tragically off, roll of carpet on shoulder, and
dragging the carpet bag after him, L door*)   360

NANCY The stupid fellow! And to think that he should be perfectly sane in all other respects! He's gone, I suppose. Well, I can't help it.
    Enter Mary, L door

MARY (*LC*) Nancy, what have you done to Jesse Pegg?

NANCY Nothing! He has taken offence and gone off to London, I suppose. 365

MARY For good?

NANCY I suppose so. He has really been quite unbearable lately.

MARY How?

NANCY Unbearably in love with me.

MARY Is that so unpardonable, Nancy? Can't you see how he 370 worships you?

NANCY I don't want to be worshipped by Jesse Pegg. I don't like common people. What luck you've had, Mary!

MARY Have I?

NANCY I should like to be in your shoes. 375

MARY Would you? (*Takes off hat*)

NANCY Yes, to be living at Tatlow Hall with pleasant, refined people. Of course you deserve it, dear. I don't grudge you. But I should like to be admired by such men as Captain Chandler instead of Jesse Pegg. 380

MARY (*goes to Nancy, puts hat on table RC*) Nancy, I'm going to give you a little advice. Jesse Pegg loves you dearly. Handsomeness very soon wears off. Kindness and goodness don't. Perhaps some day Jesse may come back again and ask you to be his wife. If he does, Nancy, take him, he's a good honest soul, take him, dear. (*Clasping* 385 *Nancy*) And thank God, (*Nancy looks up*) yes, dear, thank Him with all your heart for giving you a man that can so reverence and worship a woman that he becomes like a fool in her presence. Thank Him that though your lover seems common to you, he loves you so much that you can never become common to him. 390

NANCY Mary! I've never heard you talk like this! What's the matter?

MARY Nothing, dear. (*Subdues herself, and becomes quite calm and indifferent for the rest of the scene with Nancy. Going to C*) By the way, Nance, you've often longed for a watch—you may as well take mine. (*Taking off watch and chain*) 395

NANCY Oh no, Mary, I couldn't think of it. What will you do yourself? (*Rises, comes to Mary, C. She has left her handkerchief on table*)

MARY I shan't want it. (*Hurriedly*) There are plenty of clocks at Tatlow Hall. Come, I insist. (*Holding up watch and chain to Nancy,* 400

who takes them admiringly. Nancy turns slightly, kisses watch) There.
(*Pause*) Won't you give me a kiss for it, Nancy? (*Nancy kisses her,
then turns away again*) You don't mind kissing me, do you?

NANCY Mind kissing you?

MARY There never were two sisters who loved each other better than   405
you and I do, Nance.

NANCY Never! But you didn't come all the way from the Hall to tell
me that, did you?

MARY No. (*Indifferently*) I came to have a little gossip with father.
Where is he? (*Goes up stage a little*)   410

NANCY Gone to get something for his new kiln. He'll be back
directly. (*Looking at watch*) Twenty minutes to one! Good gracious, I've been forgetting all about dinner! You won't be going
yet? (*Going to door R*)

MARY (*following slightly*) Yes, I shall be going soon.   415

NANCY (*carelessly*) Well, good-bye. I shall see you on Sunday as
usual! (*Exit*)

MARY (*C*) You'll never see me again, Nancy. Oh, you are cruel,
Julian. To leave me without one word, to let me face this dreadful
shame alone! I can't do it! I can't! (*Comes down to fireplace*)   420
    *Enter Cyrus L, very excited, very joyful. She turns her head a
    moment*

CYRUS (*as he enters*) That's it! That's it! Why didn't I think of it
before? How stupid of me! (*Seeing Mary*) Mary! Mary, my dear!
I'm so glad to see you! (*Kisses her*) I've just found out the way to
build my new kiln! There were nineteen different ways of doing
it—all of them wrong—and just as I was coming along, it flashed   425
across me how to do it—yes—it's as good as done. In a fortnight
it will be in full work. And then I shall be able to try my new
experiment—and, who knows, I may be able to make the old china
after all.

MARY I'm sure you will. (*Kissing him. Cyrus goes up steps, and unlocks*   430
door, then comes down again. Mary goes up stage, gets L of steps)

CYRUS And Jesse Pegg has been giving me a good sound scolding.
He's very sensible, Jesse Pegg is—sometimes—and he lectured me
as I deserved. And what do you think—I'll tell you a secret—I'm
not going to be a fool any longer. I'm going to make lots of money   435
for you and Nancy. Tell me, dear, what shall I buy you when I'm
rich? (*Goes to table, takes large vase from table, and places it on the
floor by the side of the steps*)

MARY What would you like to buy me?

CYRUS Everything that's beautiful. A beautiful house, and a horse, 440
and beautiful dresses to wear, silk and embroidery and lace and
satin, and furs to keep you from the cold, and white soft dresses
in summer—(*Cyrus sits on steps*) all white like your own soul, my
Mary—when I'm rich I should like you never to wear anything but
white. 445

MARY (*Cyrus should not see Mary's face during this scene*) White—yes,
I'll wear white. But what will you buy for yourself, father?

CYRUS Never mind about me. I shall spend all my money on you
and buy you everything that you deserve. A new home to begin
with— 450

MARY A new home—

CYRUS Yes, with a corner for me—unless—perhaps some day, Mary,
you may want a new home with somebody else. (*Fondling her hand*)

MARY No, no, father—

CYRUS Don't be too sure, dear—somebody will come and take you 455
from me—and—

MARY No, no, it's quite—quite impossible.

CYRUS What! You'll stay with me always! How happy we shall be in
the future. (*Kissing her hand*)

MARY Yes, how happy we shall be in the future. (*Kissing his head*) 460
Father, (*anxiously watching him*) as I was coming from the Hall just
now, I saw poor old Mr Viner standing at his door. He seems quite
aged—quite broken—since—Mary—

CYRUS Ah, no wonder! It would have killed me (*Mary winces*) if my
daughter— 465

MARY (*quickly*) But she's dead!

CYRUS Yes, poor girl! It's a mercy her shame is hidden in the grave.

MARY Yes, it's a mercy.

CYRUS What a pity she didn't die when she had the fever three years
ago—she wouldn't have broken her father's heart then. 470

MARY Yes, death is far better than such disgrace, isn't it? (*Anxiously*)

CYRUS Yes, a thousand times better. (*Rises, goes to table RC, takes up
vase Nancy has been painting, looks at it*) There—there, don't speak
of it. (*After a thought*) And her name was Mary too. (*Puts down
vase on the table*) 475

MARY Yes, her name was Mary.

CYRUS Ah, how different from my Mary! (*Turning, sees Mary is
crying; goes to her C*) Come—come, my dear. (*Caressing Mary*)

MARY (*with apparent indifference*) Well, I must be getting back to the
Hall. 480

CYRUS And I must be getting to my work. You know, dear, I love to have a talk with you, but I can't spare the time today. Look in tomorrow, will you?

MARY No, not tomorrow.

CYRUS Well, the day after—promise you'll come the day after.   485

MARY I won't promise. (*Kissing him*) Good-bye, dear. (*Kissing him warmly*) Good-bye, my dear, dear father! God bless you! Good-bye.

CYRUS Good-bye. (*Goes up ladder to his room, opens door*) Ah, you shall see, dear. Your old father is not such a fool as they think him.   490 He's going to make a great fortune for you, dear! You shall be rich and happy, and ride in your carriage, and everybody shall look up to you! Yes, dear, we shall see! Good-bye! Good-bye!

> *Enters his room, and closes door. The ladder remains down. Mary nods and laughs, and kisses her hand to him. The moment the door is closed, she bursts into a flood of tears, and stands mechanically repeating his words*

MARY (*L of steps*) 'It would have killed me if my daughter—' 'It's a mercy her shame is hidden—is hidden in the grave.' 'Death is a   495 thousand times better.' Oh, my father, how shall I hide myself, how shall I spare you the blow? 'Death is better!' (*Suddenly*) You shall think me dead. I will go away. (*Advances a little*) You shall hear that I have died in a strange country. And it will be true, for from this time forth I shall be dead to you. Yes, Mary Blenkarn,   500 your child who never guessed what evil was, is dead. This isn't me! No, I am dead, and that is all you shall ever know of me. In a few months you shall learn that I have died—there will be no disgrace for you in that, and you shall never know how sinful and unhappy I have been. How can I save you from troubling about   505 my leaving you? I'll write—(*Goes to table*) there's a pen and ink in the next room. (*Looks round, goes to inner door R, opens it softly, calls softly*) Nancy! She's upstairs. I'm glad of that. I couldn't bear to meet her again. (*Exit door RUE*)

> *Rather long pause. Jesse Pegg enters L, sulky, crestfallen, looks all round to see that nobody is about—flings his carpet bag under bench—looks at Nancy's place, finally removes her chair, opens the roll of carpet along her bench, replaces her chair in position, till he is satisfied all is quite comfortable, sees the handkerchief she has taken off lying on her bench, takes it up, kisses it passionately again and again, puts it in his pocket, crosses to L, hangs up hat, takes off coat, sits down to work a moment, sees*

the curtain which is drawn on one side, rises, draws it across the place where he sits, so that it hides him. Re-enter Mary door RUE)

MARY (*letter in hand*) I have thought of everything. If they follow 510
me, they will think I have taken the express to London. Yes, that
will be the surest plan of getting away. Forgive me for deceiving
you, father. This will soften my departure—and when the news
comes that I am dead, you must not grieve for me, father, I'm not
worth it—(*Kisses letter, then places it on table, goes L*) 515
    Chandler enters L

MARY Mr Chandler! (*Shows great shame; turns away to R. Chandler
looks cautiously round—in a low, cautious voice*)

CHANDLER My dear Miss Blenkarn, I want a word with you. We can
perhaps speak better here than at the Hall. (*Puts hat and stick on
table*) 520

MARY (*low voiced, deeply ashamed*) Go on, sir. (*R of table, back to him*)

CHANDLER (*RC, cautious, low voice, watching her keenly*) I have been
thinking it would be wise of you to leave Tatlow.

MARY (*hurriedly*) Yes, I know. I am going.

CHANDLER You have spoken to your father? 525

MARY No, I've written to him. (*Indicating letter on table*)

CHANDLER And you've told him—

MARY Nothing, only that I have not been very happy lately at Tatlow
Hall, and not wishing to cause any unpleasantness between you
and him, I have obtained a situation at a distance and have gone 530
to it.

CHANDLER (*much relieved*) Very sensible—very sensible indeed. It
shows great consideration for his feelings. And you go at once?

MARY Yes, this morning, now. (*Going L*)

CHANDLER (*intercepting, C of stage*) You will allow me to assist you? 535
(*Takes out note-case*)

MARY No—except—there is rather over a month's salary due to me.

CHANDLER Allow me to make it a hundred pounds—a hundred and
fifty—you're welcome.

MARY No, only what is due to me. Not a farthing more. 540

CHANDLER Very well, since you insist. (*Puts note-case away*) But
I should like to have shown my generosity. (*Putting money on
table*)

MARY (*taking up money*) Thank you. (*Going*) Good day.

CHANDLER Stay, I should like to have some news of you. (*Intercept-* 545
ing her C)

MARY My father will have news of me soon. You will hear what has become of me through him.

CHANDLER At least, you will allow me to express my regret—in fact, my sorrow—at the rascally conduct of my son— 550

MARY Oh, please don't speak of it—(*hiding her head*)

CHANDLER Oh, I must—I shall write him what I think!

MARY You have heard from him?

CHANDLER Yes, no, at least, a telegram. He is nearly at Rome— tomorrow he will be on his way to Egypt. 555

MARY (*mechanically*) Rome—Egypt.

CHANDLER I shall tell him that I consider his behaviour most shameful—to ruin and betray the daughter of a man whom I respect as I respect your father—I shall say—

MARY (*crosses to L*) Oh, please, no more—let me go—(*much agitated*) 560

CHANDLER Miss Blenkarn. (*Mary stops. Cunningly*) I may rely that you will not mention Captain Chandler's name—(*Mary, at door, looks him full in the face for the first time*)

MARY Do you think it possible I could? (*Exit door L*)

CHANDLER Hum, she's a very foolish, quixotic girl! However, we're 565 rid of her. I wish she had taken a hundred pounds or so. It would have made my conscience quite easy. Well, I did offer it to her; it's her own fault. (*Takes hat from table*) Lucky I happened to come across that letter of Julian's. The young fool! He'll soon forget her. (*With a sigh of relief. Exit door L. Jesse slowly draws aside the curtain*) 570

JESSE What shall I do? How shall I tell him? I can't—it will break his heart. I'd better let it be, perhaps, then he'll never know. It's no business of mine—Nancy's sister! And that villain gone off! He might be brought back. Yes, it is my business, and if anything's to be done, it must be done now. Yes, I'll tell him. (*Goes up steps,* 575 *shouts*) Mr Blenkarn, sir, Mr Blenkarn, do you hear, sir? Mr Blenkarn.

The door at top of ladder opens, and Cyrus appears

CYRUS What is it, Jesse?

JESSE I've got some news for you, sir—(*Cyrus coming down ladder*)

CYRUS News, Jesse? Well, I'm so busy. 580

JESSE About Miss Mary. (*Comes down a little*)

CYRUS (*quickening his steps*) About Mary? What's that?

JESSE Well, sir, she's—(*Turns away LC. Cyrus comes to Jesse, examining his face. Jesse turns aside his face*)

CYRUS Not bad news, Jesse? (*Jesse nods*) But she was here just now. 585 There's been no accident? She's not dead?

JESSE No—

CYRUS Thank God! Thank God!

JESSE (*very sadly*) Worse than that, sir.

CYRUS Worse than death! (*Pause*) What do you mean, Jesse?   590

JESSE (*after a pause*) I mean, sir, that Captain Chandler's as damned
a villain as ever breathed.

CYRUS (*puzzled*) Captain Chandler! My Mary! (*Then shows he
guesses*) It's a lie! (*About to strike him*)

JESSE It's the truth, as I'm standing here! Do you think I'd tell you   595
a lie about such a thing, sir? (*Cyrus stands overwhelmed for some
seconds, then very quietly*)

CYRUS How do you know, Jesse?

JESSE I heard it from Mr Chandler's own lips just now. He offered
Miss Mary money—   600

CYRUS (*stung*) He offered her money? Where is he? Fetch him to me.
Where is he?

JESSE (*goes to window*) He left here a minute or two ago. There he
is, going to his office! (*Goes to door L, opens it and calls*) Mr
Chandler! Mr Chandler! You're wanted here! (*To Cyrus*) He's   605
coming, sir! Oh, Mr Blenkarn, you see what you've done! You've
made the father rich, and the son robs you of your own flesh and
blood! Don't spare him, sir! Don't spare him! (*Chandler enters door
L*) Mr Blenkarn wishes to speak to you, sir. (*Exit Jesse door L*)

CHANDLER (*suspicious, discomposed*) Well, Blenkarn?   610

CYRUS He says—he says—my Mary—Captain Chandler—oh, my
God! (*Staggers a little*)

CHANDLER I'm very sorry, Blenkarn—deeply sorry, I assure you.

CYRUS (*with a cry of despair*) Then it's true! And you knew! You
knew and kept it back from me!   615

CHANDLER I only learned it yesterday.

CYRUS Yesterday? But that would have been in time! He was here
yesterday, and—ah! (*Suddenly*) I took his money. I've got some of
it now. He paid me! He paid me! (*Taking money out of pocket,
dashing it on floor, trampling on it*) Curse his money! Curse his   620
money! Curse—curse—curse! Money for her innocence—oh, my
Mary! Would I'd died rather than this, my girl! My girl! My
girl! (*Sits on steps and sobs violently. Chandler after a pause goes to
him*)

CHANDLER Come, Blenkarn, don't give way! (*Puts hand on Cyrus'   625
shoulder*) I sympathize with you—I do indeed, and I'll see what can
be done.

CYRUS (*rises*) You will? I knew you would! Thank you, sir! Thank you! She's a lady—she won't disgrace your family. You'll send for him to make it right? (*Eyes cast down as if ashamed*)   620

CHANDLER I'm afraid that is out of the question, (*goes down L two steps*) but I'll do what I can for you and your daughter.

CYRUS (*looking up with dignity*) There's only one thing you can do. It's his duty to marry her! Send for him!

CHANDLER It would be useless! He's nearly at Rome by this time,   635 and he cannot come back. He's on his country's business.

CYRUS His country's business! But he's ruined my child! And she—what will become of her? You'll send for him—you'll send for him. Tell me where he is and I'll go myself! Where is he? Send for him, write, telegraph, send for him! I'll work for you! I'll slave   640 night and day! I'll wear my fingers to the bone! Every hour of the rest of my life shall be yours, only save—(*falls on his knees to Chandler, looks up for a moment or two, dumb with entreaty*) my child, save her! Yes—yes—you will—you will—you must—you shall (*rises, Chandler turns facing him*)—yes—please save her, save   645 her, save her, save her. (*Falls dumb and breathless on his knees against table*)

CHANDLER (*after a pause*) This is quite useless, Blenkarn. (*Crossing to him*) It can answer no purpose.

Cyrus, in removing hand from face, catches sight of letter on table

CYRUS What's this? A letter from her. (*Kisses it*) Oh, my dear, my   650 dear! (*Tears it open, reads*)

CHANDLER (*watching him*) Perhaps it's as well he knows! (*Going L a little way*) He's too fond of her to make it public. And it will all blow over in a few days.

CYRUS She's gone! She's gone! She's left me! Left me! (*On his knees,   655 head on table*)

CHANDLER (*crossing to Blenkarn*) Well! Well! It's better for her to be away from Tatlow for the present. The truth need never be known. Come, Blenkarn, rely on me to do everything that lies in my power for both of you.   660

CYRUS But you won't send for him? (*Intense grief*)

CHANDLER (*turns away one step*) I cannot. (*Turning to Blenkarn*) I wish to act like an honourable man—(*sneeringly*)

CYRUS But you won't send for him? (*Turns away*)

CHANDLER He wouldn't come. (*Turns away*) But I'll provide   665
handsomely for you—you shall be my under manager at the new
works.

CYRUS (*angrily*) But you won't send for him?

CHANDLER Really, Blenkarn, you make me angry! (*Turns away*) I'll
do everything in reason! I'll make your daughter an allowance—   670
any sum—

CYRUS (*pleadingly*) But you won't send for him?

CHANDLER No! (*Exit L*)

CYRUS Hear! Hear! (*Rises*) Thou that holdest the scales! Judge
between this man and me! A balance! A balance! Give justice here!   675
I've made him rich and proud—let me now make him poor and
despised. He mocks at my grief. Let me some day mock at his! Let
me hold his flesh and blood as cheap as he holds mine! Show me
some way to bring him to the dust! Give him and his dearest into
my keeping! Make them clay in my hands that I may shape and   680
mould them as I choose, and melt them like wax in the fire of my
revenge!

CURTAIN

*Curtain rises on 1st picture. Cyrus discovered alone, distracted
with grief. He gives a loud cry of anguish, and staggers towards
window as curtain descends*

CURTAIN

*Curtain rises on 2nd picture. Cyrus seated by window leaning on
table, his face buried in his hands. Jesse standing by his R
shoulder, trying to rouse him. Nancy standing C reading Mary's
letter. Both doors open. Curtain*

3.

Shed containing Cyrus Blenkarn's firing ovens or kilns. At back a door, RC, and a window, LC, giving a view of a landscape in the English pottery district at night, with kilns vaguely seen by the flickering lights their fires give out. Down stage right a kiln burning; down stage left a kiln not burning; above it another kiln burning. A truckle bed down stage LC. A stool towards the right of stage. A table up against the window. A chair close to it. Seggars° in front of kilns down R and L. The scattered remains of a heap of coal. Six months have passed.

Discover Cyrus, seated on stool, RC, gazing into the oven which throws a glow upon his face. He has aged considerably; his hair has grown quite white, his face sharper and keener set—his whole appearance much wilder and poorer than in Act 1—his dress quite in rags. He is apparently overcome with fatigue, and is almost asleep. Rouses himself with a start

CYRUS (*looking intently into fire*) The heat's going down! I must keep it up. There's twenty more hours to burn! Nancy! Nancy! (*Calling off, then goes to coal heap, scrapes up nearly all that remains, shoves it in kiln. Three shovelfuls. Flash each time coals put in*) What shall I do when this is gone? 5

    Nancy enters L between ovens. She is dressed in mourning, very plain and inexpensive

NANCY (*C*) Yes, father.

CYRUS (*R, takes trial piece from kiln*) Go to the railway yard. Try all the coal merchants. Tell them I'm firing over a thousand more specimens, and I'm bound to find out the secret at last. (*Puts iron with trial piece on bucket to cool*) 10

NANCY (*listless and despairing*) It's no use, father. You know I went yesterday. They won't trust you any more.

CYRUS Go again! If I don't have coal, these ovens will go out and all my work will be lost. Look, that oven has gone out.

NANCY Father, wouldn't it be better to give it up? 15

CYRUS (*taking up stoking iron*) Have you forgotten your sister?

NANCY Mary is dead.

CYRUS (*hard, tearless*) Yes, she is dead. But the man who betrayed her is living. And his father, his father who might have saved her, is living. They live, these Chandlers, and I live, to humble them! 20 (*Stoking lower furnace. Flash*) Where's Jesse?

NANCY Asleep.

CYRUS Asleep?

NANCY You forget he's been helping you the last three nights, and has had no rest. 25

CYRUS What's today?

NANCY (*going to him*) Thursday, and you haven't had any sleep since the night before you lighted the first oven.

CYRUS I want no sleep.

NANCY You can't keep on like this for ever! 30

CYRUS No, not for ever, but long enough—long enough.

NANCY Father, if you should break down, if you should die!

CYRUS (*with a calm, hard smile*) I can't die till my work's done. Go and get me some coal! Offer them any price, ten, twenty pounds a ton. Don't take any denial! I must have it! I will have it! (*Stoking* 35 *oven R. Flash*)

NANCY (*aside*) Poor father! Is he mad, as all the people say? (*Exit, L*)

CYRUS (*taking up trial piece from bucket, puts it in water, looks at it*) No—it won't do—it's as soft as dough, and it should be as hard as my heart! (*Todd enters door RC*) 40

TODD (*C, brisk, sprightly*) Well, Blenkarn, how goes it? What's the latest? How are we getting on?

CYRUS (*R*) Badly, Mr Todd. That fire (*oven down L*) went out yesterday. (*Crosses to L*)

TODD Well, wasn't it nearly time? 45

CYRUS No, it ought to have been kept in a dozen hours longer at least. (*Sits on truckle bed L*)

TODD Have you got any of the specimens?

CYRUS Not yet—the oven isn't quite cool enough yet. I shall be able to get at them soon. But I expect they're all spoiled, and if I don't 50 get some more coals, these will go out too. (*Rises and goes to Todd C*) Let me have five pounds more, Mr Todd.

TODD Not on our present agreement, Blenkarn. But I tell you what I'll do. I'll advance you twenty pounds more on condition that *if* you discover the secret of making the old Tatlow ware, I 55 shall have the option of buying the patent from you for five hundred pounds.

CYRUS I don't sell my patent. (*Goes to oven up L*)

TODD But, my good man—look here, Blenkarn, you're a decent sort of fellow, and I want to do you a good turn. I'll advance you fifty 60 pounds now, and give you a thousand down if you make the discovery. Come now, that's fair, isn't it?

CYRUS I don't sell my patent. (*Goes R for shovel*)

TODD (*C*) You won't come to any arrangement?

CYRUS (*returning to oven up L*) Our arrangement is made. You've lent   65
me thirty pounds, and when I discover the way to make the old
ware, you are to find some man with money to put me in business.
(*Putting on coals on fire of oven up L*)

TODD Exactly—and I've got my capitalist ready, and the moment I
say 'Go,' down he planks his ten thousand pounds and off we go   70
in a gallop. But where do I come in, Blenkarn? (*Plaintively*) Where
do I come in?

CYRUS You are to be my manager.

TODD Oh, no, it ain't good enough, Blenkarn. I must be a partner.

CYRUS A partner! (*Cyrus looks at Todd and says nothing. Goes to lower*   75
oven L)

TODD Aye, suppose you do make this discovery, you'll want working.
Everybody wants working in this age. Advertise! Beat the big
drum! Stick your name up at every railway station in England in
bigger letters than anybody else! That's what does the trick with   80
the great British public! Look what a great man I made of Mr
Chandler! And if you succeed in this invention, I can make a great
man of you!

CYRUS (*crossing to oven R*) I don't want to be made a great man by
you, Mr Todd.   85

TODD (*looking at him, aside*) If the old bird should find it out
after all! It would be all U. P.° with my friend Chandler—
especially with his big Stock Exchange specs° which always turn
out wrong.

CYRUS (*up R*) The heat is going down still! Mr Todd, let me have   90
another five pounds. I'll give you fifty for it—I'll give you a
hundred.

TODD Not a farthing, Blenkarn, unless I stand in with the profits.
What do you say? (*Rattling money in his pockets*)

CYRUS (*tempted for a moment, then firmly*) No, my profits shall be my   95
own for the future.

TODD You're a very obstinate, self-willed man. (*Chandler crosses the*
window) Chandler! Not a word to him about our little affair!

CYRUS I have no dealings with Chandler. (*Crosses to L. Todd gets R*)
    Chandler enters at back, shows slight surprise at seeing Todd.
    Cyrus sits on truckle bed L

CHANDLER (*C, loud patronizing voice*) Well, Blenkarn! (*Cyrus takes no*   100
notice) Blenkarn! (*Comes in front of Cyrus*) I hear you've got

into very low water, and just to show you that I don't bear you
any malice for leaving my employ, I've come to offer to take you
back.

CYRUS I'm not so low as that!   105

CHANDLER You were foolish to leave me after having been a faithful
servant to me for so many years.

CYRUS I served you faithfully, didn't I?

CHANDLER Yes, and you ought to have taken the position I offered
you as second manager in the new works.   110

CYRUS I've done better.

CHANDLER Come, come! You know you're in debt!

CYRUS Yes, I'm in debt. I owe you something, don't I?

CHANDLER There was a trifle.

CYRUS (*with meaning*) I shall pay you.   115

CHANDLER Oh, I'll put that in the bargain.

CYRUS What bargain?

CHANDLER (*C*) I'll take you back for a term of six years at four
hundred a year on condition that any little improvements you may
happen to make in porcelain during that six years belong to me. I   120
think that's a very generous offer, Todd? (*Turning to Todd*)

TODD (*RC*) Generous! It's magnificent! It's quixotic!

CHANDLER (*C*) Candidly, Todd?

TODD On my honour—you know I never flatter.

CHANDLER Ah well, you heard my offer, Blenkarn, what do you say   125
to it?

CYRUS (*rises*) Nothing. (*Turns his back on Chandler*)

TODD (*beckons Chandler down stage R, the following conversation
confidential*) You're very well out of that! He'll never discover the
secret of the old Tatlow.   130

CHANDLER It would be awkward for me, Todd, if he did! Here's
trade falling off, and I'm bound to go on with the new works. And
did you see there's another big fall in Cornubians° again?

TODD I should sell out.

CHANDLER And drop ten thousand! It seems as if everything was   135
turning against me.

TODD You're safe enough. Can't you see he's as mad as a hatter?
(*Winks at Chandler*)

CHANDLER (*after a look at Cyrus*) Think so?

TODD Sure of it. I've pumped him. Poor old fellow, in less than three   140
months he'll be in a lunatic asylum.

CHANDLER (*placidly*) Well, I don't wish him any harm, but taking everything into consideration, perhaps that would be best for all parties.

TODD Exactly. Suit us all down to the ground. (*Cyrus is at oven LUE taking out trial pieces*) 145

CHANDLER They're very kind to the people in such places?

TODD Treat 'em like fighting cocks. Don't you trouble any more about his blessed old Tatlow—it's a dream, a myth, a delusion, a sell! 150

CHANDLER I hope so. (*Takes out his watch*) Kempster was to be at the office at seven—you'd better go to him.

TODD Yes. Ain't you coming? (*Cyrus goes up to window and watches for Nancy*)

CHANDLER I want a word with Blenkarn first. (*Going down L*) 155

TODD (*aside*) He means to nail him, and then what's to become of me? (*Down R*)

CHANDLER (*turns round*) What are you waiting for?

TODD (*apparently surprised*) Eh? Simply absence of mind—unconsciously waiting for you—sort of wish that you would come with me. (*Aside*) Hang it all! (*Exit door in flat RC, then past window to L*) 160

> Chandler goes up RC. Cyrus dips trial piece in water, etc. Chandler looks at Cyrus. Cyrus takes no notice. Chandler fidgets with his umbrella, coughs

CHANDLER (*embarrassed*) Hm, Blenkarn! Blenkarn! This is really terrible about your poor daughter Mary.

CYRUS (*up stage L*) She doesn't need your pity. 165

CHANDLER No, but I assure you the news of her death touched me very deeply.

CYRUS (*looks at him*) Ah!

CHANDLER For the last two months I've been coming to offer you my sympathy, but I put it off and put it off! 170

CYRUS Put it off a little longer. (*Throws down broken trial piece, and crosses to R*)

CHANDLER You don't want my sympathy.

CYRUS (*R*) Not yet—I'll send for you when I want it. (*Picks up stoking iron*) 175

CHANDLER You're a strange man, Blenkarn! You don't seem to feel your daughter's loss.

CYRUS (*At R oven*) No, I haven't shed one tear. My heart has been dry, so have my eyes. I haven't thought much about her death. I've

had other business. (*Stoking fire*) When that's done, I shall have 180
time to remember that she's dead, and I'll send for you. (*Stoking
fire R*)

CHANDLER (*aside*) His favourite daughter dead, and he not troubling
about it! Gives all his thoughts to his inventions! If he should make
the discovery! I must buy him somehow! It won't do to run the 185
risk! Yes, I must make it safe. (*Gets down L*)
    Enter Nancy, L

CYRUS (*R, eagerly*) Well, what do they say?

NANCY (*C*) They won't trust you.

CYRUS Did you try all of them?

NANCY Yes, every one! I offered them any price they liked. It was 190
no use. They know we have no money! (*Cyrus, with a gesture of
despair, sinks upon stool up R, dazed and dejected. Chandler beckons
Nancy to him*)

CHANDLER (*L*) He'd better come back to me! (*Nancy looks enquiring-
ly at Chandler*) I've forgiven his ingratitude, and I've offered to 195
take him back at a salary of four hundred a year.

NANCY (*LC*) You're very kind, Mr Chandler, but—(*shaking her
head*) he won't come.

CHANDLER If he doesn't, you'll both starve. Come, you're a sensible
girl. Give him a good sound talking to! Bring him to his senses! 200
(*Crosses to C. To Cyrus*) Blenkarn, I shall consider that matter open!
I'll look in again in half an hour for your answer! (*He looks at
Cyrus, who sits absorbed taking no notice, then exit door in flat RC
and off L*)

NANCY (*LC, looking at Cyrus, aside*) Perhaps Mr Chandler is right. 205
It would mean rest and comfort for his old age, instead of beggary
and work. I'll try! (*Comes to Cyrus*) Father! (*Cyrus is still abstracted*)
Father! (*Touching his shoulder*)

CYRUS Yes, Nancy!

NANCY Suppose these thousand specimens all turn out wrong, what 210
will you do then?

CYRUS Make another thousand.

NANCY But you've sold everything—you've even parted with your
collection—where's the money to come from for fresh experiments?

CYRUS I must earn it. 215

NANCY And if *they* turn out wrong, what then?

CYRUS Begin again.

NANCY But we shall starve. Father! Hear me! I'm your only child
now. If you were to find out this invention, and make a fortune, if

you were to own all the county, you could only leave it to me. I
don't want it. I don't want to be rich! But I do want food and
clothes, and you know how many times lately I've not had enough
to eat.

CYRUS It is hard. Have patience, Nancy! Who knows? I may have
found out the secret! It may be firing in one of these ovens now!
I must find it out soon! (*Rises*)

NANCY That's what you've said all your life. You began trying to
make the old china twenty years ago, and today you're as far from
it as ever.

CYRUS No, I'm twenty years nearer!

NANCY You'll never be nearer! Father, if you love me, be wise at last.
I don't beg for myself, but for your own sake. Give up this mad
dream, (*Cyrus laughs*) and spend the rest of your life in quiet and
plenty. Take Mr Chandler's offer.

CYRUS Ah! (*Nancy drops on her knees*) Take Mr Chandler's offer! Sell
myself to the father of the man that robbed me of my dead, dear
one, and perhaps brought her to her grave. Give up my life's work!
Give up all my labour and thought! Ah! That's like you, Nancy!
You never believed in me. Mary, my Mary, you believed in me! If
you were here now! And I told you that death was better than
living shame. I didn't mean it, dear! I wouldn't mind your shame
if you could come back to me. I would help you bear it, and you
would help me with your soft, low voice and loving ways. Mary!
Mary! Mary! You wouldn't have spoken to me as your sister has
done! (*Sits*)

NANCY (*deeply touched*) Father, forgive me! Forgive me! (*Flinging her
arms round him. Cyrus repulses her*) I didn't mean it! I only said it
for your own sake! I'll never be unkind to you again! Father, let
me help you. Let me take Mary's place now she is gone!

CYRUS (*kissing her*) So you shall, dear! God bless you! God bless you!
(*Very tenderly, then looking round, remembering*) I'm forgetting my
work. (*Crosses to oven, L1E*)

NANCY And I too! What can I do? That oven! Can I help you get
the specimens out?

CYRUS No, it's not quite cool enough yet! (*Touching it*) I used such
heat, Nancy, as I never used before! And to think I had to let it
out for want of coal!

NANCY Perhaps some of the pieces may be thoroughly fired. (*Comes
to Cyrus*)

CYRUS (*embracing her*) That's right. Good girl. Call Jesse, and get 260
him to fetch some wood.

NANCY (*calling off*) Jesse! Jesse!

CYRUS He's not to touch the pieces in that oven. I want to take them
out myself. (*Looking at fires*) Going down! If they would but let
me have a little more coal—a ton only! I'll try them again! I'll go 265
myself! (*Nancy helps him on with coat*) They must listen to me!
They'll never let all my work perish for the sake of a few shillings!
Keep the fires up while I'm gone, dear. Get Jesse to help you.
Don't let them go out. They mustn't go out! They shan't! Keep
them white hot—they keep me alive! While they burn, my hope 270
and life burn too! (*Exit door in flat RC and off R*)

NANCY (*up at door*) He'll never rest till he has done it, or till he is
in his grave!
                Enter Maude L

MAUDE (*LC, uncertain, timid*) Nancy, I knocked at the door, but you
weren't in the house. You'll forgive my coming here? I came to 275
tell you how sorry I was to hear—about Mary.

NANCY Thank you. (*Restrained. Comes down C*)

MAUDE Nancy, what is this mystery about her? Why did she leave
us so suddenly? (*LC*) Why did she go away from England? There's
no doubt she is dead? 280

NANCY What doubt can there be? We received the newspaper
containing the account of her death.

MAUDE She died at sea, did she not?

NANCY Yes.

MAUDE What made her leave home? 285

NANCY Please say no more. (*Shows pain and embarrassment*)

MAUDE Forgive me. I ought to have known better than to have
spoken. But, Nancy—don't be angry with me—it was not curios-
ity. It was because I loved Mary, and—we are friends, are we not?
(*Nancy does not speak*) Won't you speak to me? (*Holds out her hand*) 290
For Mary's sake, Nancy! (*Nancy impulsively takes Maude's hand
and kisses it*)

NANCY (*RC*) Thank you, thank you, Miss Chandler, for your love
for her.

MAUDE (*C, taking out purse*) And, Nancy, you will let me help you. 295

NANCY No—I can't take any money from you, Miss Chandler.
                Jesse enters L, stolidly watching. Remains LC

MAUDE (*C*) Don't show pride to an old friend, Nancy.

NANCY (*R*) It's not pride, but I can't take your money, Miss Chandler.

> *Jesse comes stolidly down LC, stares suspiciously at Maude.*
> *Maude shows embarrassment*

MAUDE (*C, confused*) Oh, Mr Pegg, you are not in our works now?   300

JESSE (*LC, stolidly*) No.

MAUDE I hope you are well and happy.

JESSE Middling. (*Stares at her*)

MAUDE (*her embarrassment increases, goes up L—aside*) He used to be so civil. What can have happened? (*Exit L*)   305

JESSE Why didn't you take the money? Spoil the Egyptians,° I say!

NANCY (*RC*) I've promised my father never to take a favour from them.

JESSE Did you see the news in the paper this morning?

NANCY About the African expedition?   310

JESSE Yes. Captain Chandler has been distinguishing himself again. Daring act of bravery and hair-breadth escape! I wish the black devils had killed him! (*Turn up L*)

NANCY What good would that do now Mary is dead? You'll look after the ovens till my father comes back? (*Going L*)   315

JESSE Don't go, Miss Nancy! (*Runs in front of her. Abjectly*) Don't go! While you're here, this place is like a little heaven below, and when you're gone it's like a little—other place. (*Picks up stoking iron*)

NANCY And what are you?

JESSE When you're kind to me, I'm nearly good enough to be an   320
angel, but when you despise and maltreat me I feel (*vigorously stirring the furnace with poker*)—I'm a lost spirit, pitchforking other lost spirits, and (*gloating, poking fire*) I like it. Oh, Nancy, do try to love me! Do try! If at first you don't succeed, try, try again! Won't you try? (*With abject persuasion*)   325

NANCY No. (*Firmly*)

JESSE (*fiercely*) You won't? (*Glares at her*) You won't even try?

NANCY (*firmly and louder*) No! (*Jesse stands scowling at her*) Listen to me, Mr Pegg. The more I try to love you, the more I don't succeed. Now perhaps if I weren't to try at all—   330

JESSE (*eagerly, overjoyed*) Do you think so? Then don't try to love me any more!

NANCY Very well, (*composedly*) I won't.

JESSE I mean—yes do. Can you bring me any good, sound, solid argument why you shouldn't marry me? No, you can't! (*Throws   335
down stoking iron*)

NANCY Attend to the ovens. (*Jesse goes to R, stokes furnace R. Nancy crosses L*) That's right. Now we'll talk about something else. (*Sits LC*)

JESSE (*R*) No, now we're on the subject of marriage, let's argue it out.   340

NANCY No, we won't begin arguing before marriage. There'll be plenty of time for that afterwards.

JESSE Then you will? Oh, it's too much! It's too much! It can't be true! Nancy, it isn't true! Is it true?   345

NANCY (*very collected and calm*) Not at present. Listen to me. I don't love you—

JESSE That's of no consequence. I—

NANCY Hold your tongue!

JESSE (*meekly*) Yes.   350

NANCY I don't altogether dislike you—

JESSE Thank you, oh, thank you—thank you so very much.

NANCY Hold your tongue! I daresay we might get on very comfortably together as man and wife.

JESSE I'm sure of it! I'll take my oath of it. And—   355

NANCY Will you be quiet? Now if I were to promise to marry you, Jesse, would you—

JESSE (*jumping down her throat*) Yes, that I would! Anything. You shall have your own way in everything! Keep all the money! Go to Church or Chapel, just which you like! Keep the beer in the house   360 so that I shall never have any excuse for going to a public! I'll never say an unkind word to you! I'll never get out of temper, even on washing day! I'll wait on you in health and sickness. I'll let you have your breakfast in bed! There, Nancy! What more could I promise?   365

NANCY Nothing. You certainly promise enough. (*Jesse puts stoking iron down*) But I'm not thinking of myself. (*Rises*) Jesse, tell me, do you think father will ever discover the secret of the old Tatlow?

JESSE I'm afraid he won't, Nancy.

NANCY And I'm afraid too. But he'll never give it up. And we must   370 encourage him and help him and take care of him in his old age. (*Comes to Jesse*)

JESSE He's your father, Nancy. He shall be mine too.

NANCY Thank you, Jesse. (*Takes his hands*) I'm going to ask you to make a great sacrifice. I give you my word I will marry you—   375

JESSE (*with a frantic shout of delight*) Oh!

NANCY Be quiet! I will marry you—

JESSE Oh! It's too much!

NANCY Some day—

JESSE No hurry, Nancy—at least, no great hurry.   380

NANCY I know you have saved some money. (*Jesse shows disquiet*) You had nearly a hundred pounds. I want you to lend it to my father. Will you? (*Hand on his arm*)

JESSE (*looks uncomfortable*) I'm very sorry, Nancy, I would if I could, but it's gone!   385

NANCY Gone? How? (*Pause*) Where?

JESSE I've lent it to your father to carry on his experiments.

NANCY (*deeply touched*) Jesse!

JESSE He was afraid you'd be angry with him, so he made me promise I wouldn't tell you.   390

NANCY You lent it to him, though you knew it would come to no good?

JESSE I did it because I love you, Nancy.

NANCY (*very softly, very quietly, giving him her hand*) I will be your wife, Jesse.   395

JESSE Thank you, Nancy. You shall never be sorry. (*They turn up LC together*)

> Enter Cyrus at door in flat, RC. Stage has gradually grown darker

NANCY Father! What success? (*Crosses to Cyrus C*)

CYRUS (*C*) None! They refuse me! They laugh at me! They tell me I'm mad! When I came to Tatlow, it was bankrupt, its trade was   400 in ruin, its people starving. My invention, the fruit of my brain, fed it, and clothed it and brought it to prosperity. And now it laughs at me and tells me I'm mad! I suppose I am mad! I haven't fattened myself on another man's labour and tears. I must be mad! God made this world for parasites. I must be mad! A leech's mouth   405 to fasten on your neighbour and suck all his blood from his heart! That's sanity, and I'm mad, my girl, for I haven't done it! (*Frantically embracing her, then going to furnace R*) Ah, what have you been doing? The heat has gone down, and I shall never get it up again! All my work will be lost!   410

JESSE (*LC*) I'm very sorry. There's no coal.

CYRUS Some wood then! (*Jesse exits LUE*) If I could only keep these fires in for a few hours longer! Who knows I may have discovered the secret? And I shall lose it all for want of a little fuel! No, I won't though! (*Seizing chair, breaking it up and throwing it on fire*)   415

NANCY Father, what are you doing? (*Trying to stop him*)

CYRUS Let me be! Let me be! I'm not mad! Another hour, another half hour may give me the secret I've been working for all my life! (*Nancy again tries to restrain him*) Let me be, I say! They shan't go out while there's a stick or shred about the place that will burn. (*Jesse re-enters LUE*) Some wood, Jesse! The palings outside! Anything that will burn! Get it! D'ye hear? You too, Nancy—make haste. (*Nancy and Jesse exeunt door in flat RC and off R. Looking round*) All my work lost if I can't keep these fires in. If I could get at this oven. It must be cool enough by this time. (*Tearing down bricks*) Come down, will you? Let's see what you've done for me after all my labour for you. (*Taking out specimens which are melted into all sorts of shapes*) What! Couldn't you stand it? (*Taking out another*) I've shrivelled you, have I? You too? (*Taking out another*) All alike, all good for nothing. Nancy is right—I'm no nearer than I was twenty years ago. (*Another piece*) All to begin over again. All my life wasted. (*Takes out a white vase, looks at it, whispers*) I'm not mad! No, but I'm dreaming again. I've dreamed it so many times, and always waked to find it only a dream. But—(*looks at it again, bursts into a long scream of delight. Jesse and Nancy enter with a large log*) Nancy, Nancy, look, my dear! Look, Jesse, I'm awake, am I not? Look! I've found out the secret! Look! Starve? We're rich, my girl, rich! You shall ride in your carriage, for I've done it! I've found the secret at last! I've done it! I've done it! (*He kisses her, bursts into hysterical laughter, drops on bed, rocking to and fro. Knock at door. Nancy and Jesse get up stage RC*)

CHANDLER (*heard outside*) Blenkarn! Blenkarn!

CYRUS Come in.

Enter Chandler, door in flat, RC. Comes down C

CHANDLER I've been thinking things over, and I'll buy any patent that you may bring out. What's the matter, Blenkarn?

CYRUS Nothing. You'll buy—?

CHANDLER I'll buy—what is it, Blenkarn?

CYRUS Go on—you'll buy—

CHANDLER (*looking at him*) I'll buy—

CYRUS What? My body and soul? Buy back the past thirty years? Buy back my girl from her grave in the sea? Buy back the sweat of my brow and the strength of my hands that I've wasted for you? *You'll* buy! No, *I* buy now! I buy *you*! Do you know the price I've paid for you? I've given the toil of my life! I've given hunger and tears and despair and agony! I've given my child to be your son's mistress! That's the price I've paid for you, but I've got you! I've

bought you! You're mine! You're mine! You're mine! (*Cyrus,
laughing hysterically, staggers to bedside as*)

CURTAIN

*Curtain rises on 1st picture. Cyrus seated on bedstead L
alternately laughing and crying, vase in hand. Chandler amazed
R. Jesse and Nancy at back. Curtain descends*

*Curtain rises on 2nd picture. Cyrus still seated, frantically
embracing Nancy, who is kneeling before him. Jesse standing L
of Cyrus. Chandler in doorway, just going. Curtain*

4.

Tatlow Hall, as in Act 1, but there are some changes in the furniture, and it is differently arranged. Two and a half years have passed.

Discover Chandler, LC, with hands in pockets and in a despairing attitude. Enter at back Mrs Chandler and Maude crying. They are in outdoor clothes

CHANDLER Are you ready?

MRS CHANDLER Quite. I've sent everything on to Florence Cottages. Florence Cottages after Tatlow Hall! Six rooms after this! (*Sits C*)

MAUDE Never mind, mamma! We shall be all the closer to one another, and learn to love each other all the more! (*RC*) 5

MRS CHANDLER Joseph, couldn't we leave Tatlow altogether?

CHANDLER Where could we go? It costs money to move, and I've got none.

MRS CHANDLER (*weeping*) To have to leave our home the very day that Julian is coming back, to receive our hero, a national hero, at 10 that place!

MAUDE (*at back of settee*) I don't think Julian will mind for himself. He was never selfish.

MRS CHANDLER But what will his wife think of us?

MAUDE Let's hope he's married somebody very nice who'll think just 15 as much of us in our new home as if we were living here!

CHANDLER You ought to have let me write to tell him I was a ruined man.

MRS CHANDLER He'll know it soon enough. Mr Vachell might have allowed us to remain here a few days longer! Can't you ask him, 20 Joseph?

CHANDLER No. He writes I must be prepared to give up possession and to go out at twelve o'clock today. He has already kept the place going for us the last six weeks, and paid all expenses.

MAUDE It's almost twelve now. Come, mamma, let's take one last 25 look round the old place. We may never see it again.

MRS CHANDLER (*rising*) Who would have thought that it would ever come to this? (*Going off at conservatory R*)

MAUDE Won't you come with us and say good-bye to everything?

CHANDLER (*sitting C*) No. I don't want to be reminded of what I 30 was and what I am. (*Maude approaches slightly*) Go away, Maude.

MAUDE Poor papa! (*Joins Mrs Chandler in conservatory, and goes off*)

CHANDLER It's a hard world! A blackguard, cruel, heartless world! It's got no pity for a man!

TODD (*outside*) Never mind! I'll find him!   35

> *Enter Todd at back C from R., very brisk, sprightly, in capital spirits*

TODD (*LC, puts hat on LC table*) Hillo, Chandler! (*Chandler rises and shows some respect to Todd*) How goes it? Just passing, so I thought I'd give you a look in! So you're clearing out, eh? (*Cheerfully*)

CHANDLER Yes, Todd. (*Crosses to L*) Vachell is coming at twelve to take possession.   40

> *Todd, sitting at his ease in centre chair, regards Chandler for a few seconds with an expression of amused contempt, then in a cheerful, philosophic tone*

TODD (*sitting on settee LC*) You've made a pretty mess of your affairs, Chandler. (*Looks at him*)

CHANDLER You needn't remind me of that, Todd. (*Sits R*)

TODD Oh, I'm always perfectly candid with you! You know I never flatter. You should have taken my advice, Chandler, and made me   45 your partner.

CHANDLER But Blenkarn hasn't made you a partner.

TODD No. You see, Pegg being his son-in-law naturally came first. But I've got a rattling good berth! Much better than I had with you!   50

CHANDLER The business has increased a good deal, I understand.

TODD Rather! We're coining money like dirt! This new ware is knocking everything else out of the market.

CHANDLER I'm so glad! I'm delighted! I thought perhaps there might be a vacancy for an under-manager? (*Sits L of Todd. Todd*   55 *whistles*) You might say a good word for me to Blenkarn, Todd.

TODD Ah! Well—

CHANDLER The fact is things are much worse than I expected— there will be a much smaller dividend than I hoped. It's absolutely necessary for me to get some employment at once to keep my   60 family out of the workhouse.

TODD That's awkward. What the deuce made you plunge like you did on the Stock Exchange?

CHANDLER I did it to right myself when I found things were going wrong, and you know the more I plunged the deeper and deeper   65 I got in the mess. (*Rises and crosses L*) Well now, did you ever know anybody have such bad luck as I had?

TODD Bad luck? Bad judgement, you mean.

CHANDLER But you advised me, Todd. You were my right hand!

TODD Not when I saw how things were going. While Batty Todd 70
worked you, you were a big man. Now Batty Todd works Cyrus
Blenkarn, *he's* the big man. I'll tell you a secret, Chandler! It
isn't *you*, it isn't *Blenkarn*, it's Batty Todd that's the big
man. Batty Todd pulls the strings and—(*business of illustrating
marionettes*) 75

CHANDLER Oh, quite so, Todd, quite so! You know I always had
the highest opinion of you. You're quite a genius in your way,
Todd!

TODD I am, and let me tell you, Mr Cyrus Blenkarn is a devilish
lucky fellow to get hold of such a chap as Batty Todd! 80

CHANDLER When do you expect Blenkarn back? (*Comes to him
eagerly*)

TODD Can't say. We haven't heard from him for two or three weeks.

CHANDLER (*piteously*) I suppose you and Pegg couldn't give me a
situation in his absence? 85

TODD (*rises, clapping his hand on Chandler's shoulder*) My dear
Chandler, nothing would please me better than doing a good turn
to an old friend like you. But, candidly, you wouldn't be worth a
penny a month to us, candidly, you wouldn't.

CHANDLER You don't seem to admire me so much as you used, 90
Todd. (*Standing side by side*)

TODD (*shrugs his shoulders*) Well—umph.

CHANDLER What would you advise me to do?

TODD I should emigrate.

CHANDLER I don't think I'm suited for that. 95

TODD Try something you *are* suited for.

CHANDLER (*piteously*) But what am I suited for? I managed the old
works for twenty years.

TODD Excuse me! (*Sits C*) *I* managed them. *You* took the money.

CHANDLER Well, I was head of the concern. 100

TODD The figure-head, you mean.

CHANDLER I don't see what else I'm fit for.

TODD No, figure-heads aren't much use in the navigation of the ship,
are they?

CHANDLER (*very low tone, piteously*) I've come to my last shilling, 105
Todd.

TODD (*rises briskly*) Have you though? You don't mean to say
it's as bad as that? Well, I must be going—(*crosses up R and takes
hat*)

CHANDLER (*crosses to C, piteously*) You won't forget me, Todd?   110
(*Stopping him*)

TODD Rely on me. I won't forget you. (*Comes back to L of Chandler*)
By the way, don't call again at my office. I'm so busy just now. If
anything turns up, I'll let you know. Well, good-bye. (*Cheerfully*)
Keep your spirits up—hope things will turn out all right for you.   115
(*Going up C*)

CHANDLER Thank you, Todd. You were always a thoroughly good
fellow. A perfect treasure to me! I've always said so!

> *Enter Vachell at back C from R, meeting and stopping Todd.*
> *Chandler gets R*

TODD Ah, Mr Vachell, welcome to your new home! So you've come
to take possession! I congratulate you! Of course you'll live here   120
for the future? (*LC*)

VACHELL (*RC*) No, Mr Todd.

TODD No?

VACHELL No.

TODD Oh! You mean to let it?   125

VACHELL No, Mr Todd.

TODD No?

VACHELL No.

TODD Ah! I see! A little investment! Going to sell it again, eh?

VACHELL (*comes down C*) No. (*Todd is puzzled. Comes down again to*   130
L of Vachell. Vachell reading a legal paper. Todd tries to overlook.
Vachell quietly closes paper)

TODD (*confidently*) The estate won't be any good to cut up into
building lots, you know!

VACHELL You don't think so?   135

TODD Sure it won't.

VACHELL Thank you. (*Todd stands there a few moments puzzled*) I
won't cut it up into building lots, Mr Todd.

TODD No—no—I wouldn't. (*Going off at back*) What the deuce *has*
he bought the place for? (*Exit C at back to L*)   140

VACHELL Mr Chandler! (*Shakes hands with Chandler*) You received
my letter?

> *Mrs Chandler enters from conservatory, comes to Chandler's R*

CHANDLER Yes, we are quite ready to go. And I'm sure, Vachell,
we're exceedingly obliged to you for your kindness in allowing us
to remain so long.   145

VACHELL You needn't thank me. I have only acted upon my
instructions.

CHANDLER (*C*) Your instructions?

VACHELL (*LC*) I have not bought Tatlow Hall for myself. It belongs
to a client of mine.   150

MRS CHANDLER (*RC*) A client?

VACHELL It was his wish you should stay here till he could take
possession himself. Yesterday I had notice from him he would be
here at twelve today, and would require you to hand over
everything to him personally.   155

CHANDLER (*C*) And who is the new owner of Tatlow Hall?

VACHELL (*LC*) I am not at liberty to mention his name at present.
(*Takes out watch*) Excuse me; I expect him here every moment!
(*Exit C to R. Chandler and Mrs Chandler look at each other*)

CHANDLER (*C*) Who can have bought the place?   160

> *Maude enters from conservatory*

MAUDE Sir Seton and Lady Umfraville have just driven up.

MRS CHANDLER It must be the Umfravilles! They've got the money
from somewhere, and bought Tatlow Hall back again!

> *Servant enters at back and announces*

SERVANT Sir Seton and Lady Umfraville.

> *Enter at back Sir Seton and Lady Umfraville, who come down
> LC*

MRS CHANDLER (*crosses C*) My dear Sir Seton! (*Crosses to Sir Seton,*   165
then to Lady Umfraville) My dear Lady Umfraville!

CHANDLER (*LC*) Upon my word, Sir Seton, this is really noble of
you to call. It's touching! (*Shakes hands*)

SIR SETON (*LC*) Hum—yes—(*crosses back to Lady Umfraville*) the
fact is, Chandler, I ought to have come on this business before,   170
but, as it was confoundedly disagreeable, I put it off till the last
moment. But as your son is returning today—you know my
position—now don't you think it would be very imprudent on all
sides to allow this marriage between my daughter and your son to
take place—eh?   175

CHANDLER I had a letter from my son this morning in which
he—ah—ra—he tells me—that—

SIR SETON That he releases Felicia. Of course as an honourable man
he could do no less. Tell him I appreciate his conduct.

MAUDE (*at back of settee*) Sir Seton, you had better know the truth   180
from us. My brother writes that he has married abroad.

SIR SETON Has he? I congratulate him.

LADY UMFRAVILLE Most heartily.

MAUDE He asks us to break the news to Felicia.

SIR SETON We will—we will. And now it's passed off so comfortably,   185
there's no harm in our mentioning that—that—(*glancing at Lady
Umfraville*)

LADY UMFRAVILLE (*L*) Our dear Felicia has received an offer of
marriage from young Strangeways, the banker—(*Chandler and Mrs
Chandler exchange looks*)   190

SIR SETON So there's nothing more to be said in the matter except
to congratulate Captain Chandler—and—to express our sincere
sympathy in your misfortunes, our deepest sympathy. (*Shakes
hands with Mr Chandler*)

CHANDLER We have to thank you for allowing us to remain at   195
Tatlow Hall.

SIR SETON Remain at Tatlow Hall?

CHANDLER I suppose it is Mr Strangeways who has bought the
place?

SIR SETON Strangeways? No. Hasn't Vachell, the lawyer, bought it?   200

CHANDLER No. Not for himself. Only for some client, who has
allowed us the use of the place and paid all the current expenses.
(*Maude goes to door of conservatory*)

SIR SETON Indeed! Who can it be?

MRS CHANDLER We cannot imagine.   205
    Vachell enters at back. Mrs Chandler drops down R

SIR SETON (*LC*) Ah, Vachell! You can explain. Who's the new
owner here?

CHANDLER (*RC*) Yes, Vachell—who is it that has been so kind to
us?
    Cyrus enters at back C from R, plainly, but well dressed

VACHELL (*C*) The new owner is Mr Cyrus Blenkarn. (*Cyrus comes   210
down. All show great surprise*)

CHANDLER Blenkarn! Then you—

CYRUS (*C, calm*) I will take possession of Tatlow Hall if you are ready
to give it up.

CHANDLER Yes, I am ready. But perhaps you'll allow me—(*crosses to   215
Cyrus*)

CYRUS (*waves him off*) Give everything over to Mr Vachell. Mr
Vachell, please take possession of this place for me.
    *Maude and Mrs Chandler exit through conservatory R. Vachell
    crosses behind to R of Chandler. Chandler is about to speak, but
    Cyrus waves him away, and Vachell ushers him off into
    conservatory R*

LADY UMFRAVILLE (*L*) My dear Mr Blenkarn, I'm heartily glad we shall have you for a neighbour. You know I have always considered   220
you a man of the greatest genius. And I adore genius!

CYRUS (*C*) Thank you, Lady Umfraville, I'm not a genius, and I don't like being adored.

SIR SETON (*C*) If there's anything I can do for you in the county, Mr Blenkarn—you may have some idea of going into Parliament.   225

CYRUS No. (*Absorbed*)

LADY UMFRAVILLE You must come and dine with us on Wednesday at the Court. We expect Lord William Vipond and the Strange-ways and old Lady Devenish—

CYRUS I'm not used to meeting such people, my lady, and I   230
shouldn't know what to say to them. (*To Vachell R*) Mr Vachell, Mr Pegg will be here directly to go through everything with you. (*Vachell goes off R*)

SIR SETON But we shall have the pleasure of seeing you at the Court some day?   235

CYRUS (*in front of settee*) No, Sir Seton, I've had to work all my life, and I can't begin to play now. I've done the one thing I set my heart upon. They told me I should never find out the secret, but I did it! (*Triumphantly*) I did it! And now it's done, I don't know what to do with the rest of my life. I begin to wish I'd got all the   240
ground to go over again.

SIR SETON Come and see us sometimes. We'd do our best to make you feel at home.

CYRUS No, Sir Seton, let me be! Let me be! My life's done! But if you want to be kind to me, I have a daughter—(*recollecting*) I had   245
two—and it was in this room—(*giving way*) the day before she left me—(*sits C. Breaks down utterly, hides his face in his hands*)

> *Sir Seton watches him for a moment, then beckons to Lady Umfraville and very quietly and unobtrusively takes her off R. Pause*

CYRUS (*rises*) I can't stop here! I can't stop here! (*Exit C to L, dropping his hat as he goes out*)

> *Enter Jesse Pegg at window L, in high top hat and frock coat*

JESSE (*puts hat on table, speaking off at window in a very brisk,   250
business-like, but not unkind tone*) Come, come, Mrs Pegg. You're late again! Always late! Come, come! Are you coming, or are you not?

> *Nancy enters at window L*

NANCY I'm very sorry, Jesse! I couldn't help it! (*Meekly*)

JESSE (*RC, takes out watch*) Ten minutes this morning! Three   255
minutes yesterday! Seven minutes at the concert on Monday!
Twenty minutes you've wasted for me this week! It's a little too
bad! (*Shaking his head severely, but not unkindly*)

NANCY (*LC*) Ten minutes this morning looking after your son and
heir—three minutes yesterday ordering your dinner—seven   260
minutes on Monday making myself handsome enough to be seen
with you. (*Comes to him, hand on his shoulder*)

JESSE Handsome is that handsome does, and the wife who wastes her
husband's time can have very little memory of all she promised at
the altar.   265

NANCY Do you forget what you promised me before we went to the
altar?

JESSE I have no recollection, my dear, of having promised you
anything in particular.

NANCY Oh, Jesse! You promised me everything! Everything!   270

JESSE Did I? I don't remember being so foolish!

NANCY It's very seldom, dear, that I keep you waiting.

JESSE Once a year, my darling, is once too often.

NANCY You know, Jesse, I'm always studying you. I'm thinking all
day long how I can make you happy!   275

JESSE Quite right, my dear, and you do make me happy.

NANCY Then give me a kiss and say you forgive me.

JESSE (*kisses her in a very business-like way*) There! There! I forgive
you, but don't do it again. I wonder where your father is? (*Turns
up stage for a moment*)   280

NANCY To think that he should have bought Tatlow Hall! Oh, if
Mary were only alive to know it! (*Crosses to back of settee*)

JESSE (*C*) Poor Mary! It's strange your father hasn't been able to find
out any particulars of her death.

NANCY No—if she sailed in that ship, it must have been in another   285
name.

JESSE I wish we had followed the track of that young widow-lady.

NANCY The one whose baby died—

JESSE Yes. It would have been a natural thing under the circumstances for Mary—   290

NANCY (*looking off R*) Here's Mr Chandler coming! Don't let him
see, poor man! It will seem as if we wanted to triumph over him.
(*Moving away to L*)
    Servant enters, C from R, comes down R of Nancy

SERVANT A letter for Mrs Pegg, very important. It has been sent on
from your own house, ma'am.   295

NANCY Thank you! (*Reads letter, shows great surprise and joy*)
    Chandler has entered from conservatory R

NANCY (*with great delight*) Jesse! Read that! Read that!

CHANDLER (*humbly*) Good morning, Mrs Pegg. (*Holding out his
hand*)

NANCY (*while Jesse has read letter*) Good morning, Mr Chandler. We   300
can't stay, Mr Chandler. (*She snatches hold of Jesse's arm, and
hurries him off at window, letter in hand, bewildered*) Come along,
Jesse! Quick! Quick! (*Drags Jesse off at window L*)
    Cyrus enters, C from L

CHANDLER Can't stay! Afraid I want to borrow money of 'em, I
suppose. (*Going towards window*) It's a blackguard world to live in!   305
(*Cyrus comes down C from L. He picks up his hat and is going.
Chandler LC*) Mr Blenkarn! Could I speak to you for a moment?

CYRUS (*C*) Well? (*Comes down C to corner of settee*)

CHANDLER I wanted to say that I behaved very badly to you in the
past. I ought to have paid you better for your invention. I ought   310
to have taken you into partnership. I hope you will allow me to
say, I'm very sorry.

CYRUS (*embarrassed*) You have said it.

CHANDLER It was strange that I should have built the new works for
you to occupy!   315

CYRUS Very strange. (*Half turned from him*)

CHANDLER Todd tells me in a few years they'll hardly be large
enough.

CYRUS I daresay.

CHANDLER I thought perhaps you might have a vacancy in some   320
small way where I could be useful to you—some very small
way—I'm not particular.

CYRUS I don't know of any, Mr Chandler.

CHANDLER It's hard to come down in the world after having been
up in it all your life.   325

CYRUS (*turning on him*) It's hard to be kept down in it all your life
without having a chance to get up.

CHANDLER You'll find me a corner—you'll forget the past and give
me a chance?

CYRUS I've nothing for you, Mr Chandler. (*Goes up C*)   330

CHANDLER But in so large a concern, for an old friend—

CYRUS What!

CHANDLER I may call myself a friend.

CYRUS No, I think not. You might have been my friend once—you remember—   335

CHANDLER I remember. (*Crosses to R*) I'm sorry I troubled you, but in a few days I may not be able to get even a meal. You wouldn't wish me to starve—

CYRUS (*taking out note-case*) No, I wouldn't wish you to starve. (*Giving note*) That will provide for you for the time.   340

CHANDLER (*effusively*) Thank you! Thank you, Blenkarn! I'm very grateful, most grateful, I assure you. And if any little situation should turn up—

CYRUS No, no. (*Takes no notice and turns away*)

CHANDLER (*going R*) I know I don't deserve it, Blenkarn, but there's   345
one who would ask you to forgive me if she were alive. Your daughter Mary—

CYRUS Stop! Don't you mention her name. Don't *you* remind me of her.

> *Chandler exits through conservatory R*

CYRUS 'There's one who would ask you to forgive me if she were   350
alive. Your daughter Mary.' Oh, my dear, if I could call you back to me, if I could hold you once to my heart! Mary! Mary! If you were alive, dear, this would be your home! Can't you hear me, dear? (*Pause*) This beautiful home is all yours. I've bought it for you! And you will never come to it! (*Sits C*) Not all the money in   355
the world will buy you back to me for one short hour. What shall I do to your enemies, my dear? They're in my hands. Their very bread is mine to give or to refuse them. I can punish them! I can humble them to the dust! Shall I strike them down, dear, or shall I have mercy? If you were here to guide me, what would you tell   360
me to do? Would you forgive them, dear? I've got my revenge, but it doesn't satisfy me. I don't want them to suffer. I want to forgive them. Tell me, Mary! You were always kind and gentle. Yes, you would forgive them, and I'll forgive them too. That shall be my revenge! (*Rises, goes to conservatory. Calls off*) Mr Chandler! Mr   365
Chandler!

> *Chandler, Maude and Mrs Chandler appear in conservatory.*
> *They all enter R*

CYRUS (*comes to C*) Mr Chandler! You will be my under-manager at the works at a salary of four hundred pounds a year. And you can live in the house that is vacant there.

CHANDLER It's too good of you, Mr Blenkarn! I don't deserve it! But   370
I thank you with all my heart.

CYRUS Don't thank me! Thank the memory of my poor wronged
girl, that begged forgiveness for you!

MAUDE You will accept my thanks, Mr Blenkarn? (*Crosses to Cyrus*)

CYRUS Yes, my dear, for you were always kind to us. Nancy has told   375
me. (*Maude retires to door of conservatory*)
> *Noise of shouting and music outside, growing nearer. Three*
> *distant shouts and music, march*

CYRUS What's the meaning of those shouts?
> *Todd enters hastily at window L*

TODD (*down L*) My dear Mr Blenkarn, I congratulate you most
heartily! (*Warmly to Cyrus*) Delightful to find you are the owner
of Tatlow Hall! But Captain Chandler is making a mistake—   380

CYRUS Captain Chandler?

TODD Yes. Didn't you know he is returning from Africa today?

CYRUS No. And he's coming here?

TODD Yes, of course—they've given him a demonstration for his
bravery, and they're bringing him here to his father's house,   385
(*glancing at Chandler*) as he thinks.

CYRUS (*to Chandler*) Did you know of this?

CHANDLER I knew he was returning to Tatlow, but it is not by my
wish he comes here.

TODD And it seems he's bringing his wife with him.   390

CYRUS His wife?!

TODD Somebody he's married abroad. (*Looking off*) They're coming
into the house! I'd better go and stop them, shall I?

CYRUS No, let them come, let them come. (*Todd goes up stage. To
Chandler*) What did you let him come here for if you wanted me   395
to forgive you? Do you think I can bury the past now? No, I can't
do it! I can't shelter and feed those who robbed me of her, and
drove her away from me to die in a strange land. I can't do it! I
have tried, but it's beyond me.
> *Band and music nearer. Three shouts outside, louder. Julian*
> *rushes hurriedly in by window as if to escape crowd*

JULIAN I've got rid of them at last! And here I am at home! Home!   400
Mr Blenkarn! (*Meeting Cyrus*)

CYRUS (*seizing him*) My child! You robbed me of my child! My
Mary! Answer to me for her! My girl! Give her to me! Do you
hear? My child!

JULIAN (*disengaging himself*) Forgive me, Mr Blenkarn. Then you   405
  never got our letters explaining?

CYRUS Letters? No. Explaining what?

JULIAN I suppose we've got here before them. I wrote you explaining
  I'd done my best to right things.

CYRUS How? By bringing your wife here—here to the very place   410
  where—? Well, let her come and know the truth about you from
  me. (*Julian goes up to window*) Your wife! Bring her to me! I want
  to see her.

JULIAN You shall see her!

> *Music outside continued. Mary, Jesse and Nancy enter at
> window*

You shall see her! (*Presenting Mary*) My wife!   415

MARY Father! (*Holds out her arms. March forte*)

> *Cyrus cannot believe his eyes, looks at her for a few moments,
> then snatches her into his arms and cries like a child*

CURTAIN

EXPLANATORY NOTES

The Inchcape Bell

1.1.4 *the Inchcape Bell*: by legend on the coast of Scotland.

27 *this Preventive Service*: an early term for Customs and Excise.

58 *principal soubrette*: a theatrical term for the lively female servant character of the nineteenth-century stock company.

69 *sawyer*: a workman who saws timber, especially in a sawpit.

128 *mopnail*: a nail of marine use employed in the making of mops.

159 S.D. '*Blue Bonnets*': a very free adaptation of the 'Border March' from Sir Walter Scott's novel *The Monastery* (1820), with music by William Thomas Parke, 1820.

179 *lignum wity*: lignum vitae; in this case the resin from the guaiacum tree.

1.2.49 *destestations*: Beckey means 'protestations'.

51 *deal*: a plank sawn from a log, of a particular length, width, and thickness. Beckey, referring to Sampson, puns on 'deal'.

1.3 S.D. *knotted rocks on the flats*: rocks with lumps and protuberances painted onto the canvas flats depicting the exterior scene.

10 *rover*: a pirate.

1.4 S.D. *A verandah and window, practicable*: can be used on stage like a real verandah and window.

9 *clincher*: originally, one who securely fixes a nail or bolt by flattening the end of it. Sampson is using the vocabulary of his trade.

10 *peg off*: move quickly.

39 *perlite*: polite.

48 *dickament*: predicament.

49 *suspicious*: auspicious. Sampson and Beckey frequently indulge in malapropisms.

76 *hop-o'-my-thumb's head*: a slighting reference to little Jupiter Seabreeze, Hop-o'-my thumb being a folk-tale dwarf.

97 *horns*: although Sampson is not yet Beckey's husband, Jupiter already thinks of him as wearing the traditional marks of the cuckold, a pair of horns.

101 *your own cunning little Jupiter*: a reference to the skills in seduction of Seabreeze's great namesake.

114 *Heels befriend me*: Sampson is running away, or taking to his heels.

118 S.D. *Picture*: for an explanation of this visual stage convention, see the Introduction, iv.

2.1. S.D. unless he has gone below during the song and the dance, it is difficult to see how Hattock can carouse on deck and then enter from the hold.
free-trader: a smuggler.

8 S.D. *hornpipe*: following the song, at least one specialist dancer among the crew of the ship performs this lively, traditional sailor's dance, a common feature of English nautical melodrama.

36 S.D. *One of the crew hauls the boat alongside, L.* The right side of the stage is occupied by the smuggler's vessel, or part of it, lying parallel to the footlights. The boat is worked on stage—perhaps pushed by concealed stagehands, or pulled by a rope—between canvas cloths on rollers depicting the sea. It is fastened to the side of the ship, and goes off left at the end of the scene.

69 S.D. *the rest open a trap . . . shut the trap*: one of the regular stage trapdoors, postioned in the deck of the ship, is opened to admit the unwilling Jupiter.

2.2.7 *'peaching*: informing or accusing.

9 *pressed*: forcibly conveyed on board by a press gang and inducted into the crew.

51 *terrific*: frightful, terrifying.

56 S.D. *He breaks away one side of the Bell with his hatchet*: large bells, cast from bronze, an alloy of copper and tin, were highly susceptible to fracture, and could easily crack if attacked with a hatchet. Sampson is of course attacking a property bell, not a real one.

61 *Mr Boreous*: Boreas, the north wind.

89 *a hobble*: a difficult situation.

2.3.52 *turnscrew*: a screwdriver.

146 S.D. *gun heard at a distance*: a ship's signal of distress.

174 *dromedary . . . dromitory*: neither Sampson nor Beckey can come up with the right word, 'dormitory', in its meaning of a single sleeping chamber.

2.4 S.D. *As the scene changes*: the chamber flat of the preceding scene is being slid off to right and left to reveal the shipwreck, which takes up the full depth of the stage.

11 *jolly-boat*: a ship's boat.

26 S.D. *The crew . . . hurry into the boat*: it is unlikely that this boat is seen; the crew would simply go over the side of the ship.

48 *All have sunk . . . trough of the sea*: however, Guy Ruthven has just told us (wrongly, as it seems) that the crew has escaped the wreck. Or it may be that just before saying this line, he looks over the side of the ship and sees wreckage.

58 S.D. *A boat is seen leaving the shore in the background*: this would be an upstage 'profile' boat in miniature, simply a canvas and wood façade of

one side of the boat with small figures in profile attached, and drawn along by an invisible stage-hand.

60 S.D. *Re-enter Sampson, Taffrail, and Sir John, in the boat*: this time, a full-size boat, like the boat in 2.1.

Did You Ever Send Your Wife to Camberwell?

S.D. *closet*: a small room, in this instance a dressing-room.

S.D. '*We may be happy yet*': a ballad from the opera *The Daughter of St Mark* (1844), lyrics Alfred Bunn, music Michael William Balfe.

1 '*Oh, never name departed years, &c.*': the last two verses of the song (Mrs Honeybun misquotes the first line) are:

> O never name departed days,
> Nor vows you whisper'd then,
> Round which too sad a feeling plays,
> To trust their tones again.
>
> Regard their shadows round thee cast,
> As if we ne'er had met.
> And thus unmindful of the past
> We may be happy yet, we may be happy,
> we may be happy yet.

12 *sheep's trotters*: the feet of a sheep, an extremely cheap meat dish for the poor.

19 *yard of clay . . . Holds up his pipe*: Honeybun is smoking a churchwarden, a clay pipe with a very long stem.

28 *one pound one*: twenty-one shillings, or a guinea.

34 *Clements Inn*: formerly an Inn of Chancery and part of the Inner Temple, one of the Inns of Court, just north of the Strand. By the early Victorian period it had degenerated into cheap apartments.

40 '*The times are out of joint*': 'The time is out of joint . . .' (*Hamlet*, 1.5).

42 *milk account . . . a serious 'chalk' to us in that article*: until regulations prevented the practice, milk was commonly adulterated by chalk. Honeybun is also referring to the tavern practice of keeping a customer's account in chalk marks on a slate.

48 *the Thames Tunnel*: opened in 1843 as a tunnel for pedestrians between Wapping and Rotherhithe.

54 *tin*: money.

59 *porter*: a dark bitter beer.

67 *cutting*: wounding the feelings.

69 *Camberwell*: now a district of London east of Brixton, but in the 1840s a pleasant and still largely rural village in Surrey, about four miles from Clements Inn.

78 *a dunstable bonnet*: a straw bonnet.

130 *Stoke Poges*: a village in Buckinghamshire.

149 *hydro-galvanic*: there is (and was) no such word, but Crank means something like 'hydro-electric'.

171 *the broad or the narrow gauge*: measurements for the width of railway lines, $7'$ or $4'$ $8\frac{1}{2}''$ respectively. The current debate over the proper width of gauge was unsatisfactorily resolved by the 1846 Regulation of Gauge of Railways Act, which failed to adopt a standard gauge throughout the kingdom.

174 *dodge*: a clever scheme or expedient.

183 *the Terpsichorean art*: the art of dancing.

190 *the polka*: introduced in Paris in the early 1840s, the polka became a craze, sweeping Europe and America.

201 *the statty at Charing Cross*: the equestrian statue of Charles I.

217 *bobbinet*: machined cotton net, made in imitation of lace.

250 *Warren disdains to shine*: Warren's Blacking, a shoe-polish. See also Richard III, 5.3: 'the sun . . . disdains to shine'.

297 *green*: simple, gullible.

302 *What's in a name*: see Romeo and Juliet, 2.2 'What's in a name? That which we call a rose | By any other name would smell as sweet.'

314 *satisfaction*: Crank intends to fight a duel with Honeybun, which is why he rushes off for pistols.

329 *twelve gentlemen will sit upon that small child's body*: Honeybun is punning: twelve gentlemen sitting upon the baby will squash it even flatter, and a coroner's jury of twelve technically 'sits' when it considers if a crime has been committed.

373 *lighted me up stairs*: Mrs Honeybun complains that her husband did not bring a candle to the otherwise dark stairs.

427 *mum*: in this usage, 'ma'am'.

491 *I found this baby there this evening*: in the text, the words are 'this morning', but this is an obvious error since Mrs Jewell does not enter the room until it has grown dark, and Mrs Honeybun has been sent to catch the 'seven o'clock omnibus'.

512 *our uncle*: a pawnbroker.

527 *it is my intention . . . till further notice*: it was traditional at the end of early Victorian farces to appeal to the audience for a run of the piece; such an appeal was cleverly woven into the text of the play.

S.D. *Disposition of characters at the fall of the curtain*: in the curtain call plan in the text, L and R probably indicate left and right from the audience's viewpoint (although this is unusual), since a convex semicircle of actors facing the audience is an unlikely curtain-call position for a proscenium stage.

The Game of Speculation

1.21 *He's settled*: the creditor is floored or 'done for'.

53 *protested bills*: written orders for payment, or bills of exchange, or promissory notes upon which payment or acceptance has been refused.

Basinghall Street: a street in the City of London containing the halls of wealthy guilds and business offices.

66 *Van Amburgh*: Isaac Van Amburgh (1811–68), an American lion-tamer, appeared first in London with his menagerie upon the stages of Astley's and Drury Lane. He was a favourite of Queen Victoria's.

69 *post obits*: bonds securing to the lender a sum of money payable upon the death of a particular person.

106 *Soyer*: Alexis Soyer (1809–59), the famous French chef of the Reform Club in London.

120 *Christmas-boxes*: traditionally, presents given to tradesmen and delivery men at Christmas; hence Boxing Day.

129 *chartists*: generally, political reformers or agitators. The Chartist movement peaked in the 1840s.

140 *the Savings' Bank*: the first English savings banks were established in the early nineteenth century.

154 *the Iron Duke*: the Duke of Wellington (1769–1852).

157 *brass*: impudence, effrontery.

162 *the Three-per cents*: 3 per cent was a standard interest rate for stocks until the 1880s.

317 *flam*: a fabrication or deception.

413 '*The man who has a wife . . . hostages to fortune*': 'Of Marriage and Single Life', by Francis Bacon (1561–1626).

551 S.D. *Earthworm's pantomime*: Hawk has seen Earthworm tap his pockets but not heard his words.

555   *sovereigns*: gold coin worth one pound sterling.

577   *a pavement . . . barricades are impossible*: a reference to the revolutions of 1848.

580   *Governments interested in the maintenance of order*: Hawk's 'Conservative Pavement' is of course a persuasive speculative fantasy, but in order to convince Earthworm he points to the very real public disorders in several European countries in the various revolutions of 1848; his chief market for his new pavement will be Europe. There was no revolution of 1848 in England, and no comparable disorders, although in Glasgow in 1848 there had been a serious Chartist riot, the last of the Chartist disturbances of the 1840s. The great Chartist demonstration of 1848 in London, and the presentation of a monster petition to Parliament, passed off peacefully.

716   *on 'Change*: on the Stock Exchange.

720   *all my plate is—having my crest engraved on it*: his plate is at the pawnbroker's.

756   *I'll go and fetch the money*. The rapid financial machinations of Hawk are complex, and perhaps require elucidation. By the end of Act I Hawk has under false pretences obtained £500 from Earthworm, £200 from Hardcore (who has been persuaded to sell his allegedly risky shares in a mine), a promise of a delay in prosecution from another creditor, Grossmark, together with some bills of exchange in return for shares—these bills become important in Act 2—and £300 and the loan of dinner plate from Prospectus, who is able because of Hawk's bamboozling of Hardcore to buy the latter's shares in the Emerald Mine Co. cheaply. All the money raised by these devices has gone to pay debts to tradesmen and to provide a splendid show (including new jewels) so that the apparently wealthy Sir Harry Lester can be duped into marrying Julia Hawk and thus save her father from immediate ruin.

2.214   *gulled*: deceived, duped.

235   *tick*: credit.

      tiger: a footman or manservant.

253   *pigeons*: persons who can be swindled.

277   *phasis*: phase.

287   *I shall be a Protectionist . . . I shall go in for the farmers' friend*: the Protectionists were opponents of the prevailing free-trade system, and especially resisted the importation of cheap foodstuffs, which farmers also opposed.

414   *acceptances*: an acceptance of the liability to pay a bill when it is due.

417   *nabob*: a very rich man.

424   *whom he christens*: Bradshaw has invented a title for his aunt.

513   *Croesus*: the last king of Lydia, proverbial for great wealth.

527 *blown upon*: informed upon, defamed.

564 *Tomorrow I have the control of thousands*: By the end of Act 2 Hawk's financial position is desperate: Sir Harry's name and fortune are fictions, and he cannot save himself by the 'splendid marriage' he contemplated. His plan now is to stave off his creditors for a few more days, during which time—as is explained in Act 3—he will through Grossmark's agency buy hundreds of now devalued Emerald Mine shares and sell them when the market rises, thus realizing a profit of £20,000, enough to pay all his debts. At the end of Act 2, however, the audience does not yet know what Hawk's plans are, nor does it yet know that he will try to dupe his creditors by asking Sir Harry to impersonate Hawk's absconded partner, Sparrow, and pretending that a now remorseful and fabulously wealthy Sparrow has returned from the East to lavish wealth upon Hawk. All this will be revealed in Act 3.

3.56 *ducks and drakes*: in this sense, playing idly with, throwing away.

80 *cold pig*: waking a person up with cold water; in this instance Hawk's use of 'Bradshaw' instead of 'Sir Harry' acts like a bucket of cold water.

102 *the Bench*: probably a reference to Queen's Bench Prison, where debtors were imprisoned, but possibly to the Court of Queen's Bench in Westminster for the hearing of civil cases, and more generally to any court of justice.

136 *Long Acre*: a street in Covent Garden that was a centre for the coach and carriage building trade.

137 *a fur pelisse and a long pigtail*: a pelisse was a long cloak; the pigtail would have given the returned 'Sparrow' the look of one who had lived many years in the East.

320 *postchaise*: a travelling carriage.

413 *Bull the market with the Tobolsk Mines*: to 'bull' was to try to raise the price of stocks (cf. 'bull market', a market of rising stock prices); the Tobolsk Mines, like the Emerald Mine, is a fictitious company.

420 *I have moved the mountain*: Hawk's comparison of himself to Mahomet is inaccurately drawn from Bacon's essay, 'Boldness': 'If the hill will not come to Mahomet, Mahomet will go to the hill.'

495 *scrip*: share certificates.

555 *Now I do not understand*. Hawk is trying to pay off some of his debts with the £2,000 in cash that Noble brought him at the beginning of Act 3, pretending that the money and the bills of exchange come from 'Sparrow', whom Hawk believes is at that moment being impersonated by Sir Harry. While he can understand the creditors being given bills of exchange—which Hawk believes are not worth the paper they are written on, coming from an imposter—he is bewildered by the

various payments being made in ready cash, since these will leave his pressing debt of £2,000 to Grossmark for the Emerald Mine shares unpaid.

556 *Bank of Elegance*: counterfeit notes.

644 *old Weller's advice*: old Weller is probably Sam Weller's father in Pickwick Papers, but this particular advice is not contained in any of his sagacious utterances.

halter: a rope with a noose, for hanging a person.

The Lights o' London

1 S.D. *Practicable*: in this scene, the stage consists of three playing areas: the Lodge, Squire Armytage's library with French windows opening onto the lawn, and the trees and seat on the lawn. Both the Lodge and the library must therefore be 'practicable'.

S.D. *Open lively*: a cue to the orchestra.

37 *knows his book*: sees his advantage.

52 S.D. *business*: there are many such stage directions in the play—and in many nineteenth-century playtexts—and there is no way of knowing precisely what the business was. The actors, or the actors and the stage manager, would have devised the business in advance; it was not improvised during performance.

76 *the Great City*: a common term for London; as in Andrew Halliday's melodrama of 1867, *The Great City*.

98 *brick*: a good fellow.

99 *a long firm cheque*: a cheque dated a long time ahead that has not lost value.

139 *the Lights o' London*: not only the title of the play but also a song by Louis Diehl, 'The Lights of London Town' (1880), with lyrics by Sims.

183 *'The Village Beauty'*: an eighteenth-century moral narrative, and a poem and tale of the 1880s, but not a Victorian novel; none of the published items has this ending.

257 *works the oracle*: obtains his ends by dubious means.

419 S.D. *the triple action*: action will occur simultaneously in the three playing areas: the Lodge, the library, and the lawn.

2.1 S.D. *Discover*: the flats open, or the drop curtain is raised to reveal the scene behind, and the characters already in place (see note for 4.1.182).

23 *the sharpest winter we've had for many a year*: the winter of 1880–1 was exceptionally cold and snowy.

27 *a h'extra company*: an augmented company. The added 'h' ' in front of 'extra' was a standard way of rendering a feature of London working-class speech that struck middle-class observers as both distinctive and amusing.

43 *Feenonynom*: the child or Infant Phenomenon was a much advertised feature of the nineteenth-century stage, and there were several well-known ones, the most prominent fictional example being a leading member of the Vincent Crummles company in Dickens's *Nicholas Nickleby*.

64 *me a playin' Medea*: Mrs Jarvis probably played Medea, who murdered her children in the Greek legend and the Euripides tragedy, in a contemporary burlesque. There were several Victorian stage burlesques of Medea, the most popular by Robert Brough in 1856.

69 *crib*: a cheap lodging or room.

85 *chuck the bills about*: post playbills advertising the play.

103 *a tragedy for one night only . . . we couldn't announce till further notice*: 'For one night only' was a common insertion on playbills to attract an audience. Jarvis means that such a tragedy as their own murder could indeed be played only once, but that since the event and its possible timing were uncertain it could not yet be announced.

117 *Don't take him out*: don't take the horse out of the shafts of the trap or carriage.

2.2 S.D. *The Jarvis caravan seen coming along the road*. Despite what Jarvis says and what the stage directions imply, the illustrations of the first production at the Princess's Theatre in London do not show a horse. What they do show is the caravan parked on stage right, with the front of it out of sight offstage. It is quite possible, however, that a real horse, with Jarvis at its head ('*Draws caravan across stage*') crossed the stage from left to right and, once off right, was taken away by stage-hands. Horses were not uncommon on the late Victorian stage.

2 '*Tis my delight | On a starry night*': Jarvis is singing a traditional song, 'The Lincolnshire Poacher'. The third line is a variant of the more common 'In the season of the year', and it should be a 'shiny' rather than a 'starry' night.

8 *them there syrups Iago advertises in the play*: 'Not poppy, nor mandragora, | Nor all the drowsy syrups of the world. . . .' (*Othello*, 3.3).

29 *coves*: fellows, chaps.

60 *lor a mussy*: 'Lord have mercy'—an exclamation of surprise.

101 *if the ghost didn't walk*: if 'the ghost walked', theatre wages were paid; if not—a frequent occurrence—the actors and staff were left unpaid for a week's work. The ghost walked on a Friday or Saturday.

103 *sharin' terms*: a system whereby an actor received a share of the box office rather than a fixed wage.

109 *dishability*: dishabille, a state of undress.

3.1.3 *mag*: a halfpenny.

  7 *century*: £100. Jack suggests to Cutts that if he confessed to murder he should have a share of the £100 reward.

 20 *flat*: stupid, easily duped.

 32 *donah*: a woman, especially a sweetheart.

 54 *spondulicks*: money.

3.2 S.D. *Boston St., Boro'*: this street in the Borough of Southwark no longer exists, but it was just off the Borough Market (see note for 5.1).

   S.D. *slop work*: the making of cheap or ready-made clothes.

  1 *a oner*: a remarkable or special person.

  7 *right on my pins*: steady on my legs.

   a hornpipe . . . a breakdown: in contrast to the hornpipe, a lively sailor's dance, the breakdown was a shuffling dance frequently performed in minstrel shows.

  9 *the living skeleton*: a common exhibit at fairs and freak shows.

 27 *the last act of the 'Idiot Witness'*: The Idiot Witness (1823), by J. T. Haines, a domestic melodrama.

 94 *as turning money away*: from the box office, because the theatre is full.

101 *tanner*: sixpence.

104 *When he comes out of the tree . . . and begins to jabber*: in the actual Haines text, Gilbert the Idiot Witness exposes the guilt of a villain who has murdered his own son. He does not come out of a tree. Such melodramas, however, were freely adapted by strolling players like the Jarvises.

116 *Mum*: keep quiet.

117 *fly*: acute, knowing.

119 *the low comedy merchant*: low comedy was a stock company 'line of business' in which the actor specialized in farcical or broadly humorous characters; *merchant*: fellow, chap.

124 *slouch hat*: a soft hat with a broad brim partly covering the face.

249 *spotted dog*: a suet pudding made with currants or raisins.

257 *under the circus*: Mrs Jarvis should have said 'under the circs', or 'circumstances'.

261 *quartern loaf*: a four pound loaf.

   duff: a pudding or dumpling.

282 *extraditious*: Mrs Jarvis should have said 'expeditious'.

299 *benefit*: a theatrical performance of which the actor (or a group of lesser actors) received the box office revenue after the fixed costs of the evening had been deducted. Until the end of the nineteenth century this was an important supplement to the actor's wages.

326 *cans*: when beer was bought in a tavern and 'taken out', it was carried in cans with lids rather than bottles.

376 *the Gas, the Queen's or the Water*: the gas company collector, the tax collector, or the water rate collector.

379 S.D. *Two detectives . . . enter R:* in the original manuscript, the detectives in this scene are merely identified as First and Second Detective. Internal evidence reveals them to be the only detectives in the play, and the only ones in the cast list, Waters and Cutts respectively.

384 *imperence*: impudence.

385 *a h'order*: a theatrical reference: an order was a chit signed by the management entitling the bearer to a free seat. Mrs Jarvis really means a search warrant.

400 *I play one of the Princes what's murdered in the Tower*: a reference to *Richard III*.

4.1 S.D. *Open moderate*: another music cue.

80 *cut*: move quickly.

182 S.D. *Scene closes in*: Here the two flats painted with the outside of the workhouse and street as indicated in the scene direction for 4.2 close to hide the room of 4.1. By the 1880s, however, it is quite possible—at least in the West End and the more modern provincial theatres—that the new scene was flown in and the old terminology still used, since the old system of flats and wings sliding in grooves was fast disappearing. 4.2 is what was known as a carpenter's scene; that is, a scene positioned toward the front of the stage, written to a length sufficient to allow a big scene to be set up behind it—in this case 4.3, the Slips, Regent's Park.

4.2.4 *William Corder in the last Act of 'Maria Marten'*: the murderer who goes to the gallows at the end of the stock melodrama, *Maria Marten, or The Murder in the Red Barn*, several versions of which were performed in the 1830s. *Maria Marten* held the stage well into the twentieth century.

27 *remanded on my own recognizances for a week*: Jarvis has bound himself to appear in court in a week.

47 *Mister Irving when he's a going to play Othello*: Irving opened as Othello at the Lyceum in May 1881, four months before the first performance of *The Lights o' London*.

61 *kippered attics*: Mrs Jarvis's malapropism for kippered haddocks.

63 *Lawks a mussy*: see note for 'lor a mussy', 2.2.60 above.

84 S.D. *Casuals enter R and L*: 'casuals' were the indigent occupants of a workhouse's casual ward, a room providing free overnight shelter to the homeless and destitute. Here Sims and the Princess's stage management 'realized', i.e. replicated by a combination of actors, properties, and scene-painting, Luke Fildes's well-known painting, *Applicants for Admission to a Casual Ward* (1874).

85 *Trotters*: whether sheep's trotters or pig's trotters is not specified. See note above for *Did You Ever Send Your Wife to Camberwell?* l. 12.

95 *He's got 'em all on*: Percy is a 'toff' down on his luck, still wearing once elegant but now shabby clothes.

101 *stone breaking*: an arduous manual occupation necessary for road building, practised by convicts and poorly paid labourers.

128 *a shakedown*: a makeshift bed, often of straw.

138 *two doorsteps*: two thick slices of bread and butter, possibly a sandwich.

172 *the mission*: the two gentlemen are discussing a charitable contribution to a Christian missionary society active in Africa.

240 S.D. *Scene changes*: the backing flats for 4.2—the workhouse and the street—are now slid to right and left, or flown, to reveal 4.3 already set up behind them.

4.3 S.D. *The Slips*: a short section of the Regent's Canal on the north edge of Regent's Park, just below St Mark's Bridge, where the canal widens into a small pool or basin used as an anchorage for canal boats and as a place where barges could be turned around more easily to the north, in the direction of Camden Locks, or vice versa. Now Cumberland Basin, it has been partially filled in.

6 *Dreaming as you dwelt in marble halls*: 'I dreamt that I dwelt in marble halls', a popular aria from Balfe's opera, *The Bohemian Girl* (1843), with lyrics by Alfred Bunn.

7 *doss*: a cheap bed for the night.

23 *all the watches is gone home*: it is too late at night for respectable men, wearing pocket watches, to be walking through the Park.

25 *Sling your hook*: make off, get moving.

26 *ulster*: a long loose overcoat, often worn with a belt, a garment then in fashion.

32 *Mother Hubbard*: a cloak.

33 *hansom*: a two-wheeled cab with space for two fares and the driver.

60 *prig*: steal.

63 *wanderin' without visible means of subsistence*: a criminal offence under the Vagrancy Act of 1824.

64 *beak*: a magistrate.

67 *quod*: prison.

122 *Shut o' me*: rid of me.

125 *Newgate*: for centuries London's main prison, demolished in 1902.

167 S.D. *Seth drops into water*. Water on stage was commonly represented by painted canvas arranged in strips or rollers (which could be turned by handles if the sea was to be represented) parallel to the footlights, with three or four-foot gaps between the strips invisible to the audience, from whose viewpoint the water seemed unbroken. Blue and green limelights would add convincing colour. The actor playing Seth would fall safely onto mattresses concealed between two of the strips, possibly onto the top of a bridge below stage level (see Introduction, xi–xii), with the stage planking above the bridge removed. Harold would have followed him into the same padded area; their struggles in the water, kept well up stage, would have looked convincing enough to the audience.

5.1 S.D. *The Boro', Saturday night*. The large and thriving market in the New Cut, adjacent to Waterloo Road, was a prominent feature of London street life. This stage direction is unrevealing, but we can find out more about the detail of the scene from the unpublished biography of Wilson Barrett, quoted in the Introduction; see p. xxiii. The scene was considered the last word in stage realism.

1 *coster*: costermonger, a seller of produce from a street stall or barrow.

17 *taters*: potatoes.

59 *business . . . Dreadful bad . . . owin' to foreign competition*: a humorous reference to the current political controversy over free trade and protectionism.

78 *hokey-pokey*: cheap ice-cream sold by street vendors.

115 *Temple o' the Legitimate*: a fancy name sometimes adopted—rather in jest—by strolling companies like the Jarvises: 'legitimate' technically refers to traditional and respectable forms of drama like tragedy and comedy rather than the melodrama that was obviously the staple of the Jarvis repertoire.

the 'Era': a major theatrical weekly with an extensive section of advertisements.

120 *give me the tip*: tell me what's happening.

121 *as your father's got*: as your father has become.

138 *teck*: detective.

152 S.D. *Blue Pigeon*: the public house already referred to in the stage directions for this scene.

171 *idemnity*: a confusion of 'identity' and indemnity'.

180 S.D. *The rise goes up discovering scene 2*. The stage flat concealing the next scene is flown into the flies.

5.2 S.D. *Planned scene*: not a term used in stage directions of nineteenth-century plays, but possibly referring here to the stage manager's diagram of an elaborately set scene simultaneously depicting the market, the two rooms in the Jarvis apartment, and the staircase leading to the apartment from the front door of the house.

100 S.D. *Harold throws Clifford against door L which bursts open; they both get into room*: they are now in the second room of the apartment on stage left; the police are arriving at the door into the apartment from the staircase. Harold and Clifford continue to struggle in the stage left room while the police are still in the room on stage right.

106 S.D. *keeps scene going*: Harold and Clifford, fighting, do not speak. Bess carries the vocal part of the scene by these interjections.

120 S.D. *Clifford throws door open*: i.e. the door between the two rooms. Harold now jumps out of the window of the room L to the street.

S.D. *scene closes in*: the 'interior of police station' of 5.3 comes across the stage, or is flown in, to conceal 5.2.

5.3.14 *the best 'Witness' on the road*: a pun: the Idiot Witness, which Shakespeare plays (see notes for 3.2.27).

76 *poetical justice*: Jarvis means 'poetic justice'.

The Middleman

1.44 *dodge it up*: I have not been able to find this particular usage in any dictionary, but here it appears to mean 'get it up' or 'write it up'.

48 *that franchise which the wisdom of our legislature has conferred upon him*: the third Reform Act of 1885 approximately doubled the electorate, and gave to wage earners outside boroughs—such as agricultural labourers—the right to vote. Only a bare majority of men were now enfranchised, however, and women still did not have the right to vote.

58 *public*: public house.

82 *'nation gallows blues*: roughly, 'damned wicked blues'. Danks is supporting the Liberal party, whose representatives in this scene are wearing yellow favours, against the Tory blues.

83 *Epiphany Sunday*: the feast of Epiphany, anciently on 6 January, but now celebrated on the first Sunday after New Year.

91 *Nestor*: the elder Greek statesman and counsellor of the *Iliad*.

221 *the last Egyptian campaign*: the British invaded and subjugated Egypt in 1882.

230 *dunned by all the Jews in Christendom*: Julian has fallen into the hands of Jewish money-lenders, who are pressing him to pay his debts.

289 *kiss-in-the-ring*: a kissing game in which the players hold hands in a ring; one player runs around the outside of the ring and touches a player in the ring. The latter must pursue the former for a kiss.

319 *an order*: a chit signed by Chandler entitling Cyrus to the iron fittings.

409 S.D. *pomatumed*: pomatum was a scented ointment for dressing the hair.

440 *receipts*: chemical formulas or recipes for making the perfect china.

478 *felo-de-se*: suicide.

488 *Brussels carpet*: a particular kind of wool carpet with a backing of linen thread, originally manufactured in Brussels.

532 S.D. *Schottische*: a dance resembling the polka.

573 *quietus*: release from life, death.

725 S.D. *Picture*. The custom of raising the curtain after it had fallen at the end of an act to exhibit a tableau in which the actors have changed their positions but are still expressing the emotions dominant at the curtain seems to have begun in the 1860s, notably with the Bancroft productions of Tom Robertson's comedies at the Prince of Wales's Theatre, London.

2 S.D. *six or seven feet from the stage*: i.e. above the stage.

185 *the man down from the Crystal Palace*: the famous fireworks displays at the Crystal Palace, Sydenham, the pyrotechnical centre of England, drew huge crowds. Chandler is paying the fee for an expert pyrotechnist.

219 *moonraker*: a dreamer.

3 S.D. *Seggars*: casings of fireproof clay to protect ceramic ware while it is baking in the kiln.

87 *all U. P.*: all up, all over.

88 *specs*: speculations.

133 *Cornubians*: a fictitious stock.

306 *Spoil the Egyptians*: to take or accept riches from the enemy. 'And the children of Israel . . . borrowed of the Egyptians jewels of silver, and jewels of gold, and raiment. And the Lord gave the people favour in the sight of the Egyptians, so that they lent unto them such things as they required. And they spoiled the Egyptians.' (Exod. 12: 35–6.)